Confessions of a Shanty Irishman

Michael Corrigan

AmErica House
Baltimore

ISBN: 1-59129-228-x
PUBLISHED BY AMERICA HOUSE BOOK PUBLISHERS
www.publishamerica.com
Baltimore

Printed in the United States of America

Acknowledgments:

I must thank Pat Parker and Sondra Williams; both read the manuscript and made valuable critical comments. My wife, Karen, edited a section of the memoir for a public reading at the Idaho Rocky Mountain Poetry Festival, and her incisive editing sharpened the work in performance. I owe a great deal to my late uncle, Emmett Corrigan, and Ann Haley, a relative who suddenly appeared to answer questions; they provided vital historical facts about my Irish immigrant grandparents. In many ways, it is the courageous and generous spirit of Emmett Corrigan, also a writer, who drives many of these pages.

This is not really a true memoir or a chronicle of a time, but rather a collection of chapters from a notebook of one who witnessed extraordinary changes in the American landscape. I've combined characters and taken liberties with time. I hope the comic is a little sad and the sad a bit comic. Ultimately, the story of my grandparents leaving one hostile environment to make a life in another uncertain world brings the "notebook" back to the beginning. As T. S. Eliot said, we may finally "know the place for the first time."

PROLOGUE

IN DECEMBER OF 1956, FATHER RECEIVED A LETTER regarding the estate of his uncle in Ireland, John Corrigan, who had left him and his siblings some money. There was the small problem, however, of a grave marker, and could my father give some of the inheritance for the "erection of a headstone" as the bulk of his uncle's money went for John's requested High Masses and to support some Catholic convents and orphanages? The "cost of the erection" would "not exceed One Hundred Pounds." Evidently, Father and his siblings agreed to pay for the "erection" and Uncle John got his headstone.

Years later, Father had a simple plaque in the ground. Holy Cross Cemetery in Colma, California has famous names from old San Francisco—Wyatt Earp and Joe DiMaggio—so Father had good company. When Mother finally died, it seemed odd to scatter her ashes across Father's grave. They had married twice; both times, their marriage was a disaster. Why did she want her ashes scattered on his grave? He had been dead for twenty-five years. Perhaps it was part of her paradoxical mystery, this woman who relinquished me to my grandmother, Agnes, when I was three. Until I met her again at age eight, I often noticed any blonde woman in the crowd, wondering if she were the missing mother known as Fran, who loved traveling, famous people, glamour, and the best foods, and who, one day in her mid-seventies, decided to stop eating and end it.

My mother was rarely ill, but I knew something was wrong when I didn't receive a card on my birthday, a polite concession we both had accepted. Cards were often more important than visits. On holidays, Mother preferred to leave town rather than risk my sudden appearance to celebrate. Her renter, a man in his fifties secretly charging on Mother's account, answered the phone; he described a woman weighing less than her age and staying with her sister, Harriet. When I called, Harriet was unsettled.

"Christ's sake," Harriet said. "She looks like something out of them

World War II concentration camps, and she don't care what she looks like, either."

I couldn't imagine Mother unconcerned about her appearance. On the phone, she sounded strange, with a hollow lisp in her speech.

"I didn't get a card, today, so I was surprised."

"Card? For what?"

"Today is my birthday."

There was a pause. "It is? Well, I can't get out," Mother said. "So that's that."

"Why aren't you eating?"

"I'm not hungry," Mother insisted. "Everyone keeps buggin' me. What's the big deal? I'll eat when I'm hungry."

Finally, Health officials forcibly admitted her to the hospital.

Everyone, including Harriet, insisted that her health would turn around. There was no need to fly to San Francisco. She had an eating disorder and doctors could treat it. When the psychiatrist released her to a conventional dietitian, she couldn't treat it either. Mother died alone, chemical pneumonia from inhaled orange juice finally killing her. When Harriet called, I knew without being told. An era had ended. Then I called the doctor who expressed surprise.

"Who are you?"

"I'm her son. I wasn't listed as next of kin?"

"No. I didn't know you existed." The doctor quickly added, somewhat nervously, "I thought she only had a sister."

"Didn't your nurse tell you when I called last time?"

"She didn't. Sir, I'm sorry you weren't informed about her condition."

A friend wrote in a card of condolence that we feel unexpected emotions when a parent dies, and often don't feel emotions others assume we will feel. Father had raised me so Mother was a stranger, yet her death created a sudden vacuum. Sitting by the Boise River reading *A River Runs Through It* and Eliot's *Four Quartets* created an intellectual calm with the flow of language, but didn't erase the brutal fact: a door had closed forever. In a way, it was fitting. Mother had always defended her right to live her own life without a child, and possibly we embarrassed each other. Her final will carried a kind of reprimand from the other side, giving two thirds of Father's estate to my cousins. She always went against the Irish Catholic sentiments, even hating the assassinated Kennedys when Father worshipped them. When attending the funeral of Mary, Father's older sister, she felt angry no one knew her, but then, how could they? She was the outsider. If my home was a broken home, it was a crowded broken home, she argued defensively. The inevitable question still remains: Why didn't I visit during her final days?

Father died many years before, burning up his health with alcohol and cigarettes. There had been a final weekend entertaining relatives, and everyone swore Father looked like a saint, his face pale, his eyes bright and gleaming, a yellowish halo around his head. Mother remembered only drinking and loud arguments. I lived in another state, but had visited Father a few months after his heart attack. A simple walk in the park would resonate with voices and images. Emmett, Father's younger brother, would insist his last weekend was peaceful and that Mother had picked the fights.

A plump, nondescript woman in the cemetery office put the plot information on a screen, and with my wife, Aunt Harriet and cousin Dennis, we walked to the hill where Thomas Jr. was buried. Thomas Sr. and Agnes lay close by. Harriet, though legally blind, found Father's plot. Identical white crosses lined the green hills and his gravestone had faded over the years. Mother's ashes lay in a small box covered with a purple cloth, and it felt unreal that these powdery white ashes could contain the feisty woman known as Fran, who spent her whole life insisting she was Kathleen. That it should come to this—some white ashes scattered on a grave. Neighbors and relatives had looted her house, taking what they could hold and dumping photos and other items on the floor.

"Jesus, I took Fran to the beauty parlor, 'cause I thought it would cheer her up," Harriet said. "Even I could tell she looked like one of them people in famine times. She asked me if she looked good. Hell, I was nearly blind. 'You probably look fine as ever, Fran,' I says. Then she went to bed and never got up until they came and took her away. Christ's sake, what a way to go."

I scattered the ashes on the grave and placed some under a tuft of grass. White ashes clung to my shoes. Did old Celtic ghosts watch from some secret place?

"My old man's gone," Dennis said. His father had died in a skid row hotel, drinking out his final days. Dennis's hair was thinning and he had not shaved. "Your dad's gone. Christ's sake, me'n you are old timers."

Karen said nothing. We had married at the Hemingway memorial in Idaho, and it was a new beginning. Today would be a day of endings.

"Your mother was a strange one," Harriet told me, her white face small beneath thin brown hair, the glasses thick. "She was miss glamour puss and I was plain Jane—but normal."

It occurred to me that I was as old as the man in the grave. Would I become father to him as years passed and I grew older? A feeling of tenderness and finality swept over me as I stared at the worn stone plaque. I wanted just one more conversation with him sitting by the window looking out at Dolores Park, Father holding a drink, the rich voice filling the room. We finally walked down the windy hill of the dead as the sun broke through an overcast sky.

"I can't believe what those 'friends' did to her house," Karen said.

Dennis asked, "You still on the wagon?"

"Yes. I had to quit. Liver damage was beginning."

Dennis paled: "I won't quit. Not me."

"Both of my sons are drunks," Harriet agreed. "Like the old man. Like Tom, too. All of 'em! For Christ's sake, Irish drunks."

"Much of my life was spent on licensed premises," I joked. "And so much of it was a blur."

Dennis turned and called out, "Goodbye, Tom and Fran." A wind lifted and carried a few ashes. My blood relatives were disappearing. In four years, Uncle Emmett, would die from complications of diabetes leading to a heart condition. He would face his death stoically, no visitors except hospice personnel, no visiting priest, and no final words, though a last letter would reveal more clues about his Irish parents. Cared for by a wife and daughter, James—the blond, dashing youngest brother—would soon follow, also dying from diabetes, the family curse on Grandmother's side. Reclusive Aunt Veronica would live to eighty and end in a nursing home, the State revealing her secrets and finances at last as dementia robbed her memories.

We stopped at Molloy's Tavern for a drink. Framed newspapers hung on the wall, each blaring a famous headline. Some went back to

1926. One carried a headline about President Harding and how he had "succumbed" after landing in San Francisco. Drunks often peered blinking at the headline: "Harding 'Suck-umbs'? Who the hell is Harding 'Suck-umbs'?"

Father once confronted a man with a gun in this tavern. There was a 1939 photo taken here of Father after his wedding, the handsome Irishman drinking with his bride, my mother; they smile up at the camera. As I drank 7-Up, I thought of Father and my grandparents so long ago. What had occurred to my Aunt Veronica—the elusive Vee—during those lost years? On the way home, Dennis stopped and bought a jug of vodka. It kept the darkness away on a dreary afternoon, turning wild dreams into realities, but I knew the demons returned, creating a realm of living dead.

The next afternoon, I went back to the cemetery and walked over the hill to visit the graves of Thomas Sr. and Agnes. Their gravestone had a cross with a single rose, their names, and a faded inscription: In Loving Memory. The dates of birth were confusing. According to church records, the former Agnes Kennedy was baptized in 1889—but was twenty-two in 1914, the year they married. The marker confirmed she was born in 1892. Thomas was probably born in late 1887 according to immigration records, yet his gravestone listed 1879, eight years earlier. Why were the old Irish so careless about birth dates—because they had too many children to remember? I suddenly saw into the old house, again, the pot-bellied stove and the Christmas dinners and heard Irish voices lifted in songs and poetry. In the garden, a small boy acted an Irish knight sent to defeat the English invaders. In front of the house, Grandfather in his old-fashioned hat smoked, one arm across the banister. Veronica smiled with her mouth closed. Agnes and Aunt Kate cleaned the kitchen filled with blue-tinted hand-blown bottles for spices, a rolling pin and painted bowls that one day would fetch a good price in some antique shop. In the front room, Father drank an Irish whiskey and argued politics before the ornate fireplace.

The tears came without warning.

"Jesus Christ," I said to no one. I took some deep breaths. Then I walked to the cemetery office. A young woman sat behind the desk.

"Can I help you find a plot?"

"No, I found it. One of the birth dates is off, however."

After I explained, she had no answer. "That was the date we were given. Perhaps your father wasn't sure. Here's an obituary for your grandmother."

I looked at the yellowed clipping. It listed the death day, and all her loving relatives, including a brother, two familiar sisters, and a third sister—named Corrigan.

"This is even stranger."

The young woman regarded me. "What is?"

"Growing up, I vaguely remember hearing about another sister—Minnie—but according to this, her husband has the same last name as my Grandfather."

She looked: "Indeed. Was this Patrick Corrigan a brother to Thomas?"

"I knew my grandfather had a twin brother in Ireland named John."

"So Patrick was another brother?"

"It would seem that way. Another mystery."

Had Agnes followed Thomas to America to marry him since her sister had married his brother, Patrick? Was it an arranged marriage? Why did relatives often grow silent after mentioning Minnie's name? I knew of no living relatives to answer those questions. Growing up, I heard stories yet few specific details about their early lives and actual passage to America. I knew the history of "coffin ships" bringing Irish immigrants to the new world; many died on board or in quarantine. I had read tales of Irishmen replacing slaves to drain the swamps and die of yellow fever. I had seen a famous cartoon from 1846 showing an overloaded ship called the Gallway Poorhouse coming into Boston Harbor. A man in a small boat carrying dynamite sailed to greet the new arrivals.

Leaving the cemetery, I wondered if the story of my immigrant Irish grandparents might be the only family history worth exploring.

CHAPTER ONE

GRANDFATHER EXCLAIMED:

"Dermot MacMurrough—there's a black Irish name for ya. Dermot stole King O' Rourke's bride. Not only the girl but her dowry—cows, pigs! And when O'Rourke, Irish warrior that he was, took her back, Dermot the coward got help from the Norman French King of England—Henry II. Dermot was the first man to bring Anglo Norman invaders to our shores. Wasn't long before King Henry decided he was king of Ireland. It started then, my boy. Eight centuries of English rule!"

"Was she pretty?"

"The bride? Of course, lad! No Irishman worth his salt would fight over an ugly woman. Dermot stole her right outta O'Rourke's castle."

"What was her name?"

Grandfather's eyes grew soft.

"Dervorgilla. A lovely lass, prettier than that Greek, Helen of Troy. With Henry came Welsh troops called Geraldines, and the man known as Strongbow who had his eye on another pretty Irish lass. Oh, they were keen on cutting up parcels of land for themselves. They plundered, pillaged, drank Irish whiskey. They were after having a high old time."

I tried to imagine tough soldiers called "Geraldines."

"Grandfather, why were the Welsh called—"

"Their mother—and she popped out a lot of sons—was married to Gerald of Windsor. Before Henry, most invaders became more Irish than the Irish. Even the Vikings."

Arms behind his back, the old man paced beneath the wall mirror.

"Long before I left the country for good, there was the death of Parnell, a good Protestant for home rule but betrayed by slandering priests."

He seemed to catch himself.

"Don't you ever call them that. Most priests are good people. We need the Holy Mother Church."

Grandfather's face was moon-shaped and smooth, with pale blue eyes and wisps of white hair along the sides of his bald head. Grandfather always wore his hat, except in the house. "You come from Irish kings, boy. Too bad there were so many of them. They were always after fightin' each other instead of the English."

"When did you leave Ireland, Granddad?"

"Michael, me boy, how do I remember? Sometime after the second famine, that's for sure. Met your grandmother, Agnes, and here we are. After the 1906 earthquake, who do you think paved the streets of San Francisco—Meself."

"Were you born near any castles?"

"A haunted castle in Roscommon—under a Celtic midnight moon. The castle was built by Baylor of the Evil Eye—no, it was Brian Boru who drove out the Vikings but couldn't unite the Irish clans against Brits." He fished in his sweater vest. "It's an old, sad story. We are our own worst enemies." He found a cigarette. "When I come back in, I'll read the funnies to ya." Grandfather went outside to smoke.

We lived in a house with blue-colored front stairs facing the green hills of Dolores Park. There was a fuchsia bush by the stairs with red and white ballerina flowers dancing on the wind; they survived the San Francisco winters, though some argued the summers were just as cold. White fog encircled the Mission district. Later, I read in an Irish history book that Dermot died shortly after King Henry conquered Dermot's enemies and made proud Irish chieftains swear allegiance to England. Of course, when Henry sailed away, all bets were off. Strongbow got the woman he craved, a castle and some land. There were no pictures of Dervorgilla. Did she have blonde hair and blue eyes like Helen of Troy? Did Dermot free her from a tower and ride off on a white horse?

Strongbow. What would they have called me? Michael, King of Feebs?

Early memories contain many childhood images: a blonde woman in a red model A, an open rumble seat in the back, the wind blowing across my face; a summer camp for young children; my grandparents taking me in with Mother mysteriously gone; a snapshot of a two-year-old on a grassy hill; Father returning from World War II dressed in Navy blues, waving to me as I stand atop a slide, waiting to sail down;

Agnes the gentle grandmother, wearing an apron; Thomas Sr., the grandfather, wearing workman's trousers with red noserag, thick-soled brogans, work shirt, sweater vest, and hat. We lived in that house: myself, my father, my grandparents, and a mysterious aunt called Vee for Veronica. She had poor teeth and brown hair. We listened to radio in the early days, *Tarzan* or *The Lone Ranger*. I loved voices and the scenes they conjured. Even the names suggested mystery and adventure: the Whistler, the Shadow, the Phantom, Red Ryder and Boston Blackie.

We were one of the first families to buy a television with its tiny screen: Milton Berle in drag for his comedy hour, Tonto and The Lone Ranger riding again and Duncan Renaldo as the Cisco Kid.

"Television is a wonderful invention," Mr. Dooley said. He had always seemed old, a small bald man who sat by his window all night watching the park. "I'm never lonely," he told Father. "I've always got someone in the room with me. The comedy shows. Dennis Day singing 'Danny Boy.' Lovely."

"I like Jackie Gleason," Father said. "His TV family's louder than mine."

"Television is a wonderful invention," Mr. Dooley continued. "Oh, I still watch the park. If anything happens, I'll see it."

A shout always announced dinner. One late afternoon, I turned off the television as a king named Claudius screamed for some light and Hamlet, a blond prince in black tights, stuck a torch in his face.

"For the love of Mike," Grandfather said, "I heard screaming. What are you after watching? Cartoons?"

"A weird movie. *Hamlet.*"

"Eat," Father said.

I looked at him. "What happens to Hamlet in the end?"

"He's eight and he's asking me about Hamlet? Ask me tomorrow."

"Why is he wearing tights?"

"For the love of six bits, don't ask," Grandfather said. "We had a few of those—even in Ireland."

"A few of what?"

"I'll read the play," Father said.

That night, my father thumbed through the collected works of the Bard in an old gray book. "Hamlet kills the king in the end, then he

13

dies," he finally said. The thick player's edition of Shakespeare's works remained on a shelf, and I would take it down and stare at the pictures of famous actors in various celebrated roles. The costumes were elegant. The exotic language held coded secrets: *Burn but his books, for they hold magic.*

Twenty years later, I finally saw the Olivier film. Every five years, Olivier appeared in some major film or television appearance, an artistic marker for the passing years.

Lady From Shanghai was playing at the local movie house. At the end of the film, Orson Welles walked past San Francisco's Playland at the Beach after a surreal shoot-out in the funhouse. He crossed the streetcar tracks and walked toward the Pacific Ocean. Playland was a wonderful amusement park that lasted for over thirty years. As a child, I rode the roller coaster or stared at the huge clown-like "laughing lady," mechanically shrieking inside her glass cage since 1940. When Playland was torn down, they moved "Laughing Sal" to a small museum near the famous Cliff House. Sal seemed smaller, less threatening. A crater where Playland stood filled with rainwater until luxury apartments replaced the ruins.

* * *

THE politics of the house were simple: we were born democrat, baptized Catholic a week later. There were two kinds of people: Irish Catholics and the ones who wished they were Irish Catholics. Alcohol was a sacrament. Uncle Emmett took me on my first day to Mission Dolores Grammar School run by nuns. We passed a statue of the Virgin Mary. There was the big church and a small adobe California mission from 1776. Behind the mission was a graveyard. On rainy days, Grandfather arrived at school wearing a sweater vest, workman's clothes, hat, and holding an umbrella. We walked eight blocks through sheets of rain, past the green spacious park toward the house. Some nights, we watched the streetcars go under the bridge, throwing light over the rocks and broken glass. Grandfather disliked small talk, but often recited nursery rhymes and sang about a "dirty old Mick" who put overalls in Mrs. Murphy's chowder.

Vee haunts my memory, though her private life and work remained a mystery; it was Vee who took me to the store on Fridays for a paper and a Tootsie Roll, which I called a "Tootis Roll." The news vender on Mission Street was a short hunchback with crippled legs. He and Father had grown up together. Father came home from the post office and sat down to read his paper before dinner. He fumed about what evil the Republicans had recently done; his conversations often included Eleanor Roosevelt. She was the Joan of Arc of America, if an older woman.

"God, that Eleanor witch is ugly," another newsman on the corner of 18th and Castro said one night as Father paid for the paper. We drove off.

"You'll be ugly at that age," he muttered. "Your mother oughta be arrested."

That many considered Eleanor ugly only confirmed her strength and power to do the impossible. The fact she fought for blacks did not make her threatening. San Francisco blacks lived in the Fillmore District, not next door.

Grandfather also read the paper and told Agnes every night about the latest adventures of General Pickax. It seemed General Pickax was invading countries across Europe: France, Italy, England, and even Russia and countries with difficult names. Sometimes General Pickax made scientific discoveries, and even composed classical music. How could General Pickax be in so many places?

"He uses that name for any one he can't pronounce," Agnes said quietly.

Grandfather left me with a rugged image, but the nurturing image is that of Agnes. She glows and fades in my memory like an image from an old photo. Incidents are remembered, but not the heat that went with them.

There is a surviving photograph taken when I was about one year old. Father holds a toddler in the back yard while the two old folks gaze into a light now lost, the look in Agnes' eyes so like that of my father, his two brothers and two sisters.

As a child, I imagined Agnes traveled by train across America with her sister, Kate, following another sister and a brother, Pete, who settled in Montana; the two sisters landed in San Francisco early in the new century. A fourth sister, Minnie, settled in Sacramento, though her history remained typically unclear. Did Kate and Agnes come over on a crowded boat, like the ones that brought Irish indentured servants to the New World? Who sponsored them? How much money did they bring? Leaving no journals, it's buried on some ship's list along with the livestock and other cargo.

What personal history Agnes had remained private, her rare disapproval always tempered with a smile or a simple nod. Agnes cooked meals; Agnes washed clothes; Agnes wore baggy flower dresses and an apron; Agnes had a soft voice, always evading questions, never giving opinions; Agnes remained invisible while running a complex house. Anonymous, her name appears on no Ellis Island record.

The basement of the old house facing the park contained a history of the family and the five children who had lived there a generation before. Sunlight glowed in the single window. The three boys went to war and returned, leaving two rifles to hang on the wall, an Italian bolt-action war rifle with a crooked sight, and a Japanese Arasaka rifle with a chrome bore. I stared at them in fascination, waiting for the day I was old enough to shoot them, wondering if they would explode in my face. The Japanese Arasaka was wicked looking, with a short stock and a strong recoil. The Italian Carcano rifle later gained fame as the model used to assassinate John F. Kennedy, a hero and martyr to San Francisco Irish. The boys had fought in the Pacific. Who brought home the Italian rifle?

In the basement sat an old-fashioned washing machine with a dangerous pair of rollers for wringing and squeezing wet clothes. Similar rollers had already crushed and broken the fingers and arms of numerous children; I fulfilled a tradition at six by reaching up and slipping my fingers into the turning rollers, catching them on the wet cloth, pulling back, feeling the sudden pressure and tug on my left arm as I was caught, then lifted and pulled up against the loud shaking machine.

I cried out, unable to reach and turn off the switch on the other side of the round dryer. My hand was moving between the turning rollers, the clothes providing more deadly traction and pressure when Agnes walked in and calmly put the machine in reverse. Slowly, the rollers turned backwards, pushing my blue fingers out of the crushing grip.

Agnes put my hand in a bucket of cold water, then hung up the clothes on the line.

* * *

SEVEN was the age of reason, the time when awareness of sin began. The altar boys were dressed in red and white gowns. After singing "Lord, I am not Worthy", the assembled sweet-faced boys marched toward the altar to receive their first Holy Communion. The night before, each boy confessed his sins in a small box called a confessional, a priest inside. A white crucifix glowed over the dark square. The priest's profile was visible through the screen when he pulled open the slide.

"Bless me Father for I have sinned. This is my first confession."

"And what sins do you have to confess, my child?"

That was a tough question. What sins could a seven-year-old recite?

"I stole some comic books from the hunchback on Mission Street. Maybe I lied about it."

"Anything else, my son?"

"No, Father."

"Say five Hail Marys and five Our Fathers and sin no more. Be careful of bad companions. And you'd be better off reading something of depth, like the lectures of Bishop Sheen."

"I will. Father—I think I want to be a priest."

"Good boy, lad."

At the urging of Sister Helen Clare who taught the third grade, I had already sent away for literature about joining the priesthood, and enjoyed receiving thick envelopes with information. The drama of the Mass arrived when the priest lifted the white host in his hands and called down the Redeemer. Father was proud when I knelt and received the body and blood of Christ for the first time. The priest continued down the line of kneeling boys, mouths open, tongues extended. I could taste the thin wafer but didn't feel different with God inside me. We took pictures outside the church and had a big dinner at home. Everyone drank and ate. Father snapped a photo while Agnes sat on a couch, smiling at the camera. It was indeed a happy day. All those boys had been washed clean in the blood of the Lamb. The day after

17

Communion, I went back to the hunchback vender and bought the new Superman.

* * *

BY the time I turned eight, I could see over the top of the bridge looking down on the train tracks for the green J streetcar that rolled up through Dolores Park along Church Street, stopping under the bridge between 18th and 20th Streets. When I was six, Grandfather had lifted me with callused hands as light from the streetcar caught the sparkling glass and rocks between the rails. A glow burned from two street lamps on either side of the car stops, shadowed steps ascending to Church Street.

"What's Ireland like?" I asked on one of our nocturnal walks.

To my surprise, he answered my question.

"There's a bridge near my Lisacul house with a stream under it. The hills in the park remind me of home, but we had rocks on the hills, no palm trees. My father and mother, John and Mary—saints, both of them—raised me and a twin brother, plus another brother named—but that's not important. There was a sister, as well. Twin brother John stayed behind and farmed the land."

"An identical twin?"

"Good God, you don't think he'd make two ugly Micks identical, do you?" Grandfather lit a cigarette and took a few puffs. "At twenty, I took a steamer out of Queenstown in Cork. It was the last stop before the Atlantic and America."

'Cork' sounded like 'Cark.' I asked: "Will you ever go back?"

"No," he said. "What for? I'm not a farmer. I tried to run a store, but who could buy? That life is gone." He frowned. "Like the British Tans, you're after asking too many questions, lad."

He lifted his Irish shillelagh, a hard wooden stick with a round polished knob on the end. It was thick and heavy to the touch. Grandfather stared down the tracks.

"I left because of no work and troubles with the English. Got here in time for the '06 earthquake. And who gave the celebrated tenor, Enrico Caruso, a ride in a horse-drawn cart to the Ferry Building before all Market Street went up in smoke? I did! A fire burned half the town.

A truck overturned and I got hit by exploding cans of hot fruit. I heard some starving people later ate the horse. Caruso sailed back to Italy and I became a citizen the year the Titanic went down—1912. How many immigrants drowned that night?"

A rock sailed up out of the darkness and shattered the glass around the street lamp. Grandfather looked down. Another rock was thrown at the lamp, but it missed the globe.

"What do you think you're doing, young man? Putting us all in darkness? I worked for the city!"

There was a muffled shout from below.

"Who's that, Grandfather?"

"Two men who want to rob the trolley."

He leaned over the edge. "Two things will happen, tonight. I'll knock you both out with this," he said, holding the cudgel. "Then break your necks. You better skedaddle."

"Go away, old man," came a voice from the darkness below.

"I'll warn the passengers inside. They're after working."

"Oh yeah? You better run, pop."

"I can't run." He leaned down close to me. "Run home and tell your dad to call the bulls. I'll take care of these hooligans."

I ran along the path toward the house, running past a small pepper tree that resembled a miniature weeping willow, running stumbling up the stairs into the house. Father put down his newspaper. "Jesus, what happened? Where's your granddad?"

"Some men are holding up the trolley. He wants to fight them!"

Then we piled in the old Plymouth, driving down Church Street toward the small bridge. We saw a J car stop at 20th street. Had it been robbed? Father parked the car on a hill, the lights blinking, and ran to the darkened bridge. Grandfather stood alone, smoking, watching for the next streetcar. "They ran off," he said. "Cowards!"

Agnes waited at home.

"There was no danger, Agnes. None."

Without a word, she punched him.

* * *

THE entire clan gathered for Christmas dinner every year, including

Father's brother, Emmett, and Pete Kennedy, the brother from Montana, a large man with light blue eyes, white hair, and full lips. The Christmas tree glowed with lights, most of them white where the color had rubbed off over the years since buying new lights seemed extravagant. A pot-bellied stove made crackling fire sounds, warming the kitchen. The long table was set with the best china, silverware, a turkey cooking in the oven. I anticipated the plum pudding desert.

Emmett, who had lost his hair early, sat with his wife, rumored to be a Protestant. Her name was Shirley, and she had a pleasant smile, accompanied by an occasional giggle. Thomas Sr. and Junior stood before the mantle beneath a huge mirror, drinking whiskey. Aunt Kate in fierce black sat on the sofa, drinking tea, her gaunt face pale and pinched. She clucked her tongue when any remark displeased her. Aunt Kate struggled to be cheerful, even when brother Pete made crude jokes. Christmas was the one time Agnes gave orders.

"Remember, this is the birthday of Our Lord. No talk about politics or religion."

"Of course. You should've heard the sermon today," said Father. "Warning us about a Swedish art film."

"I don't want to miss it," said Emmett with a wink.

"I guess there's a lot of female nudity."

"For God's sake," said Kate, shocked. "Today is Christmas."

"I don't like films," Grandfather said, wearing his sweater vest. He said 'fillems' for 'films.' "But should the church be after telling us what movies to see?"

Aunt Kate sipped her tea. Uncle Pete spoke up: "In Montana, the priests tell us how to vote."

"That violates separation of church and state," said Emmett, cupping his wine in one hand.

"They have a right to warn us," said Kate. "It's their mission in life. Never disagree with our priests. Never!"

"The vote's no problem here," said Grandfather. "The Irish are taking over San Francisco. The Jews own it, the Irish run it. When I first came, all I saw were signs saying, 'Irish need not apply.' That's changed, at least."

"We got some Dagos running for office," Father said.

He had a deep melodic voice and a handsome face, with thick black hair combed back above chiseled features. Agnes announced that dinner would be served in a jiffy.

"I'd like to see that film before I go back," said Uncle Pete. "I haven't seen a nude woman since the last copy of the National Geographic, and she was an African native, a blue! Big lips, and bigger—"

"For goodness sakes," admonished Aunt Kate.

"Be careful," said Grandfather. He motioned. "The boy."

"He should know about naked girls by now," said Uncle Pete. "Of course, in Ireland, we don't see naked women until after marriage, and sometimes, not even after that."

"You're too busy sitting in a bar," Father said, smiling.

"Where else?" admitted Uncle Pete.

"This is disgraceful," said Aunt Kate. "Today of all days!"

"In this Swede film, I understand the man is also hanging out, buck naked," said Father. "Imagine that."

There was a moment of shocked silence. I tried to imagine this mysterious "art" film where men and women disrobed in front of a camera and crew.

"I'm not that liberal," said Uncle Pete.

Father nodded in agreement.

"A nude women is very beautiful," said Emmett. "Why not film her naked beauty if it fits the story?"

"Sure," agreed Father, "but a naked man is a bit much, wouldn't you say? He can't look anything but a fool with his pants down."

"Oh my God," sputtered Aunt Kate. "I'm after helping Agnes. I can't hear this talk on Christmas, and from good Catholics, too!"

"We must be kind to Aunt Kate," said Grandfather, lifting his glass. "She's all alone, a spinster, and the blues are after moving into her neighborhood."

"To Sister Kate," said Uncle Pete, lifting his glass in a toast. "A sister of Ireland lost among the blues."

"Why do you call them 'blues'?"

They looked at me. "It's better than jig or coon," Father said. "Or the 'N' word. Some of them are so black they are blue."

"I think 'Negro' is the proper term," said Emmett. "God knows, they've suffered discrimination."

21

"'Irish need not apply,'" Grandfather said. "I remember reading that all over town. I know all about discrimination."

"But we're white, like the Italians and others in power," said Emmett. "We can even change our names to get a job."

"What Irishman would change his name?" demanded Father. "A Jew might change his name, but never an Irishman."

I felt suddenly bold. "A black can't change the color of his skin."

Grandfather frowned. "For God's sake, son, your boy is after speaking out of turn. I think he's forgetting himself."

Father finished his drink. "Maybe I gave him too much whiskey for an appetizer. By the way, I'm famished."

Agnes entered the room and spoke: "Dinner's on."

Aunt Kate said grace before meals in her high, trembling voice. Then dinner was served, the huge turkey sitting on a metal tray, the guests waiting as Father carved it up.

"White meat? Dark meat?"

"I'll take a little bit of both," Uncle Pete said.

The gravy boat was passed around.

"Bishop Sheen was so beautiful on television last week," said Aunt Kate. Her faded blue eyes behind the thick glasses were moist with tears. "He spoke about the tragedy of our times, the losing of one's faith."

"Yes," said Father, winking at Emmett. "*Life Is Worth Living*. Good show. Go back to your blackboard, Bishop. Tune up the choir."

Aunt Kate put down her fork.

"Don't be disrespectful," warned Agnes.

Father held up a piece of meat on his fork.

"Delicious," he said. "The Pope's nose." He looked at Aunt Kate. "Oh, we all love Bishop Sheen, Aunt Kate. Even Protestants, I hear."

"Of course. Everyone watches Bishop Sheen," insisted Aunt Kate. "Even the Jews, the Christ Killers. Even them."

"Dad, sing a few bars of 'Who Put The Overalls In Mrs. Murphy's Chowder?'"

"It's a grand old song. You won't believe this but I was quite a dancer in my day." No one denied Grandfather could dance in his day. There was a pause. "Don't lose your way, young man," he said, looking at me. "Don't ask too many questions, and keep the faith."

"A true Irish Catholic would die before giving up his faith," declaimed Uncle Pete, lifting his glass in another toast. "To those who came over despite hardship. To those who died before their time. To the young girl who showed the way."

I wanted to ask, "What girl?" but Uncle Pete continued his toast.

"To those who died for a united Irish Nation, free of Protestants and Brits! May we all go back, someday—as Irish, not Brit citizens!"

The glasses were lifted. Shirley remained silent, eating, watching the family guests.

"We're Americans," said Emmett.

"Irish Americans, and proud of it," Father added.

"I think the Irish will go back to Ireland someday," said Uncle Emmett, "and everyone will prosper."

"To do what? Grow potatoes?" There was a lull in conversation. "Christmas day and no Vee," Grandfather said after a moment.

"She had other plans," suggested Father. "Off on her own, as usual. Wine, anyone?"

Father's face was red, his eyes moist, his speech affected by the whiskey and wine.

"We really do have to ask questions," said Emmett.

Father looked at his brother. "You're absolutely right."

We finished the meal. Agnes asked if it was good and everyone nodded that it was. Grandfather looked at Agnes with approval, even tenderness. We retired to the front room; Pete described Jew Jess, a Montana dance hall girl and legendary pickpocket. "Bejasus, in court she'd pick the judge's robes. Once I had a ten spot taped to my royal Irish—"

"—and wasn't I proud of my son at midnight Mass?" Father interrupted. "He cuts a handsome figure as an altar boy." I was curious about Jew Jess.

"He looked fine," said Emmett.

"We have a different service," said Shirley. "But I liked yours. I liked the singing."

No one commented on this admission.

I could remember waiting in the sacristy, then the sight of the spacious altar with its maroon carpet and ship-like pulpit, the tabernacle with its sun-like monstrance holding the Eucharist with the body and blood of Christ. All the vestments had magical names: surplice, cope, miter; the dramatic accessories: chalice, ciborium, the swung censer with its incense smoking. Music filled the big church, soft light from many candles touching the statues, the carved Stations of the Cross showing all the images of the Savior's final agony and passion. The congregation seemed to hold its breath as the priest lifted the white host and called down the Savior. It's hard to say at what point a person "loses the faith." When does the Mass become an old story with little relevance?

"You know what James Joyce called us," said Emmett.

"What was that, may I ask?" said Father.

"A priest-ridden race."

"Oh that's true," agreed Uncle Pete, looking down the hall for Aunt Kate. "If the Protestants don't kill us, the priests will."

"A little Catholicism will do you good. Aunt Kate is right," Grandfather insisted. "We must never forget the Catholic martyrs."

"We need a new Irish writer," said Emmett. "Someone to tell the story of modern Irish people. Some renegade to tell our history before we become obsolete."

"The story hasn't changed," said Grandfather. "Remember the Black and Tans. Recruits from England brought over to kill Irish lads."

"IRA Irish lads," said Emmett. "They killed a few Irish and Brits, themselves."

"The Irish Republican Army killed traitors!" Grandfather argued. "We were occupied by English invaders."

"The IRA is still brutal," Emmett said.

Father told a story: "I heard a story of two IRA men out to ambush an oppressive Ulster landlord but he was late. 'Say a prayer that nothing has happened to the poor man,' one of the gunmen said." Grandfather smiled, and Emmett laughed.

"Emmett? Aren't you an Irish writer?" asked Father.

"For a newspaper," said Emmett. "We're paid to get it wrong."

"Why were they called Black and Tans?"

They looked at me.

"The uniform," Grandfather said. "Half police, half army. The cowards."

Emmett leaned down. "You like to read. Maybe you can be the

serious writer."

It was a sudden, thrilling thought. I filed away the name James Joyce for future exploration. Grandfather lifted his glass. "Irish Poteen. Now that's a drink," he said. "You see enough pink elephants to start a zoo."

Sometimes at night alone in the kitchen, I stared at the small black pot-bellied stove, hearing the fire, watching the glow of flame through the grate, the flickering shadows on the wall. A sugar bowl filled with money for emergencies sat on a shelf. The house contained so much history, but it was mute. There were no voices in the flames or moving shadows. None of the old folks had left behind any personal journals, only a few legal documents and names on ship's lists. Thomas Sr. wasn't sure exactly when he was born, only sometime after a celebrated comet and close to yet another potato famine. One day I would discover Thomas Sr. was born in England but raised in Roscommon. Did his impoverished parents leave Ireland to work as servants of the hated English? Agnes came from a tiny village, Doocastle, in County Sligo, the place of shells celebrated by Yeats. Baptized in Bunnanadden Parish, did she pass the burial cairn of "passionate Maeve," the Celtic goddess, while on her way to Sligo Bay and a ship following her sisters to America?

"Grandmother, how could a goddess die?"

"Maeve became a Catholic and took mortal shape, lad. Then she could die like the rest of us. When a young person dies, particularly a young girl, the angels weep."

Was legendary Maeve the 'young girl' who showed the way?

"Why was she 'passionate'? Does that mean like boy-girl passionate?"

Agnes stared at me over her glasses. Some topics in the house were never mentioned.

"She was passionately angry. Maeve had an arrogant husband—oh, quite proud he was—who had a huge black bull. Maeve decided to buy a bay-colored Ulster bull to rival the black one, but one day, the bulls met and fought, tearing up the ground. Terrible, it was. It's said the dust and clods from their hooves made valleys and cut rivers in Scotland. Trolls living underground came to the surface and became Scots. The bay bull had a green emerald stuck between his eyes. Well, the black bull finally killed Maeve's bay one. She cried, but the green emerald became a lovely island in the Irish Sea." She picked up her towel and prepared to dry the dishes. "Your grandfather would say that's a lot of blarney, but I say there's a lot of bull in that tale." She threw the towel at me. "I could be after using some help, you know."

Thomas Sr. and Agnes met in San Francisco, unlike so many Irish immigrants who had settled in Boston or Butte, Montana. Exactly how and where they met was never discussed. Any romance seemed remote, yet they had raised five children. Did he learn to dance while courting her in 1914, the year they married at Saint Mary's Cathedral? Another sister of Agnes, Bessie, witnessed the wedding, and relatives always pointed out that Bessie married a Scot. Aunt Kate was destined for eternal black and impregnable virginity.

Everyone came together at Christmas, the house full of Irish voices and singing. When the singers grew tired, Grandfather had a collection of Irish record albums holding 78's in jacket sleeves. He and Father treasured a Bing Crosby collection; I heard the honeyed baritone of Crosby singing "Irish Lullaby" while Father and Grandfather listened in reverence, fighting tears. "Sung like an Irishman," Father said. No one dared mention that Sinatra—an Italian—had a wider range.

Presents lay around the tree to be opened Christmas morning. Guests would finally leave, exchanging season's greetings and warm good-byes. I stared at the tree with its predominately white lights and saw the tiny gleaming mirrors Agnes liked to hide in the branches. I stood by the ornamental fireplace, looking at the modest library, sipping a small glass of whiskey, thinking of traitorous Dermot and ancient Celtic wars and Christmas celebrations, wondering if good times would ever end.

* * *

THE Plymouth was parked on a dark wet San Francisco street. After waiting, I left and walked through the rain to Father's usual bar but Father wasn't there, so I called home and Agnes answered. "Where are you?"

I told her. Then Vee came on the line.

"He left you in the car while he went to get a drink? That dumb cluck. I'll be right down."

I sat on a red padded stool while the woman bartender served glasses of 7-Up. She had bleached blonde hair, like Mother's. Men sat drinking on bar stools, and smoke drifted through the bar. A few customers played darts.

"Don't worry, honey," the bartender said. "He'll have a few belts and turn up."

"It's a good man's failing," an old scrawny man argued, lifting a pint. He shoveled some cold cuts into his mouth. "It is. It is."

"You've been failing all your life."

"I have, I have," the man agreed.

When Vee came into the bar, I could see she was mad. "Let's go," she said.

At home, Agnes gave me some ice cream and little cookies called Lady Fingers, then put me to bed. "He'll be home," she said. Her gentle face was topped with Vee's brown hair; she wore thick glasses, and the blue of her eyes reflected the glow I saw in Father's eyes. My bedroom adjoined the kitchen.

It was late when Father came home. Vee waited for him; I could imagine her sitting there, mouth tight on bad teeth, eyes squinting against the smoke. Father sat down. I could tell when he spoke that he wasn't drunk. Vee lectured him about drinking and abandoning children. Her voice rose. "Take the pledge, for God's sake!"

"I did! Jesus, I was scared when I came back and found the car empty."

"What did you expect?"

"I didn't know I was gone that long."

"And what the hell happened?"

As Father told the story, I lay in bed, listening to his warm baritone. Though he had promised to quit drinking and raise his son, tonight he had ducked into Molloy's Tavern near Holy Cross Cemetery. Inside the bar, a man lay on the floor, shot through the abdomen, the gunman standing over him, a .38 still smoking. The shooter wore a service dog tag. Father spoke quietly: "You better put that down that gun, fella."

"Why?" He lifted the pistol. "Who are you?"

Thomas didn't answer but looked at the dying man, police sirens growing louder in the distance. "I was in the Navy," he finally said, "discharged in '46."

The gunman said nothing, staring at Thomas, their images reflected in the mirror as the bartender ducked behind the bar, reaching for his club.

"Swabbie, huh?" The gunman shrugged. "I was army." After a pause, he said, "All right."

"All right what?" Thomas said.

The gunman slowly handed over his pistol. The man on the floor relaxed in death. Thomas held the gun like it was a deadly snake. "Why did you do it?"

"Because of a woman," the gunman said.

"I understand," Thomas said. "My wife took off."

"You were better off. They're all bitches."

After the police left with the killer in handcuffs, Thomas walked through foggy streets to the car and found his son missing. When he entered the house, Vee remained awake, smoking, reading the paper, bags under her eyes. After he finished the story, he looked at her, looking for understanding, perhaps wondering why Vee still lived at home.

"I left without my Irish whiskey. Some other time, I guess."

"I hope it's not some time soon," Aunt Vee warned.

"I needed a drink, tonight. Bad! Now and then this black mood comes over me and only drink takes it away."

I lay in bed, listening to Father's resonant voice, trying to imagine the victim bleeding to death, the gunman's cruel eyes above the smoking blue revolver, Father like a handsome leading man standing calmly over the body, facing the leveled gun, reaching out for the barrel. Perhaps he felt a violent new world was opening up before him, dangerous and beyond control. Then the kitchen conversation stopped. Father looked in, his form silhouetted in the yellow light, asking the inevitable question I would never answer: "Are you asleep?"

The door closed, the sudden wash of light going black. It started to rain; I listened to the pattern on the roof, wondering if Mother was "like all the other bitches." I fell asleep.

* * *

I came home one afternoon and found the door locked. Climbing the fence, I saw the basement flooded from an overflowing washing machine. I pulled the plug and went upstairs. In the dark bedroom, Agnes lay with glazed eyes staring at the ceiling. Her face seemed to have collapsed upon itself.

"Grandma?"

She didn't speak. Occasionally her jaws worked but no sound came. The dark room was quiet except for the ticking of a clock. There was a mystery suddenly working, an intensity that would change the family forever. At a favorite spot in the park, Grandfather played cards with retired friends. I called her name but she didn't respond. Exhausted, I still gripped her hand when Father came home from work. He called the ambulance. Paralyzed, Agnes rode to the hospital where they removed a brain tumor.

The vigil began.

Agnes appeared fragile in the hospital bed, and I tried to remember what her voice was like, and what she had done after adopting me at three. How did this go badly so quickly? Had I helped her in the garden she raised despite cold San Francisco weather? Would Jesus heal her? Suddenly, I could hear her voice again as she beckoned me near the Christmas tree. Mirth glowed in her blue eyes.

"Look into the tree and you'll see something wonderful, lad. Come on. Look close."

I looked close. It was an old game and fun.

"See—something wonderful is hiding in the tree. Something magical."

Her tiny mirrors turned in the branches and I saw my face.

"Didn't I tell you, lad, you'd see something beautiful?"

At the hospital, Doctor Listretto took my father to one side. "She's also diabetic and needed insulin. All of you should be tested."

"Really?" Father said. "Diabetes, now?"

Then on a March morning, Grandfather broke into the bedroom, waking me and Father, demanding in a broken voice how we could sleep with Agnes dead.

"Jesus," Father said. "How could we know?"

We got up. In the hall, Grandfather looked like an animal that had been struck a fatal blow, yet unaware it was dying.

At the wake, I stared at Agnes in the coffin, waiting for her to move, to speak, to communicate. I imagined her a pretty Irish maiden at an Irish ball, holding a tasseled dance card, or huddled in a ship crossing the ocean. I saw something pass over her dead face, a ripple, yet the rosary continued, people kneeling, sitting, listening to the droning voice of the priest. The old Irish wore black. The stale air of the chapel was redolent with flowers, full of whispering voices. Father knelt or sat bolt upright, attentive, ready to pray, but there would be no miracle. Agnes was gone. He turned and looked at me.

"Son? Are you all right?"

"Yes," I said. The murmuring voices continued.

At the funeral, Grandfather sobbed, leaning over the coffin as they were about to close it before her final ride to Holy Cross Cemetery. He kissed her dead face. "I'll never see her again," he said. I had never seen Grandfather cry. Then I saw Father listening to Mr. Comisky, a childhood friend and the funeral director.

"There's a strike on," Comisky whispered. "We can't inter the deceased until it's over. I'm sorry." Grandfather stopped crying and glared at Comisky.

"Comisky? You're going to keep her on ice, for God's sake?"

One night, I had a nightmare. Wearing grave clothes, Grandma Agnes lay on ice in the morgue. I walked down a long dark hall with corpses in closed drawers. Reaching for the drawer marked Agnes, I woke up and I saw her standing at the foot of the bed, staring at me. She was a presence against the darkness, a force without a saintly aureole. Her eyes were kind, and I felt all the moments she had spent with me, filling the loneliness left by Mother. A barrier shimmered between us, like the river Styx in the Greek myths Father loved to read aloud. Had she come back to take me with her to the other side? Then the spirit faded and I was alone in the dark room. The house seemed to creak like an old ship and I slept without further nightmares

They finally buried Agnes in April. Grandfather cried in bed every night and Father hired Ruby, a day nurse, to watch him. Ruby cooked meals, and one day took a sliver from my hand using a needle, her fingers soft and strong with a precise delicate touch. They were black hands, but had the same gentle precision of an Agnes. When I left to play ball in the park, my playmates saw Ruby's gold-toothed smile.

"Who's the jig?"

30

"She's my grandfather's nurse."

Annoyed, I said nothing else, walking toward the baseball diamond.

Grandfather sat on his bed, face pale in the light, his head bald except for wisps of white hair, the once tough body suddenly frail. His breath came, slow and labored.

"I paved and tarred all the San Francisco streets. Now I'm looked after by a black. All she can cook is steak and potatoes."

"I like steak and potatoes."

"And I prefer boiled beef and cabbage."

"You want Dad to get rid of her?"

Grandfather was suddenly protective. "Lad, Ruby needs a job. How many times did I come home without finding any work to be greeted by five kids waiting for me to read the funnies, and Agnes with so little to feed them? But we managed."

"Tomorrow, *The Lone Ranger* and *Cisco Kid* are on television. James Dean's on the *General Electric Hour* tonight with Ronald Reagan."

"Reagan's a left-handed Irish Protestant and I won't be surprised if he becomes a turncoat Republican son of a bitch!" He closed his eyes. "Lad, I'm not after watching television anymore."

I suddenly felt I had invaded his dark, sealed room.

"Granddad? I think I saw Grandmother."

He looked at me, his expression calm. I was expecting one of his explosions like, "For the love of six bits!"

"I know," he said.

"You've seen her?"

"Every night in my dreams. Then I wake up and she's gone." For a moment, I could see his lower lip working as he tried to suppress the tears. "It's time to go," he finally said. "One day, the ship will take us both back home."

Sitting in the kitchen, Ruby said, "The agency don't pay much. I need ten cents extra for carfare."

"Certainly," Father said.

"I could get here faster with cab fare, though. It is a long way to the Fillmore District across the Market Street tracks."

"I agree."

"I have to cook for my family too, you know."

31

"Of course."

"You've been to the Fillmore District?"

"I've driven through the area, yes."

Ruby closed her eyes and smiled. "I bet you drove real fast."

"We have Negroes at work," Father said. "I like them."

"Thass good. I don't mind white folks."

"Good to hear that, Ruby."

"Down in Mississippi, my son can't even get a book from the library. His father, now gone, couldn't get a job. But I manage to find work here."

"We appreciate the work you've done, Ruby."

"Your father's a handful, but I like him."

"I agree, he's a handful."

We still had the big Irish family dinners on Sundays, with stories and songs. Ruby was never invited. Aunt Kate grew more frail, a spinster in dark clothes, always cheerful but sitting apart. Grandfather retired to his room early. The memory of Agnes filled the old house, inspiring even the less literate of our Irish clan to sing songs and recite poems. Everything began and ended with Bushmill's whiskey.

"The difference between an Irish wedding and an Irish funeral is one less drunk," Father said, toasting the guests. "To Ireland—a nation once again."

For a year, I heard Grandfather sobbing nights in the same closed room where Agnes had her diabetic stroke. How much longer could Grandfather endure being left behind without his wife of forty years? He still lay in bed after we returned from late Sunday Mass. Father rubbed his chest with medicinal oil when Grandfather sat up and gasped for breath; from the door, I saw his face suddenly turning blue. Did he see Agnes coming to take him? Looking into his eyes I had a child's view from his shoulders as the trolley came up the suddenly bright tracks. Then the train was gone. Grandfather's spirit struggled as time condensed and a door slammed. Father cursed and pushed me from the room, shouting out a number to call. As I dialed, I could hear his voice calling out, "Dad, Dad!" I paced in the front room, seeing only the image of a frightened thirteen-year-old boy in the huge mirror over the embossed mantle and hearing my father's desperate voice. Then Father came into the front room and said, "I think he's gone." I didn't witness the final moment of his passing. The number I called was for the priest house and one arrived before the ambulance. It was June 5th, 1955.

Later, I sat in the park. Why were children playing with a hose in the street, splashing each other? Didn't they know Grandfather had just passed? Had he died of a broken heart? A young boy with dark curly hair approached. He looked at my face.

"What's up? I'm new here."

"My grandfather just died."

"I'm sorry to hear that. My name's Richard. Richard Boyle."

I didn't respond.

Ruby came to Grandfather's funeral, and I think he would have been secretly pleased, with the kind of perverse rebellion that boasted of superior Irish Catholic blood one moment, and contested it the next, daring anyone to deny all Irish people were descended from black Moors who had invaded Ireland in the eleventh century.

"He was tough old bird," Ruby said. "But a good man."

A young boy who played baseball with me in the park stared at Ruby.

"Are you a nigger?" he asked, smiling. "That's what Mom said."

"No, I'm your Aunt Ruby. When yo momma's too drunk to feed you, give Aunt Ruby a call."

Startled, the boy walked over to his parents.

Outside the big church, the sun was too bright and I remembered sunlight on a palomino called Blondie, Father suddenly reining in the horse as I walked into the road, the hooves rising up, up, the mane white in the sun. We were in Sonoma for a vacation, and Grandfather—still alive—sat inside the cabin, reading the newspaper, throwing the pages on the floor as he read. Father's startled face above the rolling eyes of the horse faded and we stood again before Mission Dolores.

I waited for Grandfather's ghost to appear, but he never came.

* * *

MY formal education continued at Mission Dolores Grammar School. Sister Constancha called me to her desk. A huge rosary hung from her belt.

"I know you're feeling poorly. You may sit at your desk and read, today. I'll beat the rest of these heathens into some piety. Your grandparents were good people—Irish people."

Like a tall old bird, Sister Constancha paced before the class of young boys.

"In the beginning, God took the material for Man from the swamp, and he breathed hard on it and the clay came to life. But the man was all black, so he put him in Africa. Then he mixed the mud and clay again and breathed lightly over it, but the man was all yellow, so he put him in China. Then he mixed the best clay and breathed ever so lightly over it and finally he had—a white man at last. He called him Adam and placed him in lovely emerald green Ireland. Then he created a mate, Eve, and we know what she turned out to be. Eve was the first to eat of the forbidden fruit, and that's why women suffer the pain of childbirth, and the humiliation of the beast with two backs."

A boy raised his hand. He was the only black in class.

"What beast is that?"

The old nun glared. "Don't ask, Mr. Manny. No filthy questions in this class."

I wondered if the forbidden fruit was worth the taste. Richard Boyle wrote on a piece of paper and slipped it to me. It read: *Ireland was made by nuns dropping their diaphragms on the way to heaven.*

Sister Constancha had the wrinkled face of an old dog. When a lay teacher played a recording of *Macbeth*, we realized the bearded witches were like Sister Constancha. I thrilled to the rich language: *a drum, a drum, Macbeth doth come.* Did the old Celtic Irish have Thanes? Might not witch Constancha boil the liver of a blaspheming Jew?

"Bill Tate, stand up!" Tate was a tall, wiry youth with a bad complexion. He stood up. "Recite the Apostle's Creed, Tate." He did so in a flat monotone. "See? Bill's a Protestant, and he can recite better than you *Catholic* ignoramuses."

"We have the Apostle's Creed in our—"

"Sit down, Tate. Now class, who made us?"

"God made us," the class recited.

"Who is God?"

"God is the Supreme Being of the universe."

"And what church did God create?"

"The One Holy Catholic Apostolic Church, Sister Constancha."

"Good. Get your coats from the cloakroom."

"Sister Constancha?" It was Boyle. "Why is the closet called a cloakroom? Who owns a cloak except Dracula?"

Constancha clucked through her teeth and gums. "Always a clever answer, Mr. Boyle. And a *smirky* look. March!"

We marched from the classroom. Sisters of Notre Dame lurked outside the bathroom, listening for loud or vulgar joking; laughter was forbidden. Under loose black sleeves they carried wooden clickers that resembled close-pins, and could be used for jabbing and poking. I had nightmare visions of being caught in mid zip by a wooden beak, snapping out of the hall shadows.

"No impure thoughts or acts in the bathroom, boys," Sister Constancha shrieked. "I'm watching you. No *smirky* looks." Her voice echoed over the brown tile floors and along the curving walls. In the kitchen, white-haired Mrs. Rodney cooked Spanish rice for lunch. After eating, we played in the small playground next to the old adobe mission and its ancient graveyard.

The Mission District had changed. The Irish families moved up Mission Street, heading south where Irish slang and accents endured. The Black Barts ruled the lower Mission, though they weren't black but Latino Pachukos. They wore zoot suits: padded coats, pants belted under the ribcage, long chains and alligator shoes. The Pachukos confronted duck-tail white-shoe boys in pegged jeans and suede. Deals were made. A change of shoes guaranteed safe passage on foreign turf. In the next century, computer companies would move into the Mission, raise the rents and drive out the minorities and artists, but for now, Latino culture and benign street gangs dominated.

Boyle and I smoked Camels and drank vodka mixed with grapefruit juice. I should have gotten sick but didn't. Boyle was a startling sight: curly black hair with flaky dandruff, bad teeth, slight potbelly, nasal voice, loud, harsh nasal laugh. Everything about him reeked of arrogance and contempt. His very presence made others nervous. Outsiders, Boyle and I boxed each other to get in shape for inevitable fights. Then we both saw Lucy Bond, already sensuous at thirteen, walking to the Catholic girls' school. Charles Woods also saw her.

When Boyle made his move, Charles Woods and Doug Harry confronted us at a bus stop. Doug Harry wore short spiky hair and Woods had a handsome face, with dark eyes and pretty eyelashes. He was a star athlete and popular.

"You been lookin' at my woman, Boyle." He reacted to Boyle's buck teeth. "Jesus, check the guy for lethal weapons."

For an answer, Boyle pulled a switchblade. They circled each other like boxers in the ring. Boyle was small, but had a malevolent evil in his eyes. Charles Woods circled, fists up, amused by this skinny punk with a blade. Boyle jabbed and Woods danced while Lucy held her books and watched, excited.

"Go ahead, Boyle, use the blade," Woods said, backing away.

Lucy pushed Boyle into Woods. "Cut him up, you chicken-shit!"

It ended quickly. A young nun named Sister Ann Maureen broke up the fight and no blood flowed. Lucy taunted Woods: "You gonna kick his ass, pretty boy?"

Woods didn't answer, and Boyle carried his rebellion into class.

"When I graduate, I want to be dictator of Chile."

"Boyle, I'm calling your mother," Sister Constancha said. "I know you don't have a father. I bet you don't even know your father. Stop smirking!"

The boys in blue and pepper uniforms marched into school every morning to the tunes of John Philip Sousa. Boyle shrieked to the martial music in mock Hitlerian German. Years later, Boyle would travel as a journalist to El Salvador during a brutal civil war. His embellished adventures would become a film starring James Woods: *Salvador*.

"For God's sake, stay away from Boyle," Father warned. "The nuns called today. What the hell is wrong with him?"

"He doesn't like the nuns, uniforms, or religion class."

"What? Sounds like a nut."

I didn't dare mention I also disliked the uniforms and religion class. Nuns in black shrieked about sin. The devout altar boy weeping over Jesus had vanished. Other vistas were appearing: thoughts of young girls and the world of books "opening on the foam of perilous seas, in faery lands forlorn."

"Boyle is bright."

36

"Okay, he's bright. And he's got two arms and two legs. He still isn't normal. You need to watch the company you keep."

* * *

IN October, 1955, Father did something strange; he took me to a film that he must have known only I would enjoy, *Rebel Without a Cause*. James Dean had been dead a few days, and now glowed on the big screen, more luminous at the moment of his non-existence due to light, shadow and sound captured on celluloid. He would live on forever young, peering out from under upturned brows, the mouth open, small chin tucked in, the face caught beneath the flame-like hair. He was delivering a message to the young people from that moment forth: to be alive is to be misunderstood; to be glorious is to act in defiance of blind authority. The face said it all with its sly, elusive smile at some hidden joke, and the eyes that saw into some dark future, knowing eyes, clear above the dark bags of an insomniac who lived for the night.

"I dare you to not like me," his ghost whispered.

I sat in a theatre, more deeply moved by the glowing face on screen than by any other spiritual or physical force. During the knife fight, I remembered Boyle pulling the switchblade on Woods. I had to say it out loud: "Man, how could he die?"

"All right," Father said, driving the old black Plymouth. "He was a good actor. So what? He's like that Brando character, a little goofy. It's nothing to model your life on. I bet he's forgotten in a year. Old hat."

"I don't think so," I said, remembering the red jacket. I had an old white windbreaker that could be dyed red. I secretly smoked, and Father might even approve, since he smoked heavily. A lot could be done with a cigarette, another gesture of defiance in a world of death.

"Now Tyrone Power's an actor. A real actor."

It was an obvious choice, and Father had Power's dark Irish good looks. Still, I reacted with mock surprise.

"Dad, do you really think Tyrone Power can hold a candle to Dean? Phony Tyronie?"

Father lit a cigarette, thinking. After a pause, he said, "Don't be a wise guy."

"Do you?"

"I didn't say that, exactly."

"Dean and Brando are bad actors?"

"They're great," Father said "They just make me nervous, that's all. I wanna see pictures I enjoy."

"Will you see Dean's upcoming film, *Giant*?"

"Sure. Why not? There's still something shifty about Mr. Dean."

"Who's this Brando guy?"

"Another clown. 'I coulda been a contender.' So what?"

"You never memorized any lines by Tyrone Power."

"He makes normal pictures. They're harder to remember. Hell, I coulda been a contender. I outswam Johnny Weissmuller at the 1939 World's Fair. He starred in the movies and I ended up at the post office."

"Dean's cool. There's no other way to say it."

Father snorted. "Cool? The guy lying in the street, drunk, playing with the toy monkey? Horseshit."

"You never got drunk and fell in the gutter?"

"Never," Father insisted. He looked at me. "Oh, it's normal to have a drink taken, of course. Just don't you get any ideas about drinking. If I catch you smoking with your asthma, it's curtains."

"You drink. You smoke."

"That's different. I'm an idiot."

The Plymouth labored up Dolores Street. I thought about Dean's black Mercury and the red jacket, which was a kind of warning. That same month, a homosexual Jewish poet named Allan Ginsberg read a poem called "Howl," but no one anticipated the poem and Kerouac's subsequent *On the Road* would rip open American literature. Elvis would soon destroy the hit parade, separating youth from their parents.

Sister Ann Maureen, dubbed SAM by Boyle, taught the eighth grade. She had a strong, hard swing in softball and could slam the ball over the fence, unencumbered by the habit. Sister Ann Maureen was young and pretty, inspiring adolescent sexual fantasies; I imagined her lying on a bed, naked, the black habit and rosary coiled on the floor. How could such a lovely young woman be a bride of Jesus Christ? SAM had a genuine fondness for both of us until one Good Friday. The church was dark and the mood somber. Worshippers followed the

Stations of the Cross at the hours between twelve and three. Each carved station depicted a moment in Christ's last steps to the crucifixion site. Light glowed in the stained-glass windows. Candles burned. The class stood in the aisles of the impressive Mission Dolores Basilica with its dome and wide altar. As Catholics, we had to meditate on those last moments: the sweating of blood in the garden, the betrayal and arrest, the mock trials, the scourging and the final brutal death on the cross.

"Let's slip out the side door," dared Boyle.

"We'll get in trouble."

"So?"

We escaped. Outside, the sun was shining and we sat smoking in the park. Later, Sister Ann Maureen called the house.

"By whose authority did you leave?" she demanded. "Boyle's? Listen, I want you to have your father call me—tonight."

"I don't like the service," I said. "A man going to his execution. Barbaric."

"It's a beautiful service."

"What if Jesus was electrocuted? Would we wear electric chairs around our necks?"

"Where did you read that?"

"Though Veronica's story fascinates me," I said. "Did they ever find her veil with the imprint of his face?"

In her anger, Sister Ann Maureen couldn't answer. Good Friday was special to Father.

"If I catch that Boyle punk in this house, I'll punch his ugly face," he warned. "I know he talked you into it. How could you...on the day Our Savior is howling in darkness? That's sacrilege. Wait until the Jesuits get a hold of you, young man."

"I want to attend Lowell High School."

"It's a public school. You are going to Saint Ignatius if I have anything to say about it. Understand?"

"Do I have anything to say about it?"

"No!"

That Sunday, we attended church, Father sitting or kneeling, his handsome face in profile. The music played. The choir sang. The priest droned out a sermon. The altar boys moved stiffly like poor actors in

39

an outdated play.

Graduation ceremonies concluded with students, teachers and parents suddenly mingling in a kind of false camaraderie. Boyle wore a suit, and his mother, a small bird-like woman, walked with him. Charles Woods and Doug Harry were polite, smiling at everyone. Tom Manny came with his parents, two bothers and a beautiful older sister named Dolores. Tom was tall, muscular and confident; Dolores smiled at the white families and they nodded and smiled back, as though they were admiring exotic wildlife. Woods whispered to Harry as they passed me: "Tom's a great ball player, man. Even if he is a nigger."

"Yeah," Harry said, "that's right, but he's our nigger."

Father made the rounds, talking to other families, including Boyle's mother. I wandered off to study the mossy headstones in the old mission cemetery. There was something magical about the small graveyard where Jimmy Stewart walked in *Vertigo*. The weathered headstones and old graves held so many buried secrets from the past. It was fun to make up stories connected to the ancient dead. I thought about my grandparents. Sister Ann Maureen suddenly appeared, radiant, shaking her head, smiling. She wanted a photo; I had one from the seventh grade.

"I like this. It's a cute shot. Your tie is crooked." We glanced at the old, barely legible epitaphs. "I remember you playing by yourself on the day of your first Holy Communion. You were chasing leaves. That's a problem, young man. You daydream."

I had memorized lines that often proved effective. "I could be bounded in a nutshell and count myself a king of infinite space, were it not that I have bad dreams."

"At your age, I'm glad you can quote from *Hamlet*, but be careful that's not some phony intellectual pose."

"I heard a recording of the play at the library."

"You do have an unusual sensitivity to books and theatre."

"And I do daydream. Tell me, do you have a picture of yourself?"

She was surprised. "Why would you want a photo of a nun?"

"You're a very beautiful nun. Too beautiful."

Sister Ann Maureen laughed. After a moment, she was very serious. "I hope Sister Constancha never hears you say that."

"No danger there," I said. "But it's true, you know."

She didn't smile.

"That sounds like your friend, Mr. Boyle. He'll come to no good, since the secular world and all its evil has already corrupted him. Let the poetry inside you lead to something positive. Don't follow his lustful thoughts."

"I got a few of my own, " I said.

Sister Ann Maureen met my eyes. "I suspect that you do."

She seemed to understand the sexual nightmare of early puberty, and I looked away, embarrassed. There was a pause. She began speaking.

"I came from a rich family. I had money, plenty of men, a chance to live in luxury all my days. I'm not as square as you may think. It all bored me. Then I dedicated myself to helping people. Jesus is my man, now, and his healing work is my life. I may leave San Francisco to work in Latin America among the poor."

I was surprised at her candor. Then she took out a cigarette and lit it.

"Awful habit. Tell me. Do you miss your grandparents?"

"Yes. I used to get embarrassed when my grandfather came to get me on rainy days. He always wore those old-fashioned hats and workman's trousers and looked like he just got off the boat, even forty years later. Never lost his brogue, either."

"Are you still embarrassed?"

"No. Now I'm embarrassed I was embarrassed."

"Would they appreciate you cutting Good Friday services?"

"God no. They were devout Catholics."

"And you aren't?"

I didn't know how to answer. "I guess it just doesn't make sense to me."

"Your father's worried about your faith."

"He can never remarry because of his faith. Why should he be alone?"

Sister Ann Maureen turned her lovely profile to me and drew on the cigarette. "Good point. Tell me, do you admire Hamlet as a character?"

"I think so. What I understand. I like the sound of the words."

"Think of Jesus as another Hamlet out to save the out-of-joint world, despite personal fear. I'm curious. Where's your mother today?"

"She couldn't make it."

"I'm sorry to hear that. I'll remember you and always pray for you. Hopefully, you'll outgrow false popular idols and this cynical adolescent agnosticism."

"Is that what it's called? Big word."

"In the third grade, you wanted to be a priest."

"Yes. My father would like that. Or else, first base for the Giants."

She peered at me. "Did Confirmation and a promise to defend the faith mean nothing to you?"

I recalled kneeling and the bishop's gentle slap on the cheek to remind us about courage under persecution. "Sure. I took the Confirmation name of John," I said.

"Why Saint John?" She seemed encouraged. "Because he was the beloved of Christ?"

"No. Saint John's the only apostle not to get executed."

Sister Ann Maureen paused, then laughed. She stamped out the cigarette and we joined the others. White-haired Bishop Guilfoyle in his cope and red bishop's cap, holding the heavy staff and silver cross, walked among the nuns, students and parents.

* * *

HIGH school. Veronica bought me a ticket to see Elvis Presley at the Civic Auditorium in San Francisco; the concert was on Thanksgiving Day, 1957, shortly before Presley's induction into the army. It always puzzled me why Vee bought me a ticket for someone threatening her generation. I first heard him on a car radio; that first month, Presley destroyed the dull hit parade. He swiveled his hips and sang like a black man, and though white, barely subdued panic regarding the potential morals of white youth. There was the Presley voice, a sensuous crooning to the ear, even with the early rocking blues numbers that drove teenagers to move, to dance, to get in touch. Presley combined white and black music and created a public arena for teenagers, a new religion of rock. There would be future rock gurus with more to say, but Presley cut the first wood.

"Bing Crosby can sing," Father insisted.

"So can Elvis Presley," I argued.

"Sure he can. His smile gives me the willies."

42

Thanksgiving Day arrived. Presley with a huge pompadour and wearing a light purple suit stepped out from behind a curtain; he sang fourteen songs, the liquid baritone filling the auditorium, illuminated by thousands of screaming girls shooting flash photos. Presley moved like a cat, and shook with invisible electricity shooting thorough his swiveling, supple body. He straddled the cut-out of the RCA Victor dog on stage while singing "Hound Dog." Was Lucy Bond in the screaming audience?

The handsome god in purple strapped on his guitar but didn't play it; he bowed, the long hair coming off the scalp, the head suddenly snapped back, each shiny hair flying in place. Then, in an instant, the god was gone, the voice still echoing in young hearts, speaking to one another with an erotic thrill of abandon and sensuality.

I sat at dinner, eating turkey, fewer guests now. Veronica asked questions, disguising her bad teeth; it was difficult to explain that Elvis wasn't just another singer but a way of life. Father was only mildly impressed.

"Sinatra had them screaming too," he said. "Mice can make girls scream."

If Presley's later years made for sad reading as the musical revolution he started left him behind to die a bloated drug addict, the voice remained, signaling dramatic change. Elvis Presley also filled a void left by James Dean.

In October of 1956, *Giant* opened, and students cut classes, waiting in agony through the slow beautiful film for Dean's appearance. He finally appeared in the background, humped over a car, then in a breathtaking close-up, the familiar craggy face beneath the cowboy hat, always cool and mysterious, smoking a cigarette. The audience stirred. "There he is. Jimmy!"

The screen seemed to ripple for a moment. Elvis didn't replace Dean, only succeeded him.

* * *

WITH a learner's permit, I spent one summer with Father, driving back roads in Modesto where Uncle Emmett lived; I sat behind the wheel of the black Plymouth driving along narrow irrigation canals.

The engine hummed as dust rose behind us from the unpaved roads; the car jolted as the gears engaged.

"You have to time the clutch, son. This is a stick shift. You can double clutch this baby to make the shifting smoother. You don't want to strip gears, now."

Father sat on the right, smoking a cigarette. The back roads were narrow with open country on either side. On the main highway, cars passed us, and the black road saturated with heat stretched and turned through rows of trees. Warm air pouring in the open widow smelled of fresh tar. Orchards and pastures filled the horizon, and well-managed fields.

"I love these old cars. Everyone wants an automatic shift, but give me these old clunkers you can repair with bailing wire and chewing gum. A Chevy will last forever. You have to shoot that baby to stop it from running. Don't lean when you turn, it looks amateur. Bush league. Remember, hands at a three o'clock position. That's the safest for quick turns and shifting." The warm, intimate voice cast a spell with only simple directions.

The weekend came when I drove all the way back to San Francisco, even crossing the Bay Bridge while at the wheel; sailboats tacked on the bay. I was closer to being a man. With the eventual purchase of a Studebaker, a sleek silver-colored car shaped like a bullet, doomed to obsolescence, my education and accessories were nearly complete: car, pegged jeans, white tee-shirt with cigarettes rolled into the sleeve, suede shoes called white bucks, red jacket, and Elvis on the car radio. A suicide knob gripping the steering wheel was essential. One could turn rapidly while the other arm was draped over a girl—when there was a girl. If Dean's celluloid image remained to show us how to be cool under pressure, Grandfather's Celtic spirit still gave off a vibrant energy. His stories and the kindness of Agnes would speak for another time.

Against the basement wall leaned a painting of an old ship, the kind that carried immigrants to the new land. I created a story in my mind. I saw my grandmother at twenty leaving an Ireland that was about to explode, Agnes and her sister, Kate, sleeping on straw in abandoned animal pens while crossing the Atlantic, never telling the story of personal horrors back home. Was it terrifying to land in New York, then take a train across an America still open and wild? If the new land was violent but promising, the old one was violent and poor. Grandfather waited in San Francisco where he tarred and paved the streets. There would be little time for a romantic courtship.

I remembered a deep excavation where workers dug out ground for a new hotel off Market Street. I was eight, and Grandfather held my hand, reliving his days as an Irish laborer. Dust rose from the gigantic pit. Overhead, a huge electric Hamms Beer sign looked dark and fake. Along the cyclone fence, an old Irishman with missing teeth glared at us.

"Look at that, will ya?" He pointed, furious. "Haven't they got a black workin' there? A nigger takin' a job from a white man with a family!"

"And weren't we slaves, too, only cheaper, and doesn't the black also have a family?" Grandfather asked. He shook his head and muttered: "The Irish. What a sad race."

Disgusted, the old man backed away. He took a swig from a bottle of cheap wine. "And what kinda Irishman are you?" he demanded, wiping his mouth.

"The kind who came over on a cotton ship, who cleared a swamp and nearly died of yellow fever. The kind who broke his back paving this street for the likes of you. Aren't we all blacks, for the love of Mike?"

The old Irishman spat and walked away. On the way home, Grandfather described the three breeds of Irishmen: Lace Curtain for well-off, Shanty Irish for working class, and the extremely rich Micks called Two Toilet Irish.

"We won't ever have two toilets in our house," he said, "unless you make a killing in vaudeville. We're Shanty Irish. The neighbor woman used to look down on me when I came home covered with tar, but whose door was she after knockin' on when her lawyer husband needed a blood transfusion? Mine! Never gave blood in me life, but I did. I guess I wasn't so Shanty, then."

"Is Uncle Pete a Shanty Irish?"

"Of course," said Grandfather. "A working miner with five older sisters, the poor man."

Grandfather could see me counting.

"Minnie, Bessie, Kate and Agnes. That's four. Who's the fifth sister?"

"My mistake, lad," Grandfather said, quickly averting his eyes. "Didn't I leave not one but two sisters behind in Ireland?"

Did Grandfather forget he had another sister in the "old country" or was he changing the subject? I knew that dropped voices and lowered eyes indicated more than a lapsed memory. We walked on but before I could probe any buried secrets, he recited his favorite comic lyric in an exaggerated Irish accent:

"'Fire, fire', said Mrs. Maguire.

'Where, where?' said Mrs. O' Hare.

'Downtown,' said Mrs. Brown.

'Oh the Lawd save us,' cried Mrs. Davis."

At evening, he read the paper and tossed the pages on the floor, knowing Agnes would pick them up. The night she died, San Francisco had a rare full moon, exposed in a cloudless sky. The silver-gray light drained the garden flowers of their bright colors, giving them a ghostly look. As always, when it grew dark, we could see the electric beer mug filling up, the golden liquid lit from within, shimmering like a promise or a warning in the night.

CHAPTER TWO

"THE JESUIT MOTTO'S ON GOD'S PERSONAL STATIONERY," joked Father.

The principal from Saint Ignatius called to tell my father that there was "a desk with my name on it," even though I lacked the athletic ability the school administration expected of its new freshmen.

I said goodbye to Boyle, who was attending Lowell.

"When I get laid, I'll send you a postcard. Man, an all boys' school run by Jesuits."

"My dad went behind the scenes," I said. "I know my test scores sucked dogs."

"It might not be all bad, a college prep school. Read dead guys like Caesar and Cicero."

"It's known for the best baseball team in town. I'm not an athlete."

Memory reveals an image: standing at the plate in a windy park, waiting for a high inside fast ball to pull into right field as Father walks toward me, hoping I can drive the ball over his head. But it's a strike.

Boyle laughed, showing his black teeth. "Have fun at Saint Ignatius."

At the time, Saint Ignatius High School was on Stanyan Street near Golden Gate Park's panhandle. One day it would accept girls, grow with the times, and demote certain mortal sins like masturbation, but for now, it was like a page torn out of a prisoner's notebook. The first week was full of confrontation: initiation, lectures on being pure Catholic youth, and leering bulky seniors with athletic block sweaters. Every morning, always cold and foggy, a freshman had to run a gauntlet on the red stairs.

"This one's short and skinny. How the hell did he get in?"

"Must be an intellectual. You know Latin, Shortie?"

"He doesn't have any glasses. He can't be an intellectual. Maybe this one's smart. What's your name, four eyes?"

"Cucherie."

"A Dago!"

I watched, waiting for Cucherie to say something. Then another boy, tall and muscular, walked up the stairs. He was the only black freshman, but they said nothing, only exchanged looks as Tom Manny walked past them.

When Cucherie, who sat behind me, wrote on my jacket with a pen, I confronted him on the yard. "Why did you scrawl on my jacket, Cucherie?"

"I felt like it. You wanna do something about it?"

I felt a murderous impulse, as Cucherie, short and dark with shiny black hair and large dark eyes, adjusted his glasses, blinding him for a moment. I swung on him and connected; he went down. He got up and swung on me, and then we were surrounded by a howling mob of seniors. Both of us went down, hitting the hard surface of the basketball court. The delicate novice priest who taught Spanish broke up the fight, pushing us apart with dainty hands; tearfully, he demanded an explanation.

"Just a friendly fight, Father."

"You will speak with the vice principal," he said with a pout, "Father Carlin!"

When the short blond priest left, a senior with a blobby face leaned close to me.

"You have to fight him up at the reservoir. It's a tradition, Freshman. Otherwise, you'll both be chicken shits for the rest of the year."

The reservoir sat in the park above the school. It was not really a reservoir but a rocky amphitheater where the seniors staged freshmen fights. Concentrating in class was difficult as repeated whispers informed the student body of the impending fight. What would Father do? I slammed my locker shut and saw older boys lurking at the end of the hall. The leather gang in *Rebel* came to mind. A tall, thin youth with a narrow hatchet face, sharp blue eyes, and ducktail hairstyle suddenly appeared beside me. He could see my fear and quickly held out his hand. The boys down the hall vanished, giggling.

"John Kopp. Relax. Listen, just sucker punch the dude."

It was a long walk to the park. Students gathered in a circle around the fighting area. A few people walked their dogs along the narrow paths. Across the street, a mailman delivered mail. Cucherie stood against a big rock, taking off his jacket, adjusting his glasses. He had sweat on his upper lip. I could feel a tightening in my lungs.

"He's blind without them glasses," Kopp whispered. "But watch out a senior don't cop a sunday on you."

Ray Reed, a handsome basketball star, stood in the center of the circle. Other boys were hooting and jeering as dust rose from their stamping feet.

"We have our first fight of the season, gentlemen. Anyone who backs off will deal with us. No cowards allowed at Saint Ignatius. Are we ready?"

Cheers indicated they were.

"No weapons, knives, no kicks below the belt, no hitting when a man is down. We just want a good old-fashioned fight. When I drop my bandanna, come out swinging and kick the shit outta the guy."

Ray Reed held a red bandanna. I walked toward Cucherie.

"Hey," I said. "I can't hit a man wearing glasses."

"We don't care," somebody screamed. "Hit him!"

Ray Reed lifted his hand when Tom Manny seized his wrist. In his other hand, he raised a small crucifix.

"This is a symbol of our religion. We are Catholics. We don't believe in fighting. We believe in turning the other cheek, remember?"

There was a shocked intake of breath, then a chorus of catcalls. Breaking the grip, Ray Reed stared at Tom Manny. Reed's mouth hung open.

"What the hell are you talking about? We got a code, here. They have to fight, so get outta the way."

"Christ would not want this."

"Christ's got nothin' to do with it!"

Manny turned and faced the howling boys. "Peace," he said, holding up the cross.

"Back off, nigger!" screamed Ray Reed.

There was a deadly silence, and I could suddenly hear the birds and distant traffic. Afternoon sun filtered through the trees. Tom Manny walked up to Ray Reed. "What did you say?"

"You heard me, jungle bunny!"

Tom Manny smiled. He put down the cross. For a moment, he

seemed sad, looking around at the circle of boys waiting for a fight. He shrugged once. Then he socked Ray Reed in the stomach. It seemed the whole amphitheater erupted into a mass brawl, like those staged in westerns. Cucherie was confused, standing in a swirl of boys, now trying to pull Tom Manny off Reed as he took off his shoe and hit him again, bloodying his handsome face. John Kopp took me by the arm and pulled me toward the path. For a moment, I imagined warriors cutting into a dead beached whale, painting themselves with blood, drinking strong liquors. Ray Reed struck Tom Manny, then a group of seniors blocked the two fighters; it was getting too dangerous. They could all be expelled. Ray Reed's marked face was a mask of outrage.

"We'll meet again, nigger."

"Sure, you white piece of shit."

Tom Manny threw the restraining boys away from him.

"Wait!" I was shocked how everyone stopped when I shouted in a theatrical voice. "It's over," I told them. I handed Tom Manny his cross. "Let's all go home."

* * *

JOHN Kopp drove a shellacked custom red Chevy with a suicide knob on the steering wheel. White leather covered the seats. He smoked despite his constant wheezing.

"You better learn to smoke," he insisted.

"I smoke."

"You got a rubber?"

"Excuse me?"

He flashed his wallet like a badge, the thin circle of the condom visible under the leather.

"No. I don't wear socks in the shower, either."

"It's a prop! You know Juicy Lucy, the girl at Notre Dame High School, the one with the big tits?"

"Lucy Bond? Yeah, I know her."

"I finally copped a feel last night. You ever cop a feel?"

"Of course," I said. "In fact, I had Lucy last night."

"Yeah?"

"I had her good."

Kopp laughed.

"How good?"

"Real good. You can watch, next time."

We drove down the steep 17th Street hill toward Market Street. Fog rolled in over Twin Peaks.

"Ray Reed is a punk," Kopp said. "I'd like to hit the son of a bitch."

He threw out his cigarette and breathed off an asthma inhaler, full lips sucking air into his thwarted lungs. Like Jimmy in *Rebel Without a Cause*, smoking was cool. It was also time to buy some rubbers.

I saw Father Carlin the next day; he was a big man in a black cassock, his blue eyes cold and pale, the face clean-shaven. He had thick, short hair the color of a strong oak. His voice was soft and light, giving his authority a sinister edge. He kept a heavy wooden paddle in his small office. Afternoon light came in the window.

"I heard about the fight from Father Belcher," he said. "I don't like to see freshmen fight, but I know it's part of being a man. I really don't like to see star athletes fighting. Ray Reed and Tom Manny are two reasons we may beat Sacred Heart this year."

He glared at me across his immaculate desk. "Why are you here?"

"My father got me in?"

"Very smart, but I think he's deluded into thinking you want to study for the priesthood or get a good Catholic education. I can see you won't help us beat Sacred Heart."

"I guess not...Father."

"I've instructed Mr. Cucherie to clean your jacket, but you will have to suffer the consequences for starting the fight on the yard. Here." He gave me a whistle. "You will kneel in front of my office. You will wear this little Jew beanie with a propeller on it, and you will blow this whistle on the hour. How are your knees?"

"I don't know."

"You need to visit the chapel more. Kneel down. Learn a little humility. You can't kid the cops, and I am one, young man!"

Kneeling in front of Carlin's office, I blew on the whistle every hour until school finished. As they passed by, one by one—Ray Reed with a swollen eye, Tom Manny, John Kopp and even an amused Cucherie—I felt a certain distance. Perhaps the distance was good. I didn't want to be among their number, and even recalled a line by Lord

Byron: "I stood among them but not of them." It was a good line despite the fact the jocks would make the news, get scholarships, play in a stadium to cheering fans. The girls would love them, though there were no girls at our school then. I rode home with the school scarecrow and fellow outsider, John Kopp.

"Well, at least no one beat your ass," Kopp said.

She was waiting on the corner, and when Lucy Bond slipped into Kopp's car and lit up a cigarette, I knew some girls liked boys who weren't jocks. Older now, she had a coarse beauty. In a B picture, she'd be a slut goddess.

"Those other girls…they think I'm a slut and whore," she told us.

"Well?"

Lucy reached over and playfully socked Kopp.

"Why do they think that?" he finally asked.

"Because I ride with you and this chump, here, who locked up the school door with a tie last year."

"That was Richard Boyle," I said.

"Ugly Boyle? He tried to get into my pants and failed." She dragged off the cigarette. "Threw up on me. What a pig." She looked over her shoulder. "You still livin' on 20th Street?"

"Yes," I said.

"I don't like the other girls," Lucy said, blowing smoke through her full lips. "And I don't put out for free, either."

Kopp reached in his pocket. "Honey, how much? I'll pay for it!"

This time, the slap was hard. "You can drop my ass off right now," she said.

"Sorry," Kopp said. "A nice ass, too."

Elbows on the back seat, I could see the swell of Lucy's beautiful breasts. She crossed her legs and leaned back, her blonde curls falling over the seat.

"Why don't you get a hot rod and be cool, too?" she asked. "I bet Boyle has one."

"Can't afford one, yet," I said. "I'm not old enough to drive alone."

"Neither is ugly old John, here."

For the first time, I realized John Kopp had to be driving illegally.

"I'm fifteen," said Kopp. "I got a learner's permit."

Lucy shook her head and laughed. "Where's your grown-up?"

I wanted to touch the cleavage her uniform couldn't conceal.

"My girlfriend's lookin' for a boyfriend."

Kopp was startled. "Mary? She's a skag, a dog! She's an ugly virgin."

"So are you."

"Hell if I am."

Lucy looked at me. I remembered Mary, always wearing her uniform with long skirts; she had reddish hair, blue eyes, freckles, braces on her teeth, and was obviously shy.

"You like Mary?"

"Mary?"

We had an indirect connection. The Catholic Youth had a high school dance club called the Dolorians, and they threw dances once a month. I remembered a dance held in the Mission Dolores auditorium, and Dolores Manny stood with a few white girls, looking at the boys who looked away. No one danced with her, and she didn't ask any of the boys to dance when it was lady's choice. Tom stood outside, not coming inside, already aware of the whispers: "They're all right, but what about their black friends? What if Tom dances with a white girl? Can't he bring a black girl of his own? Dolores is sure pretty but—"

Then I walked across the dance floor as Dolores turned to see me, her black hair curled in layers, her blue dress stylish and form-fitting. She smiled.

"Dance?"

"Sure," she said.

We danced to a slow song from the fifties as the other boys and girls watched, including Mary. There was an intensity in Mary's eyes. Nuns lurked on the perimeter of the dance floor. The music stopped, and I nodded to Dolores. Our only moment was over, and I walked back to a circle of smirking boys.

"Sure, I like Mary," I said. "But I need girls with experience."

Kopp laughed through his nose, teeth closed on a cigarette. Lucy stared at me.

"Since you ain't got none, I can see why," she offered. We drove on. Lucy Bond shook out her hair. "Don't judge Mary too quick. You'd be surprised."

We talked about *Rebel Without a Cause*.

"Wasn't it cool when he cried at the end?"

"My father thought it was a goofy picture," I said.

"You comb your hair just like James Dean," Lucy observed. "Too bad you ain't him."

"I'd rather be alive," I told her, thinking it was impossible James Dean was in his grave with only one more film left to see. There would never be another Dean. Then we heard the wailing liquid baritone on the car radio, the trembling sensuous voice singing with darkness and honey about a place called Heartbreak Hotel.

"Who's the black woman?" I asked.

"Just another blues bitch," said Kopp.

"That ain't no nigger woman," insisted Lucy. "That's a pretty white boy named Elvis Presley."

"What kind of a name is Elvis Presley?" I said, listening to a raw blues voice from a bordello of the gods. "Sounds like a fruit name."

Lucy cranked up the volume and the electric guitar screamed at us in staccato bursts. "He's a Memphis hillbilly," she shouted. "And he ain't no fruit. He can touch me anywhere he wants, anytime. I'll be smiling all day."

Lucy got out of the car, furtively slipping me a note to meet her in Dolores Park that night. I felt my heart throbbing as I walked down the path to find her sitting on the swings. A bitter wind blew in from the west. She wore a short skirt and a shirt opened so I could see a curve of breast from the side. She trailed her feet in the cold sand as I sat down next to her.

"I'm in love," she finally said.

"With John Kopp?"

"Hell no! With someone you know real good."

"Really? Who?"

"Ray Reed. You go to school with him, right? I seen him practicing on the courts at night. Maybe you could set up a meeting or something." She smiled for the first time. "I could set something up with Mary."

"Ray Reed is a prick."

Lucy was surprised. "Well listen to you. I guess I got to meet Mr. Handsome all by my lonesome. You jealous?"

"Maybe."

"I like bullies. And I bet you'd take me out behind John's back."

"Maybe."

"In what? You don't got no car."

"I don't have any car. But I will."

"You roller skate?"

"Sure."

"Maybe we could meet at Playland at the Beach. Go around a few times. If I get introduced real proper to Ray Reed, maybe me'n you could spend some time together."

I remained silent. It was cold in the park, and Lucy stood up. "I'm freezing. I gotta go." She looked at me. "You still a virgin?"

"I won't say that I am, I won't say that I ain't."

She laughed. "Don't forget what they say about ugly girls like Mary. All the ugly ones put out."

"How do you know?"

"I just know, just like I know you whack off every night."

"Never. That's a mortal sin," I said.

Lucy touched my face, then slapped me gently.

"You want me?"

"Maybe."

"You gonna think of me tonight?"

"Maybe."

"Maybe every night? I bet you dream about my tits. John Kopp does. He got a feel, but nothin' else." She touched her throat. "You wanna see them?"

"Sure."

It seemed like an eternity on that freezing playground at dusk, the white fog rolling across Twin Peaks looming over the Mission District of San Francisco as Lucy Bond slowly pulled open her shirt, exposing the beautiful full breasts with pink nipples now turning blue in the sharp wind. Then she snapped her shirt tight and laughed. She called out over her shoulder: "You want more, you introduce me to your buddy, Mr. Reed."

I shouted out to her: "Why bother with me? Just show him your tits."

Her laugh came back in the growing darkness. She was right, of course; my dreams would be full of bare, glistening breasts.

55

A week later, I saw Tom Manny and Ray Reed walking together. They had the athletic swagger I came to recognize.

"Ray, I gotta talk to ya."

Ray Reed stopped. He grinned, his fleshy lips pulling back from the perfect teeth, the eyes dull, like bog water. "About what, Skinny?"

"You know Lucy Bond?"

"Yeah, I know the bitch. What of it?"

"She wants to spend time with you. Asked me to set up a formal introduction."

"I don't need your help, freshman. She's the kind of cow you just fuck. You don't talk to it." Tom Manny shook his head and looked away.

"Hey, this is a warning. She puts out for everyone. Probably has the clap."

Ray Reed laughed, but there was a moment of fear in his eyes.

"I don't need your advice, okay? I can handle it."

"Can you handle her?" asked Tom Manny.

They walked off. After another week, I saw Lucy Bond sitting on the swings in the park. She had a darkness around her eyes as she looked at me. I sat down. Quietly, she began to cry.

"What's up?"

"Nothing. That shithead, Ray Reed, stood me up. I called the son of a bitch back, but he didn't have no explanation." She wiped her eyes in the biting wind. "He said he talked to you."

"Yeah, he did."

"What did you say to him?"

"That you were really nice, and that I liked you."

Lucy looked at me with a genuine surprise. She grinned.

"You're sweet. I'm sorry I've been such a bitch."

"You're just fine," I said.

"I know I ain't smart. Why did he stand me up like that? I ain't used to men doing me that way. I mean, Kopp would die if I put out for him. He'd just die."

We sat in silence, wind blowing over grass and sand.

"I bet you'd die, too."

I grinned. "I think you're right."

"Mary's expecting you to call. Man, she'd give you the loving of a

56

lifetime. She's been building up to it for a year now. I swear, them nuns make all of us want to be whores!"

"Or else nuns."

Lucy shook her head.

"Not this ole' girl." Her voice dropped a note. "Maybe I should put out for you. Steal a car and maybe you can steal me."

I pulled up my coat collar against the cold.

"My dad's giving me some lessons this summer. Hey, for now, let Kopp be the wheel boy. I could do you in the back seat and give him a few pointers."

Lucy laughed, and then began crying, again. "I feel like shit, but I'll get over it."

"You have to."

"You're a real loyal friend," she said. "I won't forget you. Let's talk next week sometime. I feel too sick right now to even think straight."

She kissed me on the cheek and walked away. I watched her, feeling a sinking dark sadness inside. Did adolescent lovers always fail? This could have been a scene in a movie never shot starring Ricky Nelson and Tuesday Weld.

"Loyal friend," I said. "Jesus."

Father was reading his newspaper when I came home.

"Lothario returns."

"I beg your pardon?"

"How's your new girlfriend?"

"She isn't a girlfriend. She's just a friend."

"Mary sounded pretty hot to me," he said. "Aren't you a little young to be getting calls from anxious girls?" He looked up from his paper. "What's wrong?"

"Nothing. I was with someone else."

"What a rogue," he said.

"No, I'm just an asshole."

I was expecting Father to get angry, but he only stared at me as I walked to my room.

There was a store up the street from Saint Ignatius where boys met to smoke and talk in the morning fog. Smoking was against school rules, but no one seemed to care if they smoked beyond the school grounds. Boys stood in clusters, smoking, watching the morning traffic.

Ray Reed had become a hero, hitting a basket with moments to go in the championship game. He stood there, holding the ball, watching the hoop, the players frozen in a glorious moment before the ball swished through the basket and the buzzer sounded. Ray Reed was also flunking physics taught by Father Spoan.

"He's a conceited prick," Reed said. "Jesus, no matter what I do, he's out to flunk me. I can't go to college or play pro ball if I don't graduate from high school."

"You'll have to write out the physics book," someone said. "Spoan hates young boys with talent."

Father Spoan had thinning hair, a jowly face with thick spectacles, and a bulky, square body. His eyes were cold, opaque, without humor, and he had a mechanical quality to his movements. I smoked, feeling the sharp bite in my lungs, watching Ray Reed walk back to the school. I knew the smoke could trigger an asthma attack. Later that afternoon, I met John Kopp on the school roof and looked out over the city toward the avenues. There was a low wall with no guard rail but no student had ever jumped.

"We got the religious retreat next week," Kopp said. "We'll hear warnings about sex, but never any details about the dirty deed, and they'll bring up Jimmy Dean to get our attention about temporal life and sudden death. Then the speech on hell."

"The speech on hell by James Joyce in *Portrait*?"

"Who?" said Kopp.

"James Joyce."

"Who the hell's James Joyce?"

"Shortstop for Cleveland."

"Never heard of him. You like English, don't you?"

"Yeah."

I hate it—and Latin. If Cicero was such a great speaker, why did they kill his ass?"

"For his bad speeches."

The retreat began in the chapel. Kopp was right about James Dean. The bishop raged about mortality and the horrors of hell. After listing hell's torments—the demons, the fire, the stench—he described the chickie run in *Rebel*, the young boy's sleeve caught on the door handle of the death car, the plunge off the cliff, and Dean himself meeting his end on a windy highway in California. The eyes of the old bishop blazed at the young boys, driven by the sexual nightmares of adolescence.

"Where is Dean's soul, now? Where will your soul be? Will you give it all up to be Elvis Presley?" His voice thundered in the chapel. Jesus hung on the cross above his head. "Will you risk hellfire for a passing headline? Will you lose your soul for an hour of sexual pleasure?"

"How can you make it last an hour?" whispered Kopp.

Quiet and meek, we left the chapel.

Columbini masturbated daily, preferably through Father Roubidoux's religion section, and always with extraordinary discretion. Until his legend began to grow, few students even knew of Columbini, a husky youth with short blond hair and glasses who rarely spoke. He slipped his fingers into his pockets while Father Roubidoux droned on about the Beatific Vision. Would not the 'Beatific vision' in heaven grow boring after awhile was today's silent question. Columbini's other hand carried a Kleenex and his expression never changed, even at the big moment, the opaque eyes staring ahead while Roubidoux launched into his favorite lecture about human frailty.

"Self abuse is a mortal sin and must be avoided. If you succumb to this disgusting submission to bestial instincts, accompanied by loathsome fantasies, it must be confessed! Otherwise, you get a ticket to hell. Any questions?"

Roubidoux's old sagging face and bulging eyes roved the classroom. Welsh raised his hand; he had slow, deliberate speech. Columbini sat in his seat, playing pocket pool with barely perceptible movements.

"Yes, Mr. Welsh?"

"What is self abuse? Like he's hitting hisself?"

"Don't kid the cops!" shouted Roubidoux.

"I don't understand."

"Self abuse is the solitary use of the genitive faculty."

"Genitive faculty? What is that?"

"Sit down, Mr. Welsh. I will call your mother today if I hear any more of this filthy talk!"

Welsh looked around the classroom. The other boys turned away, covering their mouths.

"Well, what the hell *is* self abuse?"

Columbini shuddered in his chair, eyes suddenly intense behind his glasses. He bellowed: "Jacking off. It's jacking off!"

A hush gripped the classroom. Father Roubidoux swelled up like a cartoon blowfish. He sputtered: "Columbini, to the office. To Father Carlin's office!"

Columbini left. Father Roubidoux, his cassock always too loose, suddenly got up and followed him out the door.

"Is that what it is?" said Welsh. "I guess I'm going to hell. Shit, all of us is going to hell—on a landslide."

* * *

ONE night, Father, anxious to talk, held a class paper.

"Mr. Becker called. He said you wrote a comic short story about a young boy who gets killed in a car crash after a wild night and dies without confessing."

"The theme was the wages of sin leading to death."

"But a comic story?"

"I added the humor to make it interesting."

"Humor? Mr. Becker wanted a serious short story with a moral. When the boy's mangled body—"

"Mangled?"

"—that's how it's described...when the boy's mangled body is found with a rosary and a...a package of rubbers in his pocket, I think you're supposed to make the point that if the boy had said his rosary, he'd be alive and in a state of Sanctifying Grace."

"Right. I was being ironic."

"Ironic? Mr. Becker seems to think you're questioning why the boy had the rosary in the first place. I hope you're not suggesting he was better off with the girl instead of saying his Hail Marys in the chapel."

"Not at all."

Father watched me, holding the story between first finger and thumb. His face was pale in the kitchen light. He had spent many nights at the kitchen table solving difficult bonus questions from my algebra class.

"What do you know about rubbers?"

60

"Modern Youth and Chastity class teaches about the evils of birth control. They never specifically mention rubbers. Have you ever used one?"

"Look here, I know this is some kind of a joke. Mr. Becker found the reference to rubbers—prophylactics—very offensive."

"I'll rewrite it."

Father stared at me. "Where are you going tonight?"

"John Kopp wants to go for a ride."

"I bet he does. You stay home and rewrite that nasty story."

Father poured some vodka into a glass and added tonic.

"I thought you took the pledge."

"I need a nip."

"Aunt Vee will be mad."

"I'll take care of Veronica."

He gave me the short story.

"No rides tonight. Straighten this out for Mr. Becker. I don't want him to think I got a jokester for a son."

"I never joke with the Jesuits."

"That's a good policy. What else do they teach in that chastity class?"

"That sex before marriage is a sin, and could cause the generation of a child. They don't go into detail."

"Thank God for that."

"How could I generate a child? Can you tell me?"

Kopp gunned his motor in the street. "Don't stay out late," Father said.

John Kopp had added moon hub caps and twin pipes to his cherry red Chevy. I ran across the street and got inside the smoky car, "Sea of Love" blasting from the radio speakers. Lucy sat in the front seat, smoking, flashing her full-lipped, sensuous smile, tossing her hair back over the white leather. Mary Callahan sat in the back, her hands resting in the lap of her long plain skirt. She smiled nervously. Her eyes were guarded above the thin lips and small freckled nose.

"Hello," she said.

John Kopp palmed the dancing naked lady on the suicide knob, turning the wheel, whipping the car around, the Chevy laying a smoking twin strip of rubber going up 20th street. For some reason, I remembered a sepia-toned wedding photo of my grandparents and how innocent and serious they looked.

"Boy, I can imagine what my granddad would've said if he saw me in this car."

"Hey, forget that old time boogie. Live for now."

Kopp drove the loud souped car over steep hills. Lucy drank from a bottle while Mary sat quietly, tapping her foot to the music.

"It's nice to see you," she said.

We were driving toward Twin Peaks and lover's lane.

"I finally got Ray Reed outta my craw," Lucy shouted over the singing and the rumbling engine. "Mr. Thrill is history."

"Good," said Kopp. Some Elvis heat came on the radio and Kopp turned it up. Lucy began to rock in the seat, drinking.

"How are you, Mary?" I said.

"Sick of school. Sick of nuns."

She smiled, her braces gleaming in the light-split darkness.

"Mary's sick of a lot of things and honey, so am I!"

We drove to the top of Twin Peaks overlooking San Francisco and the distant bay. Fog rolled through the Golden Gate Bridge. On the hill, many cars were parked, windows fogged, the lights out.

"Why don't you two love birds sit in front?" said Kopp. "Give me'n Lucy more room."

Lucy was still laughing, her gleaming lips sucking from the whiskey bottle. She passed the bottle back.

"Why should I git in the back seat with ugly old you?" she said. "You skinny geek!"

"Because I'm the backdoor man."

They got into the back seat; there was a sudden draft as we got out and climbed into the front seat. Mary sat, peering through the fogged window. A pair of dice hung from the rear view mirror. Kopp's hatchet face suddenly appeared beside me, the shiny ducktail hair and mischievous eyes an image of the 50's American teenager. He held two blankets.

"Take a blanket, man. Warm you up if you go outside."

"Why should we go outside?"

"The front's a little cramped," he said with a hoarse asthmatic laugh. Lucy grinned, suddenly taking his face in her hands, kissing him.

62

Moments later, they were lying beneath the blanket, Kopp's wheezing punctuated by Lucy's occasional moans. The car began to rock.

Mary held the bottle between her legs. She licked her lips. "Want a drink?"

"Sure."

I took a drink. It burned going down.

"Boy, this is firewater!"

Mary took a long slow swig, swallowing the raw whiskey. She turned to face me, her eyes suddenly bold and defiant.

"The nuns are always warning us to save our precious pearl for a husband, but they don't go into any detail. Just what is a 'pearl'? They use words like 'penetration' and 'impure violation.' We're taught that intercourse before marriage is a mortal sin. Right, Lucy?"

There was a gurgle of surprise from Lucy, buried under Kopp's wiry body. She grunted: "Yeah, sure."

"Lucy's busy. I've been figuring out which impurities of the flesh are not mortal sins. Like, what's an impure act that's a mere venial sin? Finger fucking? Blow jobs? Up the ass?"

Mary snorted. Lucy's laughter was smothered by Kopp's loud, wet kisses. Mary's speech was slurred: "Of course, no one wants to be what they quaintly call, 'P.G.' or pregnant. Or a whore. But secretly, like most boys, I think a lot of girls question being virgins, too. You know, the nuns, in not being specific, give us some leeway to experiment." She licked a drop of whiskey from the bottle. "Have a snort?"

We sat in the close warmth of the car. I took another drink, feeling the fire rush through veins, face, brain. Mary reached over and began kissing with abandon. The braces were hard and metallic, her thin lips suddenly full and wet. She probed with her tongue, her breath strong with the whiskey. The flesh of her thighs was smooth under the long skirt; she knew when to withdraw her mouth, when to kiss lightly, when to explore. There seemed to be a voluptuous presence between us, a dark swooning fired by whiskey.

"Press in," she said, turning to kiss me.

It felt warm, wet, giving softly like delicate petals. Her hand moved down, slender fingers gently closing over cloth, sliding down the zipper, then sliding in. Mary lowered her head. Kopp's voice broke over us. "Jesus H. Christ! Lucy baby!"

63

Mary suddenly pushed open the door, taking the blanket with her. Kopp's wheezing filled the car as Lucy made a muffled cry deep in her throat beneath Kopp's animal surge. I followed Mary out into the swirling ghostly fog. Other cars were still parked, the windows steamed, a few cars rocking. I found Mary wearing the blanket and staring down the grassy hill.

"Sorry, but I can't do it in a car."

I sat down.

"We were going too far, anyway," she said. "I can't go all the way, not yet. You have any protection?"

"No."

"Jesus. A car of your own?"

"Got my eye on a Studebaker."

"A friend with a place?"

"No."

She took my hand. "You must hate me."

"No. It was exciting."

"But frustrating?"

I reached for a cigarette. It was difficult to light it in the wind. The smoke had a pungent taste.

"Gimme one."

"You don't smoke."

"Let me try."

She began coughing. "I wish I still had the bottle," she said. "I do like that."

"I like it, too."

She rubbed my shoulder. "I appreciate you asking Dolores to dance that night. None of those other punks would."

"Dolores is very pretty."

"But you never went back to the dances."

"No. I never did. I just didn't fit into that club."

"Neither did I. Maybe we can...we can experiment."

"Like how?"

The wind blew thick white fog over Twin Peaks, touching the face and hands with particles of moisture.

"Get under the blanket."

"Okay."

64

There was a sadness in her eyes. Then Mary smiled.

"I like to be in control. Let me touch you."

"Okay."

Her hand moved with delicate precision, her mouth open.

"Now touch me. Move in a circle. Kiss me...and then I'll kiss it."

We kissed, moving together, hands exploring.

"A little faster. Yes. Don't stop!"

The Chevy's springs creaked loudly as the car rushed down upon us, bouncing noisily, some muffled screams coming from inside. In the fog, it looked like a metal monster with dead eyes. We rolled away from the runaway car that turned to one side, suddenly flipping, rolling over down the grassy slope.

Mary lurched against me as I stood up and ran down the hill, carrying the blanket, others shouting from the ridge, another man appearing out of the mist, running after the rolling car. With each roll, it seemed to turn over more slowly, then finally stopped, its wheels still spinning, the crushed upside-down car yards from the winding dark road below.

Lucy appeared in the window, her face bloody, her naked shoulders and breasts pushing past the cracked glass. The man ahead reached out to her, then jumped back. "Jesus Christ," he said. He backed away, cursing again.

I was close enough to smell leaking gasoline.

Lucy struggled to free herself from the wreck when flames suddenly exploded like a car bombed in a gangster movie. Blossoms of fire appeared on her naked back and legs as she crawled clear of the Chevy, now a white hot mass with no sound inside it, save the roaring fire. I threw the blanket over her, then felt the sudden burst of heat, the blanket catching fire as well.

Someone pulled me back. People were shouting, but I never heard the voices; others ran through the glare. The car continued to burn, the flames spiraling upward into the cold, foggy night with an eerie silence. The moon hubcaps popped off. People gathered around the smoking body still rolling in the damp grass as Lucy began screaming. The sound of a fire engine siren rose, getting closer, wailing.

Father came down to the police station to pick me up after the first round of questioning, but I couldn't tell the story again. Lucy Bond went from a hospital to a burn center; John Kopp, leg broken, had burned to death inside the blazing car. Two days later, the police came to Saint Ignatius. Father Carlin stood in front of his office with Mr. Becker, wearing a spotless soutane; they watched as I passed with the police, turning as we left the school, a few boys stopping a basketball game to watch us get in a police car.

At the station, young boys stood in the police line-up.

"Please step forward." The cop looked at me. "A witness said a kid from a rival school unlocked the emergency brake as a prank. Some prank. If convicted, he'll serve some time. Take a gander and tell me if you recognize anyone."

One boy appeared nervous; his blond crew cut and poor complexion were bloodless under the harsh light.

"I didn't see anybody. We were on the hill."

The cop looked at Mary: "You?"

"No," said Mary. "I didn't see a thing."

"We have no useable prints on the brake. Take another look."

None of the boys looked familiar and we finally left the station. Mary was silent, not glaring at me, fighting tears; we embraced before she left.

"It wasn't our fault," I insisted.

"My mom won't let me go to John's funeral."

"It should be packed," I said. "Please come."

Only Mr. Becker came to the funeral. Kopp's parents sat alone in the big, empty church. I remembered how he died, and wondered why his classmates didn't attend the service as they had when another student died of leukemia. There were no student pallbearers. I sat next to Father, watching the single coffin; the priest knelt before the altar and then entered the pulpit to lament another lost generation. Mr. Becker had a pleasant face, with dark unruly hair and large dark eyes. He met me outside the church as Father stood to one side, smoking, talking quietly with the stunned parents.

"After this is over, I think you're ready for some new books. One by Hemingway, one by Fitzgerald, and a challenging one by Faulkner."

"Where is the class?"

"His death was questionable."

"Questionable? Like Ophelia's in *Hamlet*? Was there some secret order to keep S.I. students away from John's funeral?"

"I don't think so. The boy who confessed saw the Saint Ignatius decal on John's bumper, and said John and the girl were humping in the car." Mr. Becker whispered out of the side of his mouth: "Remember your clever short story? Despite that, you and the girl resisted temptation, and were spared."

"So John's in hell, is that it?"

"That is God's judgment and decision."

"Maybe you all should go to hell," I said.

Mr. Becker said nothing.

At school, I walked past boys gathered by the store, blocking the entrance, watching the traffic. Ray Reed was still negotiating with Father Spoan to pass physics.

"Hey, skinny geek, how is Mary Callahan?"

I stopped. Ray Reed strutted over.

"I haven't seen her much since the accident."

"Why not? She's a dog like Lucy, and won't put out, but she does everything else. Very talented girl." Ray Reed popped some gum in his mouth, his eyes full of a playful malevolence. "Least John Kopp got laid. If you can't score with Blow Job Callahan, you're in trouble. I hear she wants to be a nun. You might want to score before she gives it all up for God."

I reached for Reed's collar, even as he backed up.

"Whoa, our little boy is angry."

"Fuck you."

For a moment, Ray Reed seemed too startled to react. He suddenly caught my wrist.

"You want me to break this, huh?"

"Hey! You slow down, Ray." It was Tom Manny again. "What the hell is wrong with you? Leave him alone, man. He lost a friend. You best be thinkin' about passing physics."

Ray Reed backed away. "You got off easy, punk."

I spit. "You're the punk, Reed. You'll never make the pros. In two years, you'll be a drunk, delivering pizza."

I got on the bus. I wanted to see Lucy Bond, but they had moved her to a burn center out of town. Mary was in seclusion, and I wondered if I would see her again. The bus began to move.

* * *

I stood across the street from the gray Carmelite convent as they brought Mary Callahan into a stone garden plaza behind iron gates. Mary's parents also watched as one of the nuns began to cut Mary's hair, shearing away the thick locks before she would disappear into a cell for long days and nights of meditation, talking to no one but God and other nuns for the rest of her life. Stone gargoyles glared down from the roof.

The nun worked quickly; Mary had no expression on her face as they cropped her hair but stared ahead with a pleasant empty passivity. When they finished, Mary looked once through the gate at her parents. A single tree cast a manta-like shadow on the double doors. Her head looked very naked with the hair chopped. Mary's eyes may have rested briefly on those who remembered a lost night in a car parked on lover's lane, her lips wet from whiskey and kisses. The tallest nun turned Mary around and they marched into the cloister, the thick doors slamming shut. Another nun swept the hair. I stared at the brick building, wondering if the accidental death of a youth in a burning car had driven Mary to accept the harsh life of the reclusive nuns. I remembered the playful defiance in Mary's penetrating eyes, the sensual urgency of a panting adolescence that was now gone.

It was growing dark and cold in the street; after awhile, I walked away, wondering if Mary would brand me as a sinner, remembered only in her prayers. Rapid footsteps came up behind me. "Don't walk away, stranger. Talk to me."

I turned. An attractive woman in her late twenties stood in the street. She wore a modest long skirt, blouse and sweater and except for the wimple and veil, would go unnoticed as a nun. Her eyes were familiar.

"Do I know you?"

"I think so. Are you still bound in a nutshell? Most agnostics are."

"My God—Sister Ann Maureen!"

She laughed and embraced me. "You can call me SAM if you like."

"That's Boyle's nickname."

She stepped back. "I'm glad you have an interest in young girls joining the order. The Carmelites are a bit too strict for my tastes. That convent looks like a prison out of Dickens."

"I knew Mary."

"I know."

"You were teaching her?"

"No. I've been away learning Spanish, but I did counsel her one afternoon. She mentioned you. Then I read about the accident and—but why don't we get some coffee? Wait, are you allowed to drink it?"

"Coffee it is."

We walked to a nearby café. College students sat playing chess, and a hobo hunched over coffee. A few young girls from Notre Dame High School sat at a table and glanced at us. Sister Ann Maureen moved with a certain confidence and freedom. Brown hair flowed from under the veil. She spooned sugar into her coffee and met my eyes.

"You look good."

"So do you."

"You've grown, but you're still a boy. Good. I like innocence."

"I'm not so innocent."

Her face turned serious for a moment.

"Okay. You're not. You are alive. And you still like literature?"

"Yes."

"And you're going to a Jesuit school?"

"I am, and they're making me into a little enemy of the Catholic Church."

She remained quiet for a moment. "Maybe you'll outgrow your anger."

I leaned forward. "I don't want to outgrow it."

We drank coffee. Then she guided the conversation skillfully into non-confrontational subjects. She asked about Father. She was learning Spanish to work with Chile's poor. She had decided to give up the nun's habit and dress closer to the people. She realized young people had to rebel.

"Maybe I'm a rebel, too. A lot of nuns think it's scandalous to wear street clothes and go dancing. I even have a beer now and then. I don't want the Church to be irrelevant and old hat. I say dump the Latin. Speak in the language of the people."

I remembered the high Mass, the chants, the vestments and Latin.

"If you're going to have an empty ritual, why not keep the Latin?"

"Empty ritual, huh?"

She nodded to herself and looked past me.

"Tell me about Mary."

"You first," she said, smiling again.

I told her about the night of the accident.

"What a terrible thing to happen. Mary did come to me briefly. She simply confessed she was a horny young woman and what to do about it? I told her that if she became sexually active, she had to get a diaphragm."

Sister Ann Maureen noticed my surprise.

"It's against Church doctrine, but I think unwanted children in the world is a worse sin—in fact, it's a crime. She didn't indicate any interest in becoming a nun, but Mary was very intense in her feelings." It was dark outside the window. "Are you sexually active? God, I hope not."

"Are you kidding? If there's an orgy, they send me out to wash the grapes."

It was good to hear her rich laugh. "Your humor will save you."

Some Latino gang members entered the café. They went to a rival school and saw my SI jacket. Despite hostile stares, Sister continued: "You think Mary's wasting her life, right? Murmuring prayers at the moon?"

"I don't know what I think."

She turned and addressed the glowering young men in Spanish. I saw the cigarette appear between her dainty fingers.

"*Buenas tardes, guapos hombres. Puede encendedor? Tiene fósforo?*" The young men smiled and the tallest lit her cigarette. "*Gracias.*"

When they left us, she took a puff and coughed.

"I hate smoking but it seems to make friends. I feel guilty giving them away. Now, about Mary. She's probably devastated with guilt over your friend, John Kopp. But she's channeled her intense feelings into a love of God."

"Oh yes—the Supreme Being."

"That sounds like Sister Constancha, but she was right. God is the one who made us. We serve."

"A God with a million-mile-long white beard and galaxies for sandals?"

70

She put out the cigarette. Then she took our cups for a refill. When she sat down, her approach was again non-confrontational.

"How old are you? Fifteen?"

"A little older than that."

"All right. Older. You're still so young to worry about these things."

"I don't worry about it. My dad believes in all that stuff. Resurrections and virgin births. No offense, but it still doesn't make sense to me."

"Look, don't you love the story of King Arthur?"

"Yeah."

"Don't you feel bad when his dream of the Round Table is smashed by cruel knights?"

"Yes."

"When Lancelot saves Guenivere from the fire, don't you cry with Arthur when he rejoices at her rescue even though his heart is breaking that she loves someone else?"

It was a touching scene in the famous story.

"Do you believe King Arthur and Camelot existed?"

I shrugged. "I guess not."

It was her turn to shrug. "Does it make any difference? It's a great story and it moves you. King Arthur and his twelve knights out to make the world right. I'm motivated by a great story to move the world and make it a better place, even if just a little. Make sense?"

"I guess. Can you live without a man?"

Her gaze was suddenly strong and confrontational.

"Other than Jesus? God, yes."

"Could I bum a cigarette?"

Crossing herself, Sister Ann Maureen closed her eyes. "Contributing to a minor's bad habit. One who's asthmatic, yet."

She gave me a cigarette and I produced a match.

"I have to go. I'm traveling with an older nun who will be displeased to see me here talking to a young boy, smoking cigarettes and drinking coffee. Say hello to Richard Boyle if you see him. The convent will know where I am."

"If you see Mary, say hello."

Sister Ann Maureen leaned back in the chair, her face pretty in the café light.

"She's locked away from the world. I know that makes you sick, but perhaps Mary doesn't think of herself as dispossessed. She can kneel before her new bridegroom, Jesus Christ. His naked body, covered only with a loin cloth, always bleeds profusely on the cross, and with Communion, Mary can take that body and blood into her mouth. She'll swallow the pain and degradation. Isolated in her Spartan cell, Mary will be closer to God and more happiness than any she ever knew outside. Jesus can touch her whole trembling being, and taking him into her heart, Mary can love us all, and all will be redeemed."

I took a breath. "Boy, that sounds pretty racy."

Sister Ann Maureen broke out into her deepest laugh. Then she stood up.

"I hope we meet again. I know you'll keep reading and next time, we can have a real religious argument. You're more spiritual than you realize."

"Be careful in those Latin American countries. I keep hearing stories about violent revolutions."

"I'll be careful. And I'll do my work. Good-bye. I miss all you boys—even that secular Mr. Boyle."

She was moved and I felt sad shaking her firm hand. Then I was alone in the bright, cheap café. I walked home and waved at Mr. Dooley, watching the street from his window post. In another town, doctors would scrape scar tissue from Lucy Bond's second and third degree burns.

I sat up late that night, listening to Jimmy Reed's twelve-bar blues, reveling in what the Jesuits labeled, "jungle music." Something moved inside with the throbbing beat and piercing harmonica. Then I turned it down since Father slept in another room. The garden photo of him holding a toddler while his parents stood close hung on the wall. Another photo showed me at eight with Mother standing behind, grinning, as Grandmother Agnes sat smiling on a couch. I look like I'm dancing—hips out—wearing an oversize cowboy shirt, suspenders and jeans. Mother's bleached hair and white blouse with pearls fit the black and white photo, her nails dark as she tries to hold me. Agnes wears a dress with buttons down the side. As I examine the photo, it's interesting that Mother is even there. A brief visit, perhaps, or a holiday? How deceiving old photos can be, and how odd to stare at an earlier image, wondering who the laughing child is.

A streetcar rolled behind the house, rattling above the now-dead garden that Agnes had nurtured. I didn't want to think about John Kopp in his grave and the burning red Chevy.

CHAPTER THREE

SUMMER WAS THE WORST TIME.

At night, there was a silent yearning for something unseen. Keats had written about the mysterious "fair creature of an hour," and this voluptuous creature with curving thighs and full breasts invaded all dreams.

Every summer, Father took me to either the Russian River or Clear Lake resort areas. Swimming was Father's physical art form, and he swam with Olympic style. Home movies show a man with rhythmic beauty cutting through the water with powerful strokes and invisible kicking. He built his own legend of nearly being a contender in the 1932 Olympics, with Johnny Weissmuller as his arch rival, though Father was too young and Weissmuller had left Olympic competition to star as Tarzan of the Apes. In 1936, when Father was twenty and the Depression gripped the country, he had to find work and abnegate dreams of gold medals. From a childhood hero, Weissmuller became a phantom nemesis, an image of someone he could or should have been. Weissmuller's swimming in the *Tarzan* films was open for ridicule: too much splashing and grandstand head-tossing, too much water being thrown around. I often imagined Father as a handsome Tarzan on celluloid, playing one of my early heroes in books and on the radio. Only *Tarzan* aficionados knew that Tarzan spoke French; Father's life-long fascination with that language might have added a realistic touch to the movie image of the ape man.

Collin's Resort allowed Jews. The nuns called them "Christ Killers" until Pope John XXIII lifted the blame for Christ's crucifixion from them. In school Biblical texts, they were caricatured as evil-looking creatures with big noses and cruel eyes. I had never seen an actual Jew, though I grew up thinking the word 'Jew' was a noun *and* a verb. A clever customer would "Jew down" a salesman.

The tall, thin man wearing a beanie, which I discovered later was a Yarmulke, came into the resort selling fruit; he had a beard. I had never

74

seen any of Father's Irish friends with beards. The man sold some fruit, and as our eyes met, he dropped one. He seemed to sense my morbid fascination, even as I bought some tangerines.

When he left, Father told me, "That was a Jew."

"Really?"

"Now don't stare!"

I watched the gaunt man with the beanie walk down a road shadowed by trees. Facing the lake, Father turned to another guest sitting in the shade with a young girl. A heavy-set woman got up and walked back to her cabin.

"That's his first Jew," Father said. "I don't mind Jews. You might be one yourself."

"I am a Jew," the man explained. "Abe Harris. My daughter, Lynn."

"Then I guess that was his second Jew. Or third Jew."

Abe was a short, squat man with thinning hair, dark skin, legs slightly bowed, and a hook nose; he came from a place he called "New Yawk."

"That was my wife who left. She hates the sun."

Father and Abe talked, discussing horse racing, the condition of the world, and my worsening asthma. Lynn Harris had thick black hair and dark eyes. Occasionally, Abe Harris called out to people in passing boats: "How many got hurt in that wreck?" A few boaters laughed, while others seemed unamused.

"If I was born a Jew, I wouldn't have failed," Father joked.

"What is failure? Just don't live up to cultural clichés."

"The Irish are cultural clichés, but I hear ya talkin'," Father said. "You been in swimming?"

"Can't swim," Abe said. "Don't like it."

"You should like it. I was a champion swimmer, once. I even beat Weissmuller."

"Who?"

"Johnny Weissmuller, Olympic champ in 1924 and 1928."

"Before my time," Abe said. "You beat him, eh?"

"Yeah. He was undefeated but took on all challengers at the 1939 World's Fair, and I beat him by about a length. In his prime, he did fifty yards in 23 seconds and I did it in about 22."

"Twenty-two seconds to cover fifty yards? Any girls' swim team

75

could beat that," Abe said. He looked over at us and winked.

"That's debatable. Anyway, Mr. Tarzan himself got out of the pool and said to me, 'You swim faster than I ever did.' And where the hell is he now?"

"I think he's doing Jungle Jim on TV."

Father took out a cigarette. "And where am I? The mailroom."

"I was gonna be a lawyer and I sell wigs. Not noble but it's good dough. You know, I might retire in Israel," Abe said. "I think Lynn needs to spend time on a kibbutz, learn what it means to be a real Jew. Israeli Jews are so different from American Jews. More people want to kill us."

"I understand," Father said. "I've forgotten what it means to be a Mick."

"Go back to Ireland," said Abe. "Lovely country. Everything happens in a pub."

I had recovered from a bad asthma attack and sat reading while my cousin swam in the lake. Lynn sat across from me in a bathing suit, watching with her dark, luminous eyes; they were like points of light, her smile spontaneous. I suddenly laughed.

"What's so funny?"

"A drunk in this book tells a bull fighter that bulls have no balls." I stopped, looking at Lynn, who didn't blush. "Pardon my French."

"God, he's reading Hemingway."

"I met him in Spain," said Abe, "when I fought with the Abe Lincoln Brigade. He drank too much. Good shot, though."

"*For Whom the Bell Tolls* is the best," admitted Father. "The sleeping bag scene."

I put down the book. I was beginning to live in the story.

"*The Sun Also Rises* is the one I was told to read."

Father scoffed: "Hemingway's okay but overrated. Too simple. And Faulkner's all over the joint. Thomas Wolfe, now. He could write."

"A little wordy," Abe insisted. "'Oh lost' this, and 'Oh lost' that."

"I like bombast." Father lit his cigarette. "I heard Hemingway was a fruit."

Abe seemed surprised. "Really? Macho Ernie?"

"All a front." Father looked at me. "How do you like it? The book?"

Father rarely asked my opinion.

76

"It's growing on me...all these empty people drinking and eating in cafés. How can a man write like a racing form and still be good?"

"Spoken like a professor," Father said. "His dialogue is supposed to be realistic but it sounds like dialogue to me. 'Lunch was excellent,'" he continued, slipping into a parody. "'But we drank the wine to forget the cowardly bulls of Madrid.'"

"Yes," Abe said, picking up the routine. "'The bulls of Pamplona were strong, but the bulls of Madrid obscenitied in the milk of their mothers.'"

"'And with the rain came the cholera,'" Father added. He laughed and glanced at Abe, suddenly serious. "In honor of that drunk, Ernie, I need a drink."

"Good idea," said Abe. "All that stuff about Jews never drinking is a myth."

"Really? I drink only on vacation."

As they walked toward the neighborhood tavern, Abe called out to a passing luxury boat. "How many got hurt in that wreck?" I knew that Father would drink and possibly get drunk, and then the pattern might start again—his long, rambling discussions and arguments, and his potential for accidents or fights, though he wasn't a mean drunk, only an irritating one. He never missed work, and he prided himself on always being well-dressed and well-groomed. He could count the days and months spent dry.

Lynn sat up, stretching. I had felt her eyes as I read Hemingway, tuning out the conversation. She leaned forward. "Are you bored?"

"No," I said. "Well, maybe."

Lynn smiled, crossing her bare legs.

"I didn't want to come here, but maybe we can all have fun. How's your breathing?"

"Better," I said. "When it's bad, it's really bad."

"I hate my father's cigars." She slipped a pin into her thick hair. Lynn's breasts rode up as she adjusted the pin. Then she got up, reaching out her hand.

"Let's go for a walk."

We walked along the lake as it was growing dark. Lynn had a melodious voice, with a slight eastern edge.

"What's a kibbutz?"

"It's like a communal farm in Israel. Dad forgets I've been to Hebrew School."

"Oh yeah? I survived Jesuits.".

"Survived?"

"Catholics are taught that everything's bad. We love guilt."

"So do Jews."

"We're taught that sex is a major sin."

"Really? After marriage?"

"Before marriage. Outside of marriage. Maybe even *after* marriage."

Lynn seemed amused with this answer. "Then why do Catholics have so many kids?"

"Good point."

Lynn looked out at the darkening lake.

"Your cousin might like my girlfriend, Betty."

We walked on.

"Lynn? What's your favorite subject in school?"

"Science. I believe in knowledge through experimenting."

"My favorite subject is—"

"English."

"You noticed. I like theatre, too."

Lynn tossed her head and laughed. "I know. You're also theatrical."

"You notice a lot things."

A steady breeze blew off the lake, and we sat down to watch the rolling whitecaps. We were still sitting there when her mother found us. She said nothing, but Lynn nodded and they walked to their cabin. That night, I went to sleep, thinking of Lynn's eyes, the perfume of her hair and the strong feel of her hand.

In the morning, Father swam across the lake, smooth and flat. By noon, there would be many speed boats and water skiers on the lake; he swam with a steady graceful movement, disappearing like a fading mirage into the distance. Abe watched him with appreciation.

"Young man, your dad sure can swim. He was right about that."

Before I could ask about Lynn, Abe turned and walked toward his cabin.

"My God," my cousin said. "Maybe we should follow Tom, you know? He had a snootful last night."

Dennis was a small boy with a wiry frame; he was light on his feet walking with a cultivated swagger, talked out of the side of his mouth, and taunted bullies.

"He's a strong swimmer. He'll be all right."

"Does your mom know he's drinking?"

"Not yet."

Mother was coming to visit the resort.

"Lynn's cute," my cousin observed. "Her friend, blonde Betty, is really fine. Gimme a bliazond any day," he said, using Irish slang. Then he looked out at the bright lake. "We need to get some beer and both chicks in a boat," he continued. "Get 'em drunk and we'll be in like Flynn."

"Sure."

Dennis squinted at me. "How come you like books so much? What a waste of time."

"I just like to read." I saw my mother pulling up into the resort. She had a handsome face and light blonde, chemically processed hair. "I'm going for a swim."

I stripped to my shorts and waded into the cold water, then swam toward the far slope on the other side, lined with rocks and a few pine trees. I didn't think about asthma attacks, and knew my father could rescue me. The water was cold and clear, the rocks on the pebbly bottom visible at twenty feet. I swam, then floated on the surface, the lake quiet with a few spreading ripples. The sun burned bright on the mirror of water. Halfway across the lake, I felt tired. With each stroke, an ache spread across my side, and the beach appeared more distant. I struggled toward the rocky shore where Father rested, waiting to swim back. Breathing deeply, I rolled on my back as I had been taught when a rowboat suddenly appeared; Lynn sat inside, guiding it with oars.

"Hey, voyager! Are you going to make it?"

"Certainly," I said.

"Climb in if you get tired."

"I'm fine," I said, gasping to speak.

I continued toward the shore. Father sat on a rock, smoking a cigarette. I didn't know where he had managed to find one, but he smoked, watching the blue water. Then he saw me. "What are you doing over here?"

"I came to find you."

I got out and sat on a smooth rock, breathing heavily and dripping.

"Very good," he said. He saw Lynn in the boat. "You're becoming quite a swimmer. And you have a pretty escort. Good show."

"Mother is here."

"Oh boy. I guess I better swim back. You head back with Lynn."

"All right."

He waded gingerly across the rocky bottom into the deeper water and began swimming gracefully across the lake. It was a darker blue toward the center and turquoise along the shore. Lynn sat in the boat, gripping the oars.

"Want to explore this place? There's a beaver pond on the other side of the hill."

"Later," I said. I wanted to swim back with Father. I got into the water and began swimming, but was soon out of breath and climbed into the rocking rowboat.

"You can row while I read," Lynn said.

"What are you reading?"

"A sex manual. Are you circumcised? All Jewish men are."

"I never knew what that meant. Guess I am."

"Maybe I'll find out," she said, smiling.

"You're sick," I said, rowing the boat.

Father had already swum across the lake, and I knew Mother would dominate any conversation. In a rich voice, Lynn read aloud:

"'The prostate gland mixes seminal fluid with semen from the testicles. It gets as big as a walnut, then contracts to pea-size at the moment of ejaculation.' Sounds like fun. It says here you better have it checked when you get older. The clitoris is like a little penis, you know. It also gets engorged with blood during sexual excitement. You men just have to find it."

"Could you read something else?"

"You never heard of a clitoris?"

"Sounds like a rare fruit. Is it good enough to eat?"

"I hope so."

Lynn sat in the back of the boat, holding the book.

"The Jesuits are criminals for not teaching you basic sex education."

I stopped rowing. "I guess you're an expert, huh? Had herds of men?"

Lynn stared at me. Some delicate balance had been disturbed.

"No, I haven't," she said. "Jewish girls are not taught to value virginity, but I haven't had even one. Satisfied? Why don't you let me row back? I don't want you to have an asthma attack."

Angry, she took the heavy oars.

"Did I piss you off?"

"Yes," she said, pulling back hard. "And you're right, I shouldn't read subversive literature to you."

My mother stood on the dock, wearing a blue dress with gold bracelets and a gold belt. She had come back into our lives when I turned eight, and it was still difficult to think of her as a mother, but rather someone visiting who had known my father years before. Her absence from our lives was never discussed, and my mother seemed to think explanations or apologies unnecessary. She appeared bored as we rowed in and tied up the boat. Lunch was good; Father sat, drinking 7-Up. Mother wore a sweet scent and smiled at me. Then she frowned. "He's a good-looking kid. Needs a haircut, though."

"Oh, that's the latest style. Meet Elvis."

"How about a crew cut?"

"You're in the beauty business. Would your fruits at work want him to have a crew cut? He's not a Marine at boot camp."

"They're not all fruits, and I know beauty. The ducktail is ugly. Greasy! Maybe a flat top would be better. It's cleaner."

Father laughed. He didn't meet my eyes. "Okay. Clean flat top it is."

"Don't I have any say in this?"

"Thank God your grandfather isn't here to give you one of his haircuts. Remember those old clippers?"

I did remember the heavy clippers snagging hair, the sudden tug. One did not complain when Grandfather cut hair.

"Tom? I don't want a haircut."

"I'm 'Dad,' not 'Tom'."

Mother ignored us and picked up Father's drink, sniffing it.

"Don't worry, dear, I'm dry."

"I hope so. It was a nightmare in the old days. Always drunk." She looked out at the lake. "This is a nice place. Cute."

Father stretched in the tree shadows, then reached for a cigarette.

"Our boy had an operation on his nose and got some infection. His

81

asthma's been pretty bad lately. 'Tom' speaking: How's your breathing, son?"

"I'm all right, T—Dad."

"It's all in his head," Mother insisted.

"No, it's in my lungs. Allergies. I pet a dog, I'm dead."

"You'll outgrow it."

"He's sixteen. When does he outgrow it?"

"I think all those sicknesses are in the head. I never had asthma. Why should he?"

"I don't know, Fran."

"Kathleen!"

"He calls me 'Tom,' so I guess I can call you 'Fran.'"

"I hate 'Fran,'" she said. "Awful name. Sounds like a bar maid or something."

"It's a good whore's name," I said. I could feel the sudden silence. "I mean, for a story or something."

Mother shook her head. "You like to dream up stories?"

Father sipped the soft drink. His gaudy sport shirt hung out over his belted white shorts. He had a pair of old shoes long since worn out on top, the surface frayed into little whiskers; the rubber soles were worn but still thick. "Where's your friend Lynn?"

"I don't know."

"Let me get my scissors," Mother said.

* * *

THAT night, the sunset cast a copper light over the lake. As it turned dark, we sat out in back of the cabin, the bottle between us. It was a windless evening filled with a strong scent of invisible flowers. The birds were silent, but we heard crickets. Betty's hair was platinum blonde, catching the moonlight, and a halter top contained her large breasts. My cousin spun the bottle first. Lynn sat on her haunches, watching.

"I can't believe that haircut," Dennis said, watching me. "You'll get a sunburn on your noggin."

"I can't believe I'm here," Lynn said. "This is a kid's game."

Betty chewed gum, popping a bubble. "Who cares? It's something to do."

The bottle pointed at Betty. Dennis spun it again and it slowed, pointing at him.

"Hey, we get to go first."

"Go to it," I said.

They kissed and Betty seemed to enjoy it. Lynn watched me, her eyes still dark and angry.

"Keep your hands to yourself," Betty warned.

"Sure," Dennis said. "I just seen Lynn's book. Boy, it had so many dirty pictures, it gave me a hard-on!"

Betty laughed. "Gross. I learned more than I wanted to know."

Betty spun the bottle. Then she spun it again.

"Looks like I get to kiss you," she said.

We kissed. I could feel the giving lips and the press of her wonderful breasts.

"Lynn? Maybe you'll get a turn," she said.

"Maybe I don't want a turn."

"What's wrong?"

The bottle pointed at Lynn. On the second spin, it was pointing between us. Then it pointed at Dennis. They kissed and Lynn was suddenly very theatrical, moaning, shaking her head. Dennis pulled back. "Too bad we don't got no car."

"Go steal one," Betty said.

"Why don't we walk to the arcade in town?"

"Not a bad idea," Dennis said. "There's a punk there named Chickie Jensen. He flipped a cigarette at me yesterday. I'll kick his ass if he does that again."

I produced some cigarettes. We lit up, except for Lynn. She reached down and spun the bottle and it pointed toward me. With the second spin, the bottle's slender glass neck came around to her.

"Do it," Dennis said.

Lynn picked up the bottle and threw it in the trash.

"Okay," he said. "Don't do it. How about that arcade joint?"

We got up and began waking toward town. The dark road ran between rows of trees and the night felt electric, redolent with roadside honeysuckle. Lynn took my cigarette. "Don't smoke," she said.

"All right."

We approached a small square with two taverns, a tennis court, a bowling alley and an arcade with shiny, noisy pinball machines. I once worked the bowling alley as a pin boy, often barely escaping before a drunk's heavy black ball crashed into the pins. Dennis and Betty walked ahead, and Dennis smoked his cigarette without touching it, swaggering as he walked. Shorter than Betty, he could've been a younger brother. Lynn slowed down and suddenly pulled me into an alley. We kissed, and then pulled apart.

"Why'd you do that?"

"I felt like it. I don't want to be mad anymore. Maybe I pushed you." We walked on. "I'm getting used to your flat top."

"It feels awful. Fran insisted."

"Fran? Not Mom? You don't like her, do you?"

"How can I dislike someone I don't know?"

Lynn stopped. Her hands slid up under my collar.

"My folks want me home early. They'd have a cow if they knew we were all out, together. They think I'm alone at the bingo games."

"They seem to like me."

"Sure, but for the long haul, you're the wrong religion."

"What religion? And what long haul? Who said anything about being together for life?" The words didn't sound right. "I mean, who—"

"All the same, you're not one of the club," she insisted.

We followed Dennis and Betty, who entered the dark noisy arcade to play a pinball machine. The arcade was layered with smoke. Gathered shapes danced and moved inside. We stood in the neon glow outside; young boys in groups smoked while talking, occasionally glancing at us and then looking away when I met their eyes.

"Since we don't have much time, why don't we take a moonlight swim?" I asked. "Maybe take the boat."

Lynn's eyes searched my face.

"Tonight?"

"Yes, tonight. Why not? Is there a monster in the lake?"

"You're saying, sneak out when the folks are asleep?"

"Yes."

I could see Lynn's mind working. She finally smiled. "Why not?"

"My dad's a heavy sleeper."

"So's mine, but Mother lives to worry."

"How about a nude swim…I mean, a noon swim?"

"Tomorrow?" Lynn smiled. "Sure."

"Maybe experiment."

Lynn stopped smiling and looked past me.

"What are you thinking?"

Lynn didn't answer. A strong hand closed on my shoulder and spun me around. A leering dead-looking face with pimples beneath thick, shiny hair confronted me. I could see the burning cigarette, the tight mouth and the leather jacket, the dead reptilian eyes small and dark. It was a close-up in a B picture about juveniles and the inevitable bully.

"Say, man, I like your haircut. Real cool."

"Who are you?"

"Chickie Jensen, punk. You got half a haircut. Maybe we'll have to shave it all, Flat Top."

There was a hiss in Chickie's speech. Lynn pulled at me. "Let's go."

A group of girls stood behind Chickie. They had bubble hairdos, their jaws working gum.

"That's a funny name…Flat Top."

"Oh yeah? Chickie sounds like a girl."

Chickie's eyes narrowed. When he moved, I could hear the bells on his motorcycle boots. He kept the cigarette between his lips.

"Our boy's real funny. Queers are always funny. You a queer?"

"No, but thanks anyway."

One of the girls laughed. Chickie pulled out a switchblade and the girls went silent, staring at us. I heard Lynn gasp behind me. The streetlights gleamed on the sprung blade. A few more boys came out of the arcade, smoking, watching impassively.

"I don't have a knife, Chickie."

"That can be arranged. You afraid?"

"I don't even know you. Look, let's call it a night. Okay?"

Chickie smiled, revealing two missing upper teeth. He spit out the cigarette, then stomped on it. "Let's pump foot."

"Pump what?"

"You know. Kick a little. No knives, just a little foot stomping. You afraid to pump foot, huh, Flat Top?"

I could feel the pressure from the other youths, gathering around, anxious for a fight. For a moment, I felt again like we were acting in a second-rate feature with cliché dialogue, but Chickie Jensen was real.

"Leave us alone," Lynn said, shaking.

"Maybe I will," said Chickie, watching her. "If I get me a French kiss. Hey, the Jew girl's real pretty." He finally met my eyes. "You come here, you dealing with me—the man! Understand?"

"I think I do."

Chickie put away the switchblade as Betty appeared out of the crowd. A few of the boys whistled; she took Lynn's hand.

"Let's go. We got a car."

"Wait," Chickie said. "You need permission first. Better yet, you can ride with me. Forget this chump."

Betty slipped her purse strap over one fist. She had an erotic defiance in her glance but her voice went soft, even quiet. "You don't know who you're messin' with, punk."

"Oh boy, I'm so scared," said Chickie. "What kind of short you driving, bitch? Volkswagen?"

Betty ran one hand through her blonde hair and pursed her lips in a mock pout, speaking with a girlish Shirley Temple accent.

"A gweat big icky old white convertible, but it'll do good for now."

Chickie's mottled face went smooth and slack for an instant. There was the sound of a loud engine without mufflers, then a white convertible with the top down roared into the crowd, the boys scattering even as Betty hit Chickie in the face with her purse. Dennis sat behind the wheel, a raccoon tail flying from the antenna; Betty and Lynn jumped inside. Cursing, Chickie struggled to stand up. "Get in," Dennis yelled. "Lock and load, hit the road!"

I jumped in. Chickie reached for the door, his face bloody as I struck his jaw, feeling bone crunch before the car shot forward, tires screeching. Then we were driving fast down the dark highway, Dennis shrieking. Betty opened a beer and foam spurted over her face.

"I saw him go after you, so I hot wired his car," Dennis shouted over the air blast. "That punk. Tomorrow, let's git him!"

"I had some beer cans in my purse," Betty said. "They hurt."

Lynn was crying, but after a beer, began to laugh. Throttle open, we took some dangerous curves, drinking in the warm rush of air as the car's momentum pressed us back in the seats. The dark trees became a blur on the night road, the heavy car lurching on the sickening turns, then Dennis suddenly braked and skidded onto a narrow logging road. He pulled into a remote wooded area on the lake.

"Cousin, you're driving a stolen car."

"Chickie probably stole it himself. Don't worry about it. I'll park the car in the same spot tomorrow. I'll even leave a sign for the son of a bitch. We can meet anytime."

Lynn tried to speak, mumbling her words. "My dad will kill me."

"He'll understand," I said.

Betty touched my cousin's face. Her blonde hair was pale in the moonlight, the crickets loud in the forest. Then we heard the rumbling of many motorcycles echoing through the trees; the sound faded down the hidden highway. We opened more beer and drank, the taste sharp and wonderful.

"Chickie won't find us."

"If he does, we're dead," said Betty. She began laughing, clutching Dennis, who sat holding the wheel in his tiny doll's hands. Lynn wiped her eyes.

"I'm a little scared."

I touched her shoulder. "Let's go for a night swim."

We slipped from the car as Dennis slid an arm around Betty.

"Goldilocks, you is so fine. Tonight—I'm Indiana!"

Betty blinked once. "Indiana? This is California, fool!"

"'Indiana.' That's Irish for 'getting over.'"

Lynn stumbled down a rocky path toward the lake, moonlight shimmering on the smooth surface. She began to spin like a ballet dancer. I caught her as she fell.

"I'm dizzy."

"Sit down. Rest."

"No. Let's do it!"

"Do what?"

"Listen. I hear a waterfall."

We walked along a narrow rocky beach until we saw a waterfall running down a cliff into the lake. There was a small cave, and the spray was blowing in the occasional breeze. "It's so beautiful here," she said.

"Let's go behind the falls."

"Let's go in the water first."

Lynn began to undo her blouse. She kicked off one of her sandals, then kicked off the other. She pushed away a lock of hair from her mouth.

"Let's see you strip and jump in."

"You first," she said.

"You first."

"Okay."

With slow deliberate motions, Lynn removed her blouse and pulled down the cut-offs. She fumbled with her bra. "Help me," she said.

The bra came away, freeing her breasts. She was standing on the beach in her panties.

"Take off your jeans. Then take these off."

I pulled off the pegged jeans and kneeling, gently slipped down her panties, her hands caressing the back of my head as my hands moved up her smooth, warm thighs.

"Your turn," she said. "I'll help you."

I stood and she kissed me on the mouth, throat, chest, stomach, kneeling as she hesitated, then pulled down the boxer shorts. I thought I heard a woman laughing as Lynn stood up, a warm breeze blowing off the lake, lifting her hair, an image from an erotic film never shot: a naked couple free on a beach, the woman's head flung back, the man kissing her breasts, panting with the intoxication of the evening.

"Let's go in the water."

The water had a chill, the bottom sharp with pebbles, and a growth of trees lined the lake. The shadow of a hunting owl passed over us and I saw her wet female nakedness: thighs, breasts, stomach, buttocks.

"You got protection?"

"No."

"Not prepared? You were never a Boy Scout?"

"They kicked me out."

She laughed and we kissed, wet bodies pressed together. The waterfall splashed with a steady rhythm on the lake, the water lapping in waves against the shore and spilling over the roots of trees.

"We can do other things."

Moments later, we ducked behind the falls. The sound of the

rushing water echoed in the small cave, and it was a secure feeling behind the falls. We began to touch each other, softly exploring with hands and mouths.

Later on the beach, we picked up our clothes. "We better go back."

"Wait. Let me look at you."

"I like it when you look at me. Was it okay?"

"Okay? It was great!"

"You are circumcised."

"Of course."

She laughed briefly as we dressed.

"Least I won't get pregnant."

"Did you...did you...?"

"It was fine. We just need more practice."

I hesitated before speaking.

"What?"

"How did Chickie know you were a Jew?"

"Everyone seems to know. Once, my grandfather came to pick me up at public school. He wasn't orthodox, but had a beard and a black hat and when he lifted his hat, they saw the yarmulke. Then everyone knew I was a Jew. They stated calling me 'the Yid.' But how did that punk know? He just did. They always seem to sniff us out."

We stood underneath the cloudless sky bright with the radiant moon. It felt as though we were the first couple in some primeval world as we walked back to the car.

"Did you hear some motorcycles a while back?"

"I thought I heard something." We walked on. "Lynn? Wait."

We stopped, staring at the clearing. The car was gone.

"My God, what happened?"

"Look. Biker tracks."

We saw the tracks left by turning motorcycles. Twin tire tracks from the heavy car led up the road to the highway. "They found them."

"I think they got away. Those punks."

Lynn put her hand to her mouth. "Let's get out of here."

"How?"

"Let's walk along the shore for awhile."

We walked along the curving shore and up over a hill through some quaking aspens. They made a creaking sound in the rising wind, then we saw the beaver pond with a pile of sticks and small logs at one end, a narrow stream feeding into the lake.

"We're exactly across the lake from Collin's Resort."

"Let's swim it."

We waded into the dark waters. I felt the weight of the water soaking into the jeans and then felt a tightening sensation, like sand slowly filling my lungs. Lynn was a strong swimmer but turned around. I was gasping for breath, feeling suddenly weak.

"Float. I can tow you for awhile."

I felt her strong hand cupped under my chin. After awhile, I began swimming, drawing air into my swelling lungs. Lynn's head was wet and shiny; she stopped, treading water, looking ahead at the red and blue police lights. An officer stood on the dock.

"We got a welcoming committee," she said.

We swam into shore, a full moon bright on the water.

The officer pulled me up on the dock. "Are you all right, son?"

"I need my asthma medication. It's on a table in the cabin."

Molly Harris stared at her daughter, who ran past her on the way to my cabin. Father appeared on the dock, tipsy. "What the hell happened, son?"

"Just went for a swim," I said, wheezing. "Where's Dennis?"

"We arrested him after a wild chase," the officer said. "We have an injured biker. We also have a warrant for Charles Jensen."

"For what—assault with a deadly weapon?"

Lynn came back with an inhaler. I felt the wonderful sudden rush as the spray opened up my closed lungs and I sucked in pure air. Abe walked onto the dock under a string of lights and looked at us. "Well," he said. "The Wild Ones return."

"Did your cousin steal Jensen's car?" the policeman asked.

"I guess. It was our getaway car."

"Getaway car? I see."

Lynn stood, not looking at her mother, who finally spoke.

"Officer, can I take my daughter back to our cabin?"

"Sure. But don't leave the area."

"Where's Betty?" said Lynn.

"Jail," the officer said. "They were both drunk."

Her mother's eyes seemed to die in the large moon face.

CONFESSIONS OF A SHANTY IRISHMAN

"We'll talk later," she snapped. "Let's go inside. Now!"

"Relax," Abe said.

"Relax?"

Defiant, Lynn kissed me before leaving with her mother. Abe waved good-bye and followed them.

"Busy night, officer," Father said. "These kids today."

"See you in court tomorrow," the policeman said, handing me a ticket.

Mother had trashed the cabin. Father's driver's license was torn in half, and as he explained Mother ripping it, I taped it together until a duplicate arrived. I could see her raging at him, for once again, she had caught him drunk. It seemed like a cycle they both embraced.

"We were just sitting there at the tavern, me and Abe, and in she walked. I offered to buy her a drink and the beef started. Your mother has this German temper."

"Why is that a surprise? I almost got killed because of this stupid haircut," I said. "Why are you seeing her again?"

"Why do you ask? You blaming her for your debacle tonight?" Father drank some coffee. He was shaking and the swim had sobered me.

"Okay. Why did you get drunk?"

"Was I drunk? Hm. Actually, that's none of your business. You're the one in trouble, wild man. Drinking, stealing a car. You realize you could get charged with a felony? I hate to ask what else you did."

"Maybe I had an excuse to get drunk," I said.

"We always have an excuse."

"We? What's that supposed to mean?"

"It runs in families and you got all the signs, young man."

Father looked away.

"Oh yeah? Did your brothers drink? No! Did your sisters drink themselves into a coma? No!"

"True," Father finally said. "Actually, your grandfather wasn't much of a drinker, either. Did smoke, though. The fact remains, you have all the signs of a problem drinker. I bet tomorrow, everyone's sick except you. For that matter, I worry about Dennis."

I wanted to shout a denial but didn't. The beer had tasted wonderful, and had added a glow to our adventure. Trying to sleep that night with

91

violent and erotic dreams was difficult; in the morning, we had breakfast, Father sitting quietly, sober now. Trembling, he took out a pack of cigarettes and I watched him light one.

"You think I'm a drunk?"

"Maybe not. How do you feel, son? Hung over?"

"I feel all right."

"High tolerance...a bad sign," he said. "I can tell you something, excuse or not, your mother helped drive me to drink."

One weekend when I was eight and Father visited Mother after they met by chance, her Siamese cat disappeared while they were out and I slept. I woke up with a flashlight in my face and saw only shadows.

"Where's George?" Mother demanded.

"What?"

"You heard me. What did you do with my cat?"

I tried to shield my eyes. "I didn't do anything with the cat."

"Then where is it?" Mother asked. "In Siam?"

"Something happened to George?"

"Son," Father said. The light went away. "When did you see the cat last?"

I sat up, rubbing my eyes. "I think the cat was running up and down the hall, playing with its image in the mirror. Yeah. Before I sacked out."

"Did you strangle George?" Mother asked.

"Strangle George? Why would I—"

"I'll check the garbage can," Mother said. "He probably dumped the body in the trash, thinking we wouldn't find it."

Father sat down on the bed. "Maybe the kitty just ran away," he said. "I don't blame her."

For two days, tension gripped the apartment on Hyde Street. Down the hill, we heard the cable cars going up and down the slick tracks. The kitten had disappeared and I was a suspect.

"Maybe he's just jealous," Mother said. "I can understand him being jealous of Dennis since he's such a wonderful man's boy—but a cat?"

"I didn't touch George," I insisted. "And why did you name a female cat George?"

Mother only shrugged, and when we left that Sunday and went home to the house on 20th Street, I hoped we wouldn't see her again, but she lay down and the cat stirred, hidden under the bed, hungry now and tired of hiding.

Years later, I looked at Father.

"Why didn't you and Fran apologize for accusing me of snuffing George? Why would I kill her cat? I like cats."

Father seemed puzzled, then remembered and shrugged.

"Your mother's...a nutcase. She can be very kind with strangers but ugly to relatives. I think when it comes to trusting or liking people close to her she's a little...a little blind." He stubbed out the cigarette. "I guess we better go, son. Leave your guns here."

Abe Harris waited outside the court, dressed in slacks and a sport jacket; he reached out a welcome hand. I was afraid to look at Lynn.

"I support you guys," he said. "Believe me, I know fascists."

The judge quickly slipped on his black robes; he had canceled his fishing for a day. Tourists filled the small courthouse, including Mr. Collin, who wore a gray suit. Father was dressed in a navy blue suit and didn't make eye contact with other guests. Dennis wore his best casual clothes, sitting on the stand, speaking in the cramped courtroom that was used for small claims, AA meetings, and occasional drunk driving and assault cases.

My cousin's voice went on, gathering strength as though he enjoyed telling the story of seeing his cousin and girlfriend in trouble, how he hot wired a car to save them and they escaped to the country for a quick swim before being caught by Chickie's biker pals, then the subsequent wild ride back to town, only now police were involved in the chase. His Mission District accent and Irish expressions flavored the story.

The judge sat above the rapt, white faces. "Why didn't you pull over?" he asked.

"They'd book us at the cop shop, so I just drove there."

There was scattered laughter.

"I guess I coulda stopped and let the bulls drive me."

"Were you drinking?"

"I had a glass of wine with dinner but wasn't stewed. I never get a snootful and drive."

"How much beer was in Mr. Jensen's car?"

"I seen two six packs."

"You drank some of it? Most of it? All of it?"

"God no! It was already done drunk up. Holy moley, the guy's got a drinking problem. A fireman! Fire one, fire two!"

"What happened to your cousin and the other girl?"

There was a quiet intake of breath. Lynn sat, her mother glaring at Dennis. Staring ahead, Betty had spots of rouge on her cheeks and wore blue lipstick.

"Like I says, the other doll wanted to go home. My cousin thought a quick swim would sober...wake them up. We was sittin' enjoying the stars when them bikers tore up the joint, so me'n Betty lammed outta there. I clipped one guy and he goes ass over tea kettle into the bushes. Next, we was on the highway, and I seen Chickie coming up real fast on my ass. He's on one side, a biker's on the other. Aye diddle, diddle, I'm in the middle, so I stomped on the gas." Dennis paused. "The thing of it is, judge, Chickie's a dangerous man. How do I know he don't got no piece or somethin'?"

"Piece?"

"Gun."

The judge looked at the visitors crowded into the small, hot courtroom. He glanced down at the case file.

"This is a hearing to determine if any further action is needed. Mr. Charles Jensen's statement is on record. Does anyone have anything to say for this defendant here before I rule?"

Father stood up. "This was all just youthful irresponsible misbehaving," he said. "I'm sure alcohol had something to do with it."

Mr. Collin stood up, his white face suddenly red. "Your honor, my guests have been tormented by Chickie's hoodlums for two summers now. Last year, Mr. Jensen had a canary colored-car and ran over one of my dogs. What kind of a man drives a canary-colored car? This year, his biker hoodlums have been making noise, drinking, taunting guests, and generally causing a lot of trouble. It's impossible to sleep when they're around terrorizing the resorts! I ask that you be lenient with these boys. Frankly, I am shocked Mr. Jensen's car wasn't already stolen."

There was a murmur of approval in the court.

Abe Harris stood up. "Your honor, I fought against the fascists in Spain with the Abe Lincoln Brigade. I fought against fascists in this country. Chickie Jensen and his bikers are fascists. In my opinion, these kids did a reckless thing, and my daughter was involved, but I'm only sorry this boy didn't run over Mr. Jensen and drive his car into the lake."

Lynn sat, staring ahead. The judge called me.

"Young man, you were threatened with a knife?"

I stood up. "Yes," I said. "We both were."

The judge wrote something in the file. Then he addressed the courtroom.

"I am dismissing all the charges except for reckless driving. I want you and your cousin to attend a traffic school in San Francisco. I want proof of that attendance sent to this court. You will pay damages for the boy who got hurt. I am also issuing a restraining order. You are not allowed near the village."

Mr. Collin stood up again. "Your Honor, what about those hooligans?"

"Charles Jensen will face assault charges. I will issue a restraining order against them to stay away from the resort area. I also understand the fish are biting today. Court is adjourned."

The judge got up and left the bench. We walked down the aisle past the upturned faces, passing through the door and outside where Chickie Jensen, in a black suit with a pink shirt, smoked, standing on the steps. He wasn't wearing the usual bells on his boots and grinned, flashing missing teeth, then spit out his cigarette.

"I'll be lookin' for you guys on the outside, dig?"

Dennis advanced a step. "You and what army?" he asked.

"Hey, let's move on," the bailiff said.

Chickie stepped back as Abe and Father walked past him.

"Maybe daddy can protect you cherries."

Father stopped. He didn't look at Chickie. "What did you say?"

"Nothin'," Chickie said. "They better not be here when you ain't around."

I pulled at Father's arm. "Let's go."

"Here, Greaseball," Father said. He took out some bills and tossed them at Chickie's feet. "For any damage to your car."

Abe snorted. "That tin can?" He looked at Chickie. Some boys gathered around, pressing close. "Frankly, I preferred the canary-colored car."

"Move on," the cop said.

Fender bashed, the white convertible sat in the street.

"How many got hurt in that wreck?" Abe said.

Chickie smiled, lighting up another cigarette.

"No one but your daughter, Jew. And she only got banged up a bit."

Chickie was laughing around his cigarette when Abe hit him, Chickie's head snapping back. A gang member tried to slug Abe and Father decked him. Then I was knocked down, the bailiff calling for help as bodies pressed around us; other police converged on the scene.

"Stop this. Stop! You're all under arrest. Stop!"

Later that afternoon, it seemed unreal as we sat in a small power boat, Lynn telling me that she was going home. The lake water was choppy in a steady wind.

"I think Father spent most of his vacation money on bail," I said. "How do you feel?"

Lynn clutched her temples. "Awful. I'm still sick from drinking. You?"

"No, it tasted good. Too good."

"What do you guys do in the city—burn buildings?"

We sat in the hot sun, the boat lifting and falling on the gentle swells. Many other boats plowed by towing skiers.

"I can't believe it. Daddy getting arrested with your dad for assault on teenagers. Mother is furious with all of us."

"I think it's kind of funny."

Lynn wasn't looking at me. When she spoke, her voice was low.

"How do you feel about converting to Judaism?"

"I can't convert to anything."

"If I see you, my father won't care. He's an old secular radical, but Mother will forbid it. I keep getting this pressure to live on a kibbutz in Israel. We'll have to meet on the sly."

"Sounds exciting."

Lynn stared at the bright water and the distant aspen forest.

"I can't believe all this happened. Going to jail to bail out our parents. I guess that is funny."

Laughing, she took my hand. There was a sudden urgency in her face. "Let's make love. I want you to come inside me."

"I'm even prepared."

"Except we got an audience of water skiers." The boat was drifting close to the dock. "And Mother's got her damn ole' binoculars."

"Let's move a ways down the lake."

I pulled on the line, starting the engine. We moved beyond sight of the dock, then slipped under a soaked, fish-smelling blanket, fumbling with each other's clothes. For an absurd moment, I imagined writing a novel in the distant future beginning, "It all began that tragic summer of..." only to hear a siren from the lake patrol and an officer demanding we move. We rode back. On the dock, her heavy-set mother, wearing a dull baggy dress, waited to claim her own.

In the cabin, Abe and Father cut the cards; Abe Harris paid for Chickie's broken jaw and Father paid for the biker's leg broken in the chase.

The next day, Lynn had to leave. We touched hands and said good-bye, her mother watching, then Lynn climbed inside the vehicle to be driven out of our lives as though she had never existed, and the waterfall and brief night of attempted love were only dreams with no substance. Abe stood in front of the van as a breeze came off the lake.

"I won't let those punks push me or my child around."

"Right," Father said. "But these kinds of vacations will break me."

"Me too," Abe said. "Tom? It's been a pleasure."

"All mine," Father said.

Abe looked at me, a kindness in his eyes. "Young man? Her mother wants her with her own people. She's becoming orthodox in her old age." Abe's dark face broke into smile wrinkles. "I'm against tribalism, but some time with real Jews might be good for Lynn."

"We have a date for the junior prom."

"That will be just fine," Abe said, laughing. "Dancing with all those Catholics. Molly will love it."

Father walked off as Abe got behind the wheel. I saw Lynn through the window, softly weeping; then they drove away. The vacation was finished. We drove back to San Francisco, fog rolling over the Golden Gate Bridge.

* * *

IT was a long wait for the junior prom, with endless calls never returned or intercepted by Lynn's mother, but after renting a white tuxedo, we finally attended the dance. The music was dull, the couples turning on the dance floor without passion or conviction. Jesuits watched from the shadows. No other boys approached us. Lynn smiled or sat at the pre-prom dinner looking elegant, a young woman attractive but distant from the proceedings. I felt the same distance. At times I thought of Clear Lake and shadows on dirt roads and the lake and touching Lynn's naked body behind the waterfall and feeling her lips.

We drove home, her house near Saint Ignatius church and school. Standing outside, a light drizzle began. We found shelter under a ledge.

"You didn't talk to anyone. Don't you have friends at school?"

"Not really. Any friends I have are outside of school."

"That's too bad. You know, I'm going to Israel this summer."

"I guess this is good-bye for awhile."

Lynn nodded. "Yes. It's not the same, is it?"

"No. But this can't be the end."

"I hope not. You know, I thought about getting us a room. I'm on the pill now."

"You are? Why don't we take a room?"

Molly Harris' square shape hovered in the window, and she peered out through the blinds.

"That time is past. I feel a little sad."

"So do I."

I began to see the moment as a farewell scene in a play.

"Listen, this boring decade is ending. I don't mean to sound like Tony in *West Side Story*, but I think something is coming to blow away all the boring crap."

"Like what?"

"I don't know."

"I'm seeing Mother's choice…his name's Ivor Moskowitz."

"See him. I'm the first person to ever touch you."

"Maybe he doesn't care. A frolic among the Goyim."

"Goyim? I knew a Jew who became a Goy and changed his name from Goldberg to Gold. He even sold his Rubens for a Goya."

Lynn suddenly laughed, putting her arms around me.

"That's an old joke." I placed my hand on her breast. She closed her eyes. "Kiss me good-bye."

"Okay, but that's risky with Shanty Irish."

We kissed and her mother rapped on the glass wet from the rain. Lynn glared at the window, her face handsome in the light. "You better go," she finally said.

"Be careful. Israel could be dangerous."

"When three world religions claim one area as sacred, anything can happen—but I can take care of myself. Hey, I'll be all right." For a moment, her eyes seemed to be looking past me into another world. "Maybe one day we'll have another chance."

I nodded, then ran toward the car, a heavier rain blowing across the street. I didn't look back and never saw Lynn again. Years later, I heard rumors she died in a suicide bombing attack in Jerusalem, but her parents had moved and it was never confirmed.

That summer, I drove back to Clear Lake in the old Studebaker. Mr. Collin had died and strangers ran the resort. The waterfall was dry and developers had cleared the aspen forest, though tree frogs still called out of the darkness. A mist came off Clear Lake and acrid smoke from controlled burns mingled with flower scents. The arcade had disappeared and the tennis courts lacked a net, though sullen teenagers crowded a dance hall and what was then called a creamery or drug store. They seemed tougher and older than their years, and with Elvis in the army, popular music had lost its magic. A merchant claimed a visiting drunk and overweight Johnny Weissmuller demonstrated Tarzan yells at the local tavern and was evicted. Eventually, he died in Mexico. Chickie Jensen's story had a sad ending. One evening, Chickie and a girlfriend missed a turn and drove his new car into the lake, the automatic windows suddenly going dead; air running out, Chickie broke the glass, letting in a rush of dark water. Drunk, they failed to escape.

I drove away from Clear Lake, thinking of F. Scott Fitzgerald and that American green light that always recedes before us.

CHAPTER FOUR

STUDY CONTINUED AT SAINT IGNATIUS. MR BECKER proved there was a magic alchemy in words, even the overheated prose of Thomas Wolfe and Poe. He turned note cards with each writer:

"Hemingway's neat but small, Fitzgerald's bright but innocent, and Faulkner towers over them all. William Faulkner was a Greek tragedian of the Old South."

I knew Faulkner's prose was "difficult," then read *The Sound and the Fury* in four days. This impressionistic tragedy of the gothic South would stay with me for a lifetime; I thrilled to stories of friends finding Faulkner drunk, passed out on the floor, the thick manuscript lying on a table. Was self-destruction typical of the great artist?

Mr. Becker pushed his favorite poets, as well:

"Forget the other romantic poets, John Keats beat the masters at their own game," Mr. Becker insisted, his voice getting tighter as he wrapped a lecture. "He could take the techniques of Shakespeare, Dryden, Wordsworth, Milton, and mine them for his own work. There's a sensuous musical sweetness in the verse that talks about death and despair—'where youth grows pale and specter-thin and dies;'—class, it's like singing a beautiful Italian aria while slitting your wrists. Taste that fire, 'turning to poison while the bee-mouth sips.'" The rhythm of the class approached high drama as the period came to an end. "That is a poet." The voice dropped to a whisper. "That…is…John Keats."

The bell rang and Mr. Becker seemed to collapse, sitting down suddenly. A few students smirked as they left his class, but others appreciated the dramatic touch.

Down the hall, Father Spoan herded students into his class.

"Pick up your feet. Pick them up, dolts!"

A school legend suggested Father Spoan had electrified the back wall of the football field to keep the boys from pissing against it on the way home. It was a unique experiment, using a hidden tin plate, demonstrating how electricity climbed up fluids containing salts. No one could find the hidden wires and battery. At times, there was no current. Other times, a student felt the sudden jolt of electricity to his exposed penis. Did Father Spoan sit in the priest house at night, finger poised over the nipple of a remote control? Boys could choose to aim at the ground, but to be zapped was a badge of honor.

Father Spoan stood, block-like in his white lab coat, glaring at the students as they trudged into class. He resembled pictures of Nazi doctors touring the camps, inspecting victims for future experiments. In another era, he might have been a cruel character in a Dickens novel.

"Don't shuffle like horses," he droned, in a hoarse voice unnaturally loud. It was amplified with a tiny microphone; with laryngitis, Spoan demonstrated a living physics lesson.

"Pick up your feet and sit down. Today, we will talk about your final grades. Your final experiments."

Father Spoan's large, cold eyes behind the spectacles seemed to glow brighter, even warm for a moment. He was going to write his name on every boy's soul before June graduation. The classroom was like a movie set for bad science fiction: charts on the wall, systems, circuits. What is a molecule? $E=MC^2$. Explain. How does a telephone work?

"I don't get it," Cucherie once said. "You speak. Your voice is turned into electricity, then picked up on the other side?"

Father Spoan stood over Cucherie. He glanced at the ceiling.

"He doesn't get it. Vibrations turned into electrical impulses traveling through wires creating vibrations on a receiver someone then hears via eardrums. Mr. Cucherie, where there's no sense, there's no feeling, right? So I could hit your thick skull with this heavy magnet, and you would feel nothing—correct?"

Father Spoan faced the class, his desk covered with models, miniature universes, scattered tubing.

"The final. It's really quite simple. You make something, perhaps a wheel turned by a battery, I test it. It works, you pass. It fails, you spend your summer writing out the entire physics book. Questions?"

"What about our other grades?"

"I'll take them into account," the harsh voice boomed, "but if your experiment doesn't work, you haven't used your knowledge well, which is being quite stupid. I don't pass stupid people."

"Will you test our experiments in class?"

"No. I test them alone."

Welsh raised his hand. Spoan's eyes touched him lightly, lingering with the fierce empty quality of a shark's. "Mr. Welsh?"

Welsh stood up.

"We don't get to see it or nothin', maybe talk about it—do the thing over if it don't work?"

"No."

"How come?"

"You mean, 'why'?"

"Yeah, 'why'?"

Father Spoan walked down the aisle to Welsh, sitting now.

"Because I run the class, Mr. Welsh. If your experiment can't stand on its own merit, it's not worth much." Father Spoan paused for a moment. "Mr. Welsh? You're not suggesting I would deliberately fail you whether or not the experiment worked?"

Welsh slumped further down in his seat. "No," he said.

Halfway through class, a freshman messenger entered as Father Spoan proved the existence of God through the human eye.

"Anyone who thinks the human eye was created without a Supreme Being is an ass—an utter ass!"

I raised my hand.

"Yes?"

"What about evolution, Father? Perhaps the first eye wasn't so good but evolved."

The class tittered, then quickly grew silent. Turning away, Father Spoan grabbed the note and read it; he pointed. "Well, Mr. Darwin, I'd answer your stupid question but you're wanted in Father Enright's office. Go!"

I got up and passed Father Spoan standing near the door. His jowly white face was suddenly close to mine, the eyes narrow and unwavering.

"Father Enright is our spiritual adviser. I think you need to see him. You certainly don't need to see me about science." I remained silent. "However, despite your attitude, I don't want to just flunk you. Perhaps you'll demonstrate that even you are capable of abstract thought, and create an experiment that works."

Father Spoan turned and addressed the class.

"It's really quite simple, but I'm sure all of you can make something with a battery. That is, if it's not too strong and burns your experiment up as Mr. Reed's did last semester."

"I want to make an electrified tin plate," I told him.

Father Spoan caught my arm, his hand light but strong; I could feel the tightening fingers. "Are you making a joke, young man?"

"Never."

"Never, 'Father Spoan'!"

"Never, Father Spoan."

I left his class and walked down the long, clean hall. Footsteps echoed. Photos hung on the wall showing past students looking older and somehow ghostly.

Father Enright was a small, elfin man with graying hair and a youthful face, the lines soft and almost elegant. He had a plush office in a separate building; he got up from a padded chair to shake hands, the soutane swishing.

"Sit down. This won't take long. Relax."

Outside, the sky was gray and overcast. Father Enright walked to the window, talking about the weather in his level but cordial voice. "San Francisco is always so cold. Mark Twain was right, the coldest winter he ever spent was a summer in San Francisco."

Father Enright turned and looked at me, his eyes not unkind. He continued to speak about the school and the difficulties of living in a secular world. My mind began to drift, thinking about that summer with Lynn. It seemed part of a dream. In my mind, we were eternal virgins, innocent and drifting through a lost magical time. I heard Father Enright's voice without listening to it until I realized he was addressing me.

"Well, I am prattling on. All this is just small talk. We have some serious things to discuss."

"We do?"

"You don't like to say, 'Father,' do you?"

"Yes, Father. I mean, no, I don't mind."

Father Enright sat down, his delicate fingers touching the top of his desk.

"You like our new Pope?"

"Pope John? Yes...yes, Father."

"He's progressive. Liberal. Welcomes the Jews." He leaned forward, his face suddenly highlighted. "Father Roubidoux says you haven't been going to confession. He can't reveal what's said in confession, of course, but he knows who goes and who doesn't. Anything wrong?"

"No, Father."

"I understand the boys call him 'Rubber-Ducks.'"

The joke was appreciated.

"I know it's tough to maintain a state of grace. I deliberately called you during Father Spoan's class. I know you're having difficulty with him. Your father is concerned."

I sat up, meeting his eyes. "I think he has it in for me."

"Oh, Father Spoan's from the old school of strict discipline. I'll talk to him about being more gentle. His techniques can breed toughness."

"All the same, he decided to give me an 'F' long ago."

"Your other grades are fine."

I did not want to discuss my feelings about Father Spoan.

"It's faith I am concerned with. What is our Jesuit motto? A.M.D.G. *Ad Majorem Dei Gloriam*. For The Greater Glory Of God." He waited for a comment. "That is why we are here. To serve God." His eyes were filled with urgency. "You agree?"

"That's what we are taught, Father."

"Taught, yes. Do you agree? Your father agrees. Where is he?"

"In Hawaii with my mother."

"A vacation together? That's good!"

"That's bad."

"You don't want them reunited?"

"It will be bad for both of them."

"It is important in our faith that marriage vows never be broken." Father Enright's voice was suddenly strained. "We don't recognize divorce. Your father can't remarry, unless it's to your mother." Father Enright continued. "Surely, you want him to be happy."

"Yes, I do."

"Well, there you are. We agree."

"They fight all the time."

104

CONFESSIONS OF A SHANTY IRISHMAN

"Then pray for them."

Father Enright stood up, as though fatigued from the discussion.

"I'll offer up a Mass for you. Mr. Becker thinks you have a literary gift. That's wonderful, but ultimately, I want to save your soul, young man. Believe me, nothing grieves me more than to think we have lost another one to the devil. You might read Thomas Merton's wonderful book, *The Seven Storey Mountain*, about his conversion to the true church. I feel helpless when a student strays from God. Don't make my life meaningless."

I was getting embarrassed. Father Enright went to the heavy door and when he opened it, he took my hand and held it for a long time as though we had a secret pact.

"I understand your father was a champion swimmer. Have you considered the swim team?"

"I don't have the speed, Father."

"But it's so exciting. All those boys stripped down, cutting through the water."

"I look like a geek in trunks."

"Then overcome that shyness. Build up those sleek muscles. Give it a try. And most important, you have to attend Mass and take Communion before graduation. Think hard about what you would lose if you lost your faith."

I went back to class and sat down; Father Spoan ignored me. The class was quiet. Richard Bloom, sitting across from me, whispered softly, "You got to be the stupidest asshole that row." I didn't reply. I knew Bloom wanted to fight, his cyanic eyes bright with contempt. "Ain't that right?"

Father Spoan walked toward us. "You have something to say, Richard, to our little friend?"

"No, Father Spoan. I like wise guys."

Richard Bloom relaxed his sinewy body in the chair. Holding a pointer, Father Spoan smugly turned away. After school, I walked out and descended the steps; the overcast sky seemed to be lower. Mr. Becker walked across the wind-blown football field and stopped when he saw me.

"How's it going?"

"Fine."

105

"My spies tell me you're having a hard time with Father Spoan."

"Your spies are right."

"Everyone has a hard time with Spoan. Make sure someone else sees your experiment."

"That's a great idea. I'm thinking of putting someone in a tiny electric chair that lights up when the figure sits down."

Mr. Becker laughed. "Just don't make him look like Father Spoan."

"Mr. Becker?" He stopped. "Why do you want to be a priest?"

"Three squares a day and a chance to serve people," he answered.

"Not God?"

"He's part of the bargain. Keep reading."

He walked on. I called out.

"Yes?"

"I'm reading a book called *The Stranger* by—"

"Oh God," Mr. Becker said. He used the French pronunciation. "Alber Ca-moo. It's a good book, but so many young men think they're the hero and become militant atheists in a world they insist is absurd."

"Oh, we don't need a book to reach that conclusion."

I wasn't sure why the book fired my imagination. Albert Camus had created a simple, even banal white African French citizen who simply wants to live his life until life begins to stalk him. After unintentionally shooting an Arab on the beach with the blinding sun in his eyes, an anti-Arab society condemns him to execution for not crying at his mother's funeral and sleeping with a woman the next day. He faces his end with scorn.

"French Existentialism is a fad. I don't believe life is basically meaningless, but Camus died young in a car crash, so he's the perfect martyr. Just what you teens need, another artist who died too soon like Jimmy Dean."

"That is a writer, that is Albert Camus?"

"Good parody of me, but I'm right. Camus is good, but there are other writers."

I watched Mr. Becker walk across the empty, windy field.

* * *

ONE day, Dean simply appeared.

106

He was handsome: a square face, high cheekbones, firm jaw, and blue eyes with long dark lashes. They were intelligent eyes, large and full of wicked humor. He had an athletic build, though he hated sports, particularly on television. We met on a bus when I was returning from a rehearsal for a high school production of *Paint Your Wagon*. The musical, set in a western mining town, was forgettable, but with the glow of make-up under hot lights, the amateur production took on a new life with the rush of music and soaring breaking voices; a full house created an exciting opening night. I played a gunslinger and shot a man on stage. The roar of the gun stirred the audience. Something happened with this theatre art form; it was a new world to be explored, conquered, and used for serious purposes. It also got Father's attention. On closing night, he came dressed as a western bartender with a string tie, vest and fake handlebar mustache.

Dean and I had our first adventure at Playland at the Beach. There was a fierce wind blowing off the Pacific Ocean. Dressed for the bitter cold, people walked past a record booth toward the roller coaster. Some standard questions were listed above the hidden microphone of the do-it-yourself recording machine.

"Where are you now?" I asked.

"In a record booth, where else?"

"Who are you with?"

"Some dickhead named Wrong Way Corrigan."

"What is your name?"

"J.R. Dean, but call me Dean for short."

"What will you do after we make this cheap recording?"

"Hunt for pussy, what else?"

After we finished the homemade recording, I recited a soliloquy from *Hamlet* into the hidden microphone while Dean made snoring sounds. Outside, the wind howled.

"Enough art," Dean said. "Let's snag a piece of ass."

The skating rink was full, couples and singles skating in a monotonous circle to slow organ music. A supervisor skated backwards, watching for reckless skaters. An occasional beautiful young girl floated by, hair lifted in the artificial breeze of movement. Dean had picked out a girl with a round, pretty face and curly dark hair. We joined the human herd circling the arena.

"'Peggy Sue' is the song we need," Dean said.

"That can be arranged." I skated to the observation booth. A fat youth sat inside, eating a candy bar. "Play some Buddy Holly, okay?"

The fat face stopped chewing for a moment. "It will be my job," he said. "Joe will kill me." He placed some forty-fives on the turntable. Rock and roll records were piled in a corner of the booth. I skated away.

Dean was talking to the young girl with curly hair; her name was Diane.

"You got a friend for this geek?"

Diane looked at me, smiling. "He's not a geek, but no—I don't."

"I'll pick one up," I insisted.

"I have a girlfriend, but she's an army brat." Diane looked at me again, her eyes suddenly sharp, metallic. "You thinkin' about joining the army?"

"Hell no," I said. "I'm asthmatic. If I joined, they'd ask, 'What side?'"

Diane enjoyed the joke. I saw the fat boy leave the booth. I winked at Dean and skated across the rink after the trick skaters finished their exhibition, waiting for a moment when all the skaters moved back on the slick, brightly lit surface. Diane and Dean slipped into the crowd, and I entered the booth, looking through stacked records. I found "Peggy Sue" and slipped it under "Tea For Two." Then I skated out into the moving crowd.

Joe skated backwards, controlling crowd speed with occasional whistle blasts. The Buddy Holly song suddenly hit the speakers, drums pounding a rocking beat with the hot rhythm guitar rumbling underneath.

Joe seemed to be frozen, whistle dropping from his mouth as faces and bodies pressed in on him. The wild moving mass on roller skates surged around the deadly curves of the rink. Joe managed to slow a few skaters, then went down beneath more crowded speeding bodies than seemed possible, Holly's rhythmic lead with its crashing chords rolling over the drums, driving the skaters in the key of A. I skated off to the side, watching Dean and Diane roll by in a mad rush. Joe skated to the booth, but got knocked down again; he got up and entered. There was a violent scratch across the record, just at the final moment of Buddy's plaintive vocal calling out to Peggy Sue.

"This will be investigated," Joe's voice boomed over the loudspeaker. "This will not be tolerated!" Joe began to break and dump the rock records.

Later, I sat in the rink fountain, drinking a Coke. As the doleful sounds of organ music began, Dean and Diane entered the creamery laughing.

"Let's go," Dean said, grinning. "I think someone saw you."

I saw Joe coming toward the shop. Outside, the wind was blowing from the Pacific Ocean. We took Diane home, driving along Golden Gate Park to stop at a sedate house in the avenues. Dean walked her to the doorstep; they kissed in the shadows, then she was inside the door. We drove back toward 20th Street.

"She's fine," Dean said. "What lips. We'll get her girlfriend next week, and maybe do some damage."

"I have to pass physics," I said.

"Forget physics," Dean said. "The only philosophy is seek pleasure and avoid pain. Physics is pain."

I explained about the experiment.

"Why don't we do an experiment on him?" suggested Dean, his classic face in profile as we came down the 17th Street hill. The city spread out before us, sparkling; the distant electric beer mug filled with golden liquid.

"If I get caught, I flunk—and my father will kill me."

"We can be clever enough to outwit this priest. He likes boys?"

"He hates boys."

"That's not what I meant."

Mexican music filled the cafés in the Mission District. Dolores Park was empty and dark. I dropped Dean in front of his house where he lived with his mother, Evelyn, a Marxist and militant atheist. She had light blue eyes, Veronica Lake hair and a rich laugh. She also demonstrated for what she called "Negro rights" and told stories of FBI agents coming to her work, asking questions, demanding why she had joined left-wing organizations. "The Democrats seem liberal but they're reactionaries, just like the Republicans," she argued. "And all religion is the opiate of the people."

"Really? What's a reactionary?" I once asked.

"A fascist who hates change," she replied. Dean's father had disappeared when he was two.

It felt unsettling sleeping in the old empty house at night, with Aunt Vee gone and Father in Hawaii. If it was a house with ghosts, they were silent. The tinted wedding photo of Thomas Senior and Agnes looked down from the bedroom wall, Grandfather with light-colored hair and Agnes looking so young and vulnerable wearing quaint clothes from another time. I suspected she was the last sister to arrive in America. Sometimes I couldn't read and didn't listen to music. It could make me feel more alone. I remembered the way Diane held Dean's hand in his lap and stared into his eyes. One night, I walked down to the bridge and watched the J streetcar coming up through the park, remembering Grandfather. A mist covered the moon. I could still hear the voices:

"Here comes the trolley, lad!"
The trolley shoots under the bridge.
"All gone, car."
Grandfather smells of cigarettes.

I heard someone walking onto the bridge and felt afraid.

"It's been a long time, stranger."

It was a woman's voice. I looked and saw Lucy Bond, a bit heavy and older now, smoking a cigarette and looking down the tracks. Her face had a hard flatness, and the eyes seemed older and tired. She wore a cheap imitation leather coat.

"My God, it has been a long time. Lucy, how are you?"

"Doing all right. I have a kid with no father, but I'm getting by. Never thought I'd be in this situation. The State helps out. You doin' okay?"

"I suppose so. You still in school?"

"No."

We talked about old times, about childcare and how silly past attitudes and styles now seemed. Fractured gray clouds drifted overhead. After all small talk ended, we didn't discuss the accident.

"Sometimes I walk in the park late at night when I can't sleep. I know, it's dangerous—a lotta wackos are out. Hey, I guess you're still at your parent's house?"

"Yes, I still am. Drop by and see me."

"Sure. I could do that."

In the streetlight, I could see the darker area around her neck where the fire had burned. A safety barrier had been constructed over the low bridge.

"I gotta go. My kid's alone. Maybe I'll see ya around. We can talk."

"I hope so," I told her, wondering what we'd say.

Lucy turned and walked off the bridge toward the street. The sensuous young girl from high school had disappeared, replaced by a single mother on welfare. Then she turned back again. There was a dead space between us.

"You ever think of John?"

"Yes I do," I said. "And Mary."

Her face was in shadow, but I could feel her isolation and regret.

"We was so happy that night. God, we had a good time, me'n John, until that damn accident. Then everything changed." She looked at her watch. "Jesus. I gotta go. You come by, you hear?"

No one else lurked in the park, and ancient Mr. Dooley observed me from his window when I returned home. I waved. He didn't acknowledge the wave but simply stared down from his post.

The days at Saint Ignatius progressed like a prison term. Even when Tom Manny went around left end, catching a pass and scoring the winning touchdown on Thanksgiving Day, and Saint Ignatius won the championship, it meant nothing to me.

"Why do you call our final work in your class an experiment, Father Spoan? It's really a project, not an experiment."

Father Spoan looked at me with cold, opaque eyes.

"Good question. An experiment suggests it is a first time, and in your case—in everyone's case—it will be a first time. Possibly, a last time. With the exception of Mr. Bloom, I don't know anyone who is capable—without help," he added.

"I showed Father Enright my project. Experiment. He thought it very clever, but wondered if it was in questionable taste. He consulted Mr. Becker, who found it amusing."

Father Spoan said nothing, remaining silent; light bounced off his spectacles and bright white coat. Finally he spoke: "Didn't I instruct you to show your projects to no one but me? I shall have to dock you a grade."

"Father Enright asked to see the project, Father Spoan. I wondered myself if it was bad form—but he insisted."

Father Spoan could stare ahead with empty eyes, containing fury that only a slowly building vocal intensity revealed. He leaned against his desk. "I shall check with Father Enright," he said.

Richard Bloom shook his head. "What an asshole," he whispered.

It would be easy to clip Bloom with a left hook, though he could take me in a fight.

"You should be more polite," I said.

Bloom glared at me. "What?"

"Bloom the kiss ass."

"What did you say?"

"No talking," Father Spoan said.

The Jesuits herded students to confession. I knelt in darkness beneath the white crucifix, waiting for the screen to slide open and confession to begin. The priest's profile suddenly appeared. "You may begin," he coached. "'Bless me Father for I have sinned.'"

"I have nothing to confess."

"What?" It was a sputtering, wet sounding voice. "What is it you say?"

"I said, I don't have any sins, Father, and if I did, I would not be sorry for half of them—particularly ones of impurity." There was a deadly pause. "Every night, I dream of naked tits."

"Give up this foolish sinful lust, young man. Pray to the Virgin Mary who watches your every filthy move— "

"Mary's a voyeur?"

"—and repeat the Confiteor. You can't take Communion without absolution."

"Then I'll be struck dead at graduation Mass?"

The voice had a tight hysteria: "It's a possibility!"

"Father, I am concerned about a certain unnamed priest who teaches physics," I said, my voice suddenly louder. "I passed the priest house and through the window saw him reading a girlie mag."

"What?"

"That's not the bad part. I believe this priest was abusing himself."

"Young man, this is a place to confess your sins, not act like an arrogant hooligan."

"Sorry."

I left the confessional quickly, passing young penitents. A few smirked and looked at each other. Richard Bloom glared at me, not smiling. Puzzled, Father Enright saw me leave the church.

* * *

WE met at Mel's Drive-In, a restaurant that would become a celebrated relic of the fifties. Diane and girlfriend Kitty sat inside. Though she carried herself with a sophisticated dignity, Kitty endured a cute name; she looked at the gathered teenagers with a haughty distance. Kitty's face resembled a classic film star's, the hair dark, her eyes a shocking brown in a pretty, talc-white face. She was tall, thin, well-dressed, smoking with an Audrey Hepburn elegance.

A carhop skated to the gleaming custom cars, lined up like piglets in a half circle around the neon drive-in, boys hollering orders from the windows. I thought of John Kopp's asthmatic laugh and shiny red Chevy. Dean repeated the Buddy Holly story.

"So you little boys like to roller skate?"

"That's right, Kitty."

"You like rock and roll?"

"Sure," I said. "What else is there, except for Negro blues?"

"Opera," Kitty offered. "Rock and roll is for kids."

"What are you?"

"I'm twenty."

"Her father is a lieutenant," Dean said.

"Lieutenant Colonel," corrected Kitty.

Diane sucked root beer through a straw. "So what? Kitty, we're out to have fun."

"Maybe she doesn't approve of fun," I said.

Kitty glared at me. "I do," she insisted. "With men."

There was a moment of silence. Dean glanced at Diane and theatrically cocked one eyebrow.

"Since we have Daddy's car, why don't we take the boys...the men, for a ride," suggested Diane, laughing nervously.

"Right. Let's go to Twin Peaks."

"I had an accident there—not so long ago."

"Tell us about it."

"No," I said.

"Anyone hurt?"

I looked at Diane's round, sensuous face.

"Yeah. I don't want to talk about it."

Kitty dragged off her cigarette, watching me. For a moment she relaxed, her eyes serious.

"Let's go up and check it out," said Dean. He playfully socked me on the shoulder. "Confront a few demons."

We drove to Twin Peaks in the colonel's Cadillac. The small identical peaks overlooking San Francisco were unchanged; the fog rolled over them, reminiscent of that fatal night with John Kopp and the fire. Other cars were parked in the curved lot overlooking the city and the distant Bay Bridge. We sat in the car, windows steaming up.

"This is like a scene out of *Rebecca*. Or *Wuthering Heights*."

"Our boy can read," Kitty observed.

"Lay off," said Diane.

"I can speak for myself," I said.

Dean reached over and stroked Diane's hair. Then his hands closed on her tight, thick, dark curls. They kissed.

"I'm going for a walk," I said.

The night air was cold, and the swirling fog created its own magic of mist and San Francisco ambiance. Kitty followed me.

"Sorry I was so rude. I am a little defensive."

"It's okay. I'm a brute myself."

"I like Diane, but I've outgrown her. How do I wean her away?" Kitty stopped, hands thrust in the pockets of her coat. "I know that sounds pretentious. Tell me about the accident. If you don't mind, that is."

"Why do you care?"

"I lost a friend in a car crash."

I told her about the burning car with John Kopp and Lucy inside. I felt her watching me.

"Listen, I tend to be rude when I'm nervous."

"What are you nervous about?"

Kitty stepped closer. She knew she was beautiful, and the light from the street lamps cast a magical foggy glow on her shining skin. Grass and weeds were blowing in the steady wind. The cold penetrated through jackets and coats.

"I'm nervous about you."

"Really?" I was surprised. "Why?"

"Because you represent everything my military father considers the enemy. I find that attractive and scary." Her voice had a melodious resonance. "I also know I could destroy you, and that turns me on."

Kitty suddenly laughed, then covered her mouth with her hand. "See, I'm warning you up front. Believe me, in two years, I'll be barefoot, pregnant and living with a Marine on some barracks."

"Sounds awful—to me, at least."

"You'll grow a beard and live in some garret with an ugly beatnik girl wearing long stringy hair, black dresses, no make-up, and no bra. She'll have a stupid drawl. Creepy, creepy."

"You have a vivid imagination."

Kitty lit another cigarette and offered me a puff. I recalled the scene in *Rebel Without a Cause* when Natalie Wood turns Dean's filter cigarette around, a cute cinematic moment over tobacco. Now I wanted to quit but was addicted, despite asthma attacks and trips to the emergency room for adrenaline shots.

"I think you're running ahead of yourself. And I doubt you could destroy me. I've been around the block. No woman burns me down."

Kitty exhaled smoke into the cold air. "Really? A tough guy?" Then she said, "Be careful."

"Why are you telling me this?"

"I don't know."

"I probably will end up in some artist's garret, writing protest songs against war or novels about greedy capitalists buggering humanity."

"Ick," Kitty said. She stamped out her cigarette. "We have to slow down."

"But nothing's started yet."

She looked at me again, something in her eyes hard to read, then she held my face; I felt her lips. It was a cinema kiss, long and sensuous. "It will," she said.

"Let's get out of this freezer and back in the car, assuming they're not humping. Okay?"

"Or finished humping."

I nodded. We saw two shapes in the car breaking apart. Inside,

Diane closed her shirt, her face empty but happy. Then they began kissing. Diane's head disappeared from view as we sat in the back, kissing gently without passion. Sometimes Kitty stopped, staring into my eyes, apprehensive. She was trembling and I felt moisture on her cheeks.

* * *

ONE afternoon, Kitty came by in her town car.

"Get in. I want to show you something."

Kitty drove fast across the Golden Gate Bridge toward the Russian River Resort area, another favorite vacation spot where Father took us many summers. It was late fall and rains had swollen the river; soon, vacationers of a different sort would enjoy the Russian River rainy season. I imagined renting a small cabin with this beautiful woman to watch the flood between the banks and listen to the rain. Then we would make love on a white rug before a roaring fire. We took a road through groves of trees, and leaves blew across the highway. A distant forest of redwoods remained, untouched.

"Where are we going?"

"To meet someone."

Kitty held the wheel in one hand and glanced over at me. Her face was clear and pristine like porcelain, and the wind through the window lifted her rich brown hair. Her skirt had moved up her spread slender legs.

"You're a bit young for me, but I think we connect on some level. Maybe you're older than your years."

"Who is this mysterious person?"

"I'll tell you when we get there." There was something in her voice, and she averted her eyes. "I'm going to reveal something about myself. Relax."

"Sure. Are you relaxed?"

"I feel a bit nervous but I'm okay. Do you like to drink?"

"I'm a cliché Irishman," I answered. "I love to drink."

"I was afraid of that."

We pulled off the highway onto some grounds with wide lawns and another grove of trees. There was a large house made from logs surrounded by bungalows. We parked and walked into a gray lobby where a number of people sat playing cards, reading or watching television. They had the pale look of patients who had survived some ravaging illness, and now they moved slowly, as though even movement could trigger an attack. A sign with AA's twelve steps hung above the desk. Kitty talked to the clerk and then motioned to me, and I followed her down a narrow hall.

"It's understood you won't talk outside about these people," Kitty said.

"Understood."

In a small sedate room, an attractive middle-aged woman sat by the window. She looked like an older Kitty and smiled warmly.

"Mother, this is Michael. Michael, meet Dorothy."

Dorothy extended her hand. "Hello, Michael. Pleased to meet you."

"Hello. Nice place, here."

"For twenty-eight days," Dorothy said. She glanced around the clean room. Photographs of a younger Kitty stood on the desk with another photo of a military man. "I'm here to meditate and dry out," she continued. "I'm a drunk."

For a moment, I thought about Father staying in such a retreat. When I said nothing, she turned to Kitty. "How are you, daughter?"

"Fine. Thinking about college."

"Take something practical. Finance. Business."

There was a long silence filled with a clock ticking. Kitty stared at the rug, and her mother smiled at me. Then Dorothy took out a fresh pack of cigarettes, tapping them. The sound seemed unusually loud. The quiet residence, unlike a hotel, carried a feeling of hidden terror. I had grown up thinking a "drunk" implied a certain honor. I also wanted a beer and felt guilty for the thought. After a moment, I stood up. "Maybe I should leave you two to catch up."

"You can walk around our lovely grounds," Dorothy said. "Are you in college, young man?"

"Thinking about it."

"To study what? Business?"

"Theatre."

Dorothy betrayed nothing with her expression. I walked down by the river and watched the swirling surface. The air was cold but vibrant.

The subdued panic in Dorothy's eyes lingered; I had seen it in Father's eyes. Could he endure a month without drinking? What would happen to Dorothy when she left? A few residents passed, watching me with some curiosity. Perhaps they could feel I was a civilian, an outsider. I waved and they waved back, then walked on. I returned and sat in the lobby with the television tuned to a soap opera. Beautiful people were having romance problems. A woman's lover was in the hospital with a spinal cord injury, and the handsome doctor, her unfortunate lover's best friend, was furtively looking down her blouse. An Indian woman in the lobby watched impassively. Kitty and Dorothy appeared, both smoking. Dorothy again held out her slender fingers.

"It was a pleasure," she said. "You take care of yourself."

"I plan to," I said, thinking of shot glasses filled with amber whiskey.

Dorothy had beginning tears. "Take care of my little girl," she said.

"Oh, Mom," Kitty said, smiling. "I can handle just about anything."

Moments later, it was twilight and we were driving back down the narrow road.

"Your mother's a nice person," I said. "Elegant. I know it must be difficult."

Driving, Kitty nodded to herself. "I felt I could trust you. Most people are ugly toward drunks. Mom's a princess, drunk or sober."

It happened suddenly. Kitty's voice broke and she pulled off the road and parked. Autumn woods lined the highway, and the pungent smell of redwoods came through the window. The tears seemed to burst from her face as I held her against me and she sobbed, crying like a wounded animal.

The next day, we went with Dean and Diane to a beach near the Golden Gate Bridge and drank beer while Kitty sketched, seated on white sand. With thin pink clouds overhead, we didn't think about treatment homes for alcoholics.

* * *

DEAN and Diane made love in the other room. We could hear her hoarse voice breaking with her orgasm as the bed pounded. Kitty got up and stood by the window, nervously smoking. Then she came over

118

to the gold couch and sat down. I touched her face and kissed her, and she touched me and then pulled away. Diane had peaked, and then grown quiet. Occasionally, we heard giggles from the other room.

I'm sorry," Kitty said. "I just can't do it yet. I want to and I don't want to. One minute I feel like a whore and the next, I'm a candidate for the nunnery."

"You would not be a good nun."

She touched my cheek. "I'm getting used to your tiny but scratchy beard."

"Good." The Jesuits had allowed it for a school play.

"I don't know any other boys—men, who wear them."

"Even better."

We sat in silence. Kitty wore a white dress with blue spots, her brown hair tied back. Then Kitty got up and turned on the television. Richard Burton was bellowing his way through *Alexander the Great* in his rich Welsh voice. I loved to hear him speak. He recited his lines with a rich ringing authority. Burton was always acting; walking through a scene with a conquered general, Alexander looked at statues of naked men and demanded where these physiques had been when his soldiers defeated the fallen general's army. The Shakespearean voice squeezed and elongated vowels with a bony resonance.

"I've seen this," Kitty said. She turned the channel and we saw a man walking through an empty, dark square when a car circled near the pedestrian and two men got out. They screamed at the man, whose face resembled that of a pug fighter, though the features expressed a poetic sensitivity. Wearing thick coats, both men were angry.

"Stay way from the girl," a burly man named Charlie screamed. "It's an unhealthy relationship."

The pug had a look of pain in his eyes, the frustration of a bewildered child, and his speech was halted. There was a slow fade but the face remained—haunting.

"This is really interesting," I said.

"I don't like him," Kitty said. "He's too bestial looking. Icky."

"Icky? Who is he?"

I should have known the actor, for I had heard his name often when my parents complained about his pictures, though they rarely missed any. I had experienced my father's nasal imitation of the actor's most celebrated lines.

"Marlon Brando, of course."

"That's Brando?"

Why I had never seen the actor myself was a mystery, but moments later, the pug was sitting in a taxicab while Charlie offered him a bribe to keep his mouth shut. So he took a dive in the past? He saw a little change, and what was the problem? Brando held up his hand Hamlet-like and said the lines I had heard mimicked so many times: "You don't understand, I coulda been somebody, I coulda had class, I coulda been a contender—instead of a bum which is what I am...it was you, Charlie. You were my brother. You shoulda looked after me."

The theme was a brother's betrayal, and Charlie crumpled.

"My God," I said, feeling tears. "So that's the famous taxi scene."

"Let's watch the other movie," Kitty said. "This one's too depressing."

"He's beautiful," I said, realizing the thrill of a new discovery.

"Burton's beautiful. Brando's a little scary," Kitty said. "He's weird."

"That's what my mother says. She wants to take a bath every time she sees him."

"I wouldn't go that far."

Kitty turned the channel; Burton was orating about Persians and young Greek boys. I looked at Kitty's face. For the first time, I imagined us breaking up, going our separate ways, meeting by chance one day as strangers. She caught my eyes.

"What?"

Dean and Diane, dressed and happy, came into the room.

"Nothing," I said.

* * *

FATHER Enright called me into his office. As I crossed the threshold, he looked serious, sitting in his chair and reading Thomas Merton. He looked up.

"Father Spoan is very upset about your exhibit. I did think it a bit strange...the man sitting in the electric chair...is that all students, or just you?"

"Just a figure, Father."

His face brightened. "You called me 'Father'. That's a step."

"What's wrong with the exhibit?"

"It sends a strange message. Perhaps you might make another project...one that is more appropriate."

"How about a boy pissing against a wall and getting electrocuted?"

Father Enright stepped forward.

"Now you listen to me, young man! I have asked Father Spoan to dismantle that electrified plate. It served a purpose."

I didn't want to comment.

"Ultimately, I am more worried about spiritual matters. Father Roubidoux mentioned that a boy refused to give his confession and walked out. I need to know if Satan is taking one of my boys under my nose." He leaned close to me and stared into my face. His lower lip trembled. "Was that boy you?"

"Yes."

"What is happening here?"

"I'm having problems with the school; with religion class, with physics, with Father Spoan, and—"

"With a woman?"

"Woman?"

I could see Kitty on New Year's Eve, tipsy, lying on the bed, nervous to be suddenly alone when Father should have been home but wasn't; slow kissing led to groping hands, a bare breast, an awkward fumbling with clothes, a sudden penetration between gaping thighs while an announcer counted down to the New Year:

"—four, three, two, one, zero. Happy New Year!"

A car backfired in the street outside. Cheers and horns came through the radio as I began a new year no longer a virgin.

Father's Enright's voice cut into my memory.

"Answer me!" he demanded. "Problems with a woman?"

I looked into his worried face. "No," I said.

For a moment, Father Enright seemed to hold his breath. He whispered: "With a boy?"

"God no."

"With your faith?"

I shrugged. "I guess so."

"Let us kneel and pray together."

"I feel funny doing that, Father."

He knelt down. "Do it!"

I dropped to my knees. Father Enright prayed silently, his lips moving. Then he stood up, lifting me with him.

"I want you to attend Mass with your father this Sunday. I told him of our little problem. I want you to ask Jesus Christ for an answer. We have no atheists here, and I know you're a boy with great potential to serve the gospels."

I walked to the door.

"Can you try, for me, just this one time?"

Father Enright seemed to grow smaller and age in the afternoon light coming through the window. His eyes were moist. "Do all these earthly things matter so much?"

I remembered Albert Camus' hero. "No," I replied.

He seemed relieved. "Then we have a start. Your Father is a very devout Catholic."

"I know."

He stopped at the door. "I'll talk to Father Spoan about accepting your project." Father Enright touched my shoulder. "Say hello to your dad. Let's hope his prospective wedding plans work out."

I looked at Father Enright. "What?"

"He hasn't mentioned it to you?"

"No."

I turned and left the office. Mr. Becker, dressed in black, again walked across the field. He stopped. "Play the game, young man. You think you got a corner on rebellion? Nietzsche, a lot smarter, beat you to it."

"Good for Nietzsche."

Mr. Becker was not smiling.

"I'm warning you. Don't be too clever." He walked on, stopped. "If you really wanted to be an egotistical asshole, you could've had a fat physics teacher sitting on the electric chair. Or maybe the Pope." He turned and continued toward the priest house.

Some boys in football jackets walked toward me. They had rugged faces and block-like bodies, all jaws and sinews. They stopped, gathering around, closing in. "We got a winner here, boys. Dork city."

"Ouch," I said.

"I hear Richard Bloom's gonna kick your ass."

"Good for him."

I could see contempt in their eyes. Tom Manny broke through the circle.

"Leave him alone. He's in enough trouble with Spoan."

"So? He's got this superior attitude."

"Who isn't in trouble with Spoan?" Manny asked.

"He's flunking my ass," another boy agreed.

The athletes left. I walked to the Studebaker and stopped. Someone had slashed a tire. Cursing, I opened the trunk for a tire iron and jack.

* * *

WE sat in Mel's Drive-In. Dean told a funny story:

"We were humping in the shower when her folks came home. Her dad stuck his head in but didn't see me or my clothes. Diane got a towel, kept them talking in the front room while I slipped out a window and ran around the block, dressing while I ran. I felt like a fool, half naked, skipping, hopping down the street, trying to pull on my pegged jeans, which practically need a zipper to get on or off. Some neighbor's dog barked his ass off."

We laughed. Kitty met my eyes. Our last time, we had made love in her father's apartment while he was away, but his dog barked in another room, and I felt the wheezing begin as we lay naked on the sofa. The asthma inhaler worked for a while and then made it worse, with labored breathing and tense nerves. Sex should have brought us closer, but daily I saw her pulling away. Was I failing her somehow?

Sipping coffee, Dean reached in his pocket. "We need more rubbers, Sport."

We left and drove to a drug store next to the Castro Theatre on Mission Street. As a child, I saw in that old theatre a sword and sandals epic, *The Black Shield of Falsworth* starring Tony Curtis. The hunchback no longer sold newspapers on the corner. The store smelled of medicine and lotions, and we heard piped-in music. A woman worked behind the counter; it was always embarrassing to ask a woman for rubbers. She disappeared to be replaced by a Latino druggist. The request for condoms was quietly repeated.

"*No habla inglés, Señor.*"

"We need Patrician Rollskins. Condoms. Trojans. Rubbers?" He blinked at us. "Here, for this," I said, pointing. "*Para esso...mucho grande*. Big Dick!"

"I don't think so," the druggist said. "*Muy pequeño*. Little dick."

We bought the rubbers and left. It was a story that would grow in the telling. Diane and Kitty waited in the drive-in. They glanced at one another.

"You guys need a place. We don't like to do it in a parent's house, or in a car, or at a cheap motel."

"My mother's a Communist," Dean said. "She doesn't mind. They're immoral atheists, anyway."

"I think she's very moral," I argued. "She'll be an activist at seventy."

Kitty didn't comment, but lit a cigarette, keeping her distance, smiling occasionally.

"We need a touch of class," she finally said. She looked at me. "We're elegant ladies, not whores, right?"

"Let's drive to my place. Father's working nights, and will probably stay with my mother. She's got a new place on Green Street."

I didn't want to think about their wedding.

We drove to the house on 20th Street. I wondered what Grandfather would have thought, the man who built the house he died in, knowing his grandson and a friend brought their girls home for a night of drinking and quick sex. It always seemed to be hurried sex. In the room where Grandfather and Grandmother had slept for forty years, we closed the door and faced each other. Then Kitty was undressed, her body long and statuesque, lying on her back now, staring at nothing; her long, dark hair spilled out on the white pillow, her dainty hands covering small breasts and the dark V between her legs. She looked away.

"Have you got that thing on?"

"You could help, you know. Be a part of it. Lynn wasn't afraid of touching and exploring, even if that's all we ever got to do."

Kitty stared at the ceiling. Diane gasped in the front room.

"Why don't you go track this Lynn down? Finish your business?"

124

Then she looked at me. "Just what did you have in mind?"

"Nothing."

"I won't take it in my mouth. Never."

"Why not? I could get you off that way."

"It's disgusting, that's why."

I sat on the bed and finished a quart of beer.

"You drink too much," she said.

I put down the beer. After fumbling with the rubber, I straddled her body, gently holding and spreading her wrists. It was like climbing onto a beautiful living statue. Kitty was contained, waiting to be serviced. There was something mechanical and furtive about the lovemaking, a quick penetration and rush to climax. Later, I heard Father's key in the door and his unsteady footsteps coming down the hall. In the front room, Dean spoke: "Good evening, sir." I imagined Diane pulling a sheet over her lovely breasts.

"Good evening, Mr. Dean," Father said. "Like your towel."

Quickly dressed, we sat at the house bar drinking, smoking, Father politely making conversation while mixing more drinks. "Your girlfriend's lovely."

"Thank you, sir," Dean said. "Meet Diane Morini."

"An Italian girl. Delightful."

Diane smiled, nervously sipping her drink. Father examined Kitty.

"Lace curtain stock, I can tell. A thoroughbred filly."

"My father's a lieutenant colonel," Kitty said. "In the military!"

"Seaman," Father said, saluting. "Third class. Had a delightful evening?"

"Yes," I said. "Very…delightful."

"I had a delightful evening," Father said, "with your mother. So delightful, I decided to have a nightcap. I'm drunk."

"I'm Dean. I think we better take the girls home, sir."

"Certainly."

"So long, Dad." We left Father drinking at the bar.

"You have to meet my daddy," Kitty said, before I dropped her off.

"Meet the colonel? Sure. That's only fair."

We briefly kissed, and then she pulled away.

"How's your mother?"

"Still dry," Kitty said. "Thanks for asking."

When I returned, Father had passed out on the couch; I knew we had to talk. My getting into Saint Ignatius was important to him, and graduating even more important. We went to Mass that Sunday, and walked both ways along Dolores Street. Cars drove up the hill, rows of palm trees growing in the divider.

"Father Spoan's a tough old bird. Father Enright sounds like a crying girl, at times. Can you work it out with those two? I'm paying good money for you to get the best college prep education you can with solid religious principles." He stopped, breathing heavily, looking at me. "Are you dropping away from the Church?"

"I do have a lot of questions."

"Of course, you have questions. We all become amateur atheists at times. Your cousin's going to a public school, and he doesn't go to church at all. The Irish were formed by the Catholic Church."

We walked on.

"Are you going to remarry mother?"

"I have to if I call myself a Catholic."

"Maybe you should lose your faith."

Father stopped.

"Don't say that," he said. "And don't be hard on her. It was tough raising a child as a single mother with a drunken father, and I was...probably still am, a drunken father."

"Grandmother raised me...and you sobered up."

"Right," he said. "For a while. Right now, I need a drink."

"Let's go home."

We walked up the path toward the house and the grassy hill where Father, at dinnertime, had whistled me in from baseball games.

"I'd like to study acting in New York," I said.

"Acting? What kind of profession is that? You're not Clark Gable."

"I don't want to be Clark Gable."

It was a frightening dream, to plunge into New York and pursue theatre against strong odds, the lonely artist making drama into a religion. Father caught his breath. "I'm too old for these hills," he said.

The next day, I promised to try harder. Father Spoan listened to my apologetic words, his eyes revealing nothing, then made a startling announcement to the class: "I'll have all the exhibits on display. You can see your projects tested at an open house for your friends and

126

parents. Why not show them your progress, days before graduation?"

The students seemed to agree.

The weekend arrived when I finally met the colonel, a tall man with a dry voice, crew cut, and dark brown eyes in a lined face. He stood erect, dressed in a brown suit. I felt uncomfortable in a tweed suit. His dog was locked in the bedroom, but I carried my asthma inhaler.

"I hear you're allergic to dogs."

"I am," I said.

For a brief moment, he seemed to frown.

"There's a swimming pool outside if you two want to swim. Care for a drink?"

"Sure," I said.

"You're old enough, I suppose?"

"He can have one," Kitty insisted, spots of color in her cheeks, hair woven into a swirl over her head, her suit modest. "Me too."

I took the drink. The colonel sat down. "Are you going to college?"

"I'm graduating from high school," I said. "Then, I may go to college...after a trip to Europe."

The colonel didn't respond for a few minutes. "High school?"

Kitty laughed. "He's grown up, daddy. Old for his years."

The colonel smiled, showing a row of gold-capped teeth.

"I'm a little old myself," he said. "Standards are different. We have a pinko liberal running for President, John Kennedy. I think it's proof we are witnessing the decline of western civilization."

"My dad loves Kennedy," I said. "But then, he's an Irish Catholic."

The colonel sipped his drink; we sat on a white couch.

"I see. A liberal Democrat." He leaned forward, asking questions with a level voice that carried authority. "How are you fixed with the Service?"

"Asthma kept me out, sir."

"Oh that's right. You're allergic." He shook his drink. "Asthma. You could've worked around that," the colonel said.

"Yeah, I guess that's right." I tossed down the drink. "I didn't want to join the Service."

I remembered the military physical, and walking to the "Reject Desk" manned by a handsome soldier with a Burt Lancaster smile. He had stamped "Unfit for Service" on my papers while half naked young boys went through another line.

"1 A," an old sergeant shouted. "Cannon fodder. Prime beef!"

The handsome soldier's face had slight contempt as he handed me my rejection papers.

I heard the colonel's voice: "You don't want to serve your country?" The colonel watched my face, waiting for my answer. In the other room, the dog barked, and I could feel a tightening in my lungs.

"Yes, I do want to serve, but in another way."

"I think he'd look silly in a uniform, don't you, Daddy?"

"Any man looks good in uniform, even a shabby one. It breeds character. I fought in Korea in the winter." He glanced at a samurai sword on the wall. "Then again, if you can't cut the mustard, getting cashiered out of the service is painful, and leaves a permanent mark on your record."

The phone rang and Kitty answered. "Hello? Who? Frieda?"

The colonel waved 'no' to Kitty. He looked at me, no longer a commanding officer. "She's a German widow who keeps eyeing me. Nice lady, but I don't know if I'm in the mood to see her today."

"He's not in," Kitty said, smiling at us.

"We'll cover for you, Colonel."

"Why don't you take a swim? I'll go for a drive."

We were in the pool when the colonel drove out, stopped suddenly by a thin white-haired woman, running to catch him. She climbed into his car as he drove off.

"I don't think I passed his tests," I said.

"You still look like a bohemian, even in a suit. You're not what he expects...military material."

"He's right," I said.

Kitty was treading water, her wet face close to mine. "What about me? What if I'm pregnant?"

"How could that be?"

"The first time we did it," she said. "Daddy would die."

"When? Before, during, or after the shotgun wedding?"

"He might shoot you first."

Kitty's dark eyes were suddenly afraid. The end of our affair could have started there, for even with the colonel's approval, the separation seemed inevitable. We were different people. Would there be much crying with red eyes and noses running?

"Why don't we go in and make love while I can still breathe?"

"Not today," she said, moving her graceful hands in the water. She looked away. A group of noisy children came into the area and jumped into the pool.

"Did you know I had a child and gave it up?"

"No. You never told me that."

"Well—now you know."

There were no more explanations. Later that afternoon, she drove me home in silence.

"Kitty's a snobby bourgeois," Dean insisted. "A sophisticated housewife. You need a beatnik girl with stringy hair who gives good head. Romance? Who needs it?"

"You're a sick mother," I said. "You don't understand love."

"What's to understand?"

Understand, I thought. Understand those quick couplings in the night. Understand images of certain favorite streets somehow changed. Understand her face in the glow of fogged over streetlights. Understand her wet pubic hair in the lamplight. Understand an innocent time passing. And what might have happened if we had a child?

The final goodbye came at a windy bus stop, her voice reciting the words: "I want you just as a friend...please understand." She cried dramatically as my bus arrived. "I'm not right for you." Then I got on the bus and sat with strangers, riding away.

"Pain of separation," I said, to no one. It was deeper and sharper that what had happened with Lynn. The road to our dreams was never fully explored, would remain in some romantic limbo. Kitty had been real for too long, the road now a dead end, our romantic film over. "It had to end sometime," she kept saying. "Remember the night on Twin Peaks? I warned you right at the beginning."

Open House marked the final days of school; parents gathered in the gym to watch a talent show and observe the various school projects. Father Spoan rigged a spotlight to fall on the exhibits of his physics class, when suddenly, as my little man sat down on the tiny electric chair, the project began to smoke, then burst into flames. The faceless little man melted.

"Your project has gone up in smoke," Father Spoan said, using his fire extinguisher. "What a pity. It seems you had a size D battery. Much too strong. They can cause a fire. Don't you know that, Mr. Scientist?"

I walked over to my father. "That son of a bitch sabotaged my project. I did not use oversize batteries!"

"Let it ride for now," Father said. Father Enright came over and took Father aside. Mr. Becker was watching me. "Don't worry," he said. "I saw it work."

April ended with a birthday celebration. Ruby attended, an old woman now, serving drinks. Kitty and the colonel arrived, with Dean bringing his mother. She was still a thin, attractive woman with flowing 1940's Veronica Lake hair and a rich laugh.

"Don't drink too much," she warned Father.

"I won't," Father said. "Just enough to keep me off the ceiling."

"And you should consider giving up meat. It's the first step toward capitalism."

"But I am a capitalist—an imperialist pig dog."

"This is my father," Kitty interrupted.

"Call me Colonel," the colonel said. Father saluted. Dean's mother backed away.

The birthday party survived on film, giving everything a happy glow, hiding the anxiety and desperation: my cousin, Dennis, dancing drunk, smoking, waving at the lens, and Mother mugging for the camera—yet somehow remote, distant. Uncle Emmett sat in a corner with his movie camera and nodded, smiling. Mr. Dooley nursed a drink and stared out the window, detached. He had grown very old and was heartbroken. The night before, someone had released hundreds of baby chicks in Dolores Park.

"For twenty years, I've watched the night traffic from that window, and the one time I leave my spot to hit the can, someone dumps baby chicks in the park!"

"The stories you could tell, Mr. Dooley," Father said.

Dooley looked through his thick glasses. "I could tell you a few stories about that boy of yours and his girl," he said. "But I'm a gentleman."

"And a gentleman needs a drink," Father said, pouring champagne.

I stood in the hall and caught Kitty's eyes. We met in the bedroom where once we made love; we could hear muffled voices in other rooms.

"Where's your mother today?"

"She fell off the wagon and went back to the treatment center. She liked you."

"I liked her."

"She and Daddy are through." Kitty began crying. "I feel something wonderful is ending."

"That's right," I said, "but maybe it's for the best."

Kitty suddenly glared at me. "I mean, you and I are ending."

"Right again. Unless you want to change your mind."

She dabbed her eyes. Music filtered through the door. Now was the time to kiss her nipples, work the small breasts out of the top of her garment, tear her away from a programmed existence. Something wild fired her eyes.

"Let's run off, together. Elope—now!"

"Okay. I'll have the Studebaker running outside."

But later, as Diane and Dean kissed behind the bar and the drunken colonel pawed Dean's mother, Kitty smiled from across the room, her exit already prepared. It was time to leave behind a trivial romance and return home. As the guests finally left, she helped the tipsy colonel to the car. Kitty would be a military wife, and her sad little wave from the street was touching and sweet. I felt something sick turning inside.

"Let her go," Ruby said. "She's got her life. You got other things to do."

* * *

AT graduation, each boy received a diploma. On the lawn, Mother took photos as the priests greeted the boys and parents. Father was appropriately happy.

"You've finally made the grade," he said.

Mr. Becker walked toward me. "I'm sorry I gave him those books to read," he joked. "He reads *Paradise Lost* and identifies with Lucifer."

"I'm just glad he passed physics."

Mr. Becker lowered his eyes. "The final grades come out tomorrow.

A lot of boys received blank diplomas and might spend the summer copying out the physics book to pass."

Father said nothing. I opened the folder with the diploma. It was blank. I looked around for Father Spoan but he was gone. "I think I'll have to postpone my trip to Europe," I said. My voice sounded strange, flat in my ears. Father looked over my shoulder.

"Jesus Christ," he whispered. "Close that!"

Father Enright stood under a tree with visiting parents, and I took him to one side.

"Do you know about this?"

"Yes," he said. "I can't change the final grade. However, I have given Father Spoan a warning about harassing the boys."

"I'm taking this to court."

"Don't do it," Father Enright said. "It won't do you or the school any good."

"He deliberately destroyed my project, and I can prove it. I have the battery he tried to wedge into the slot I made for a smaller one. Mr. Becker said he'd testify for me."

Father Enright looked at me, suddenly quiet. Other parents were approaching.

"I'll talk to Father Spoan about rethinking his final grade. At least be thankful you're in a state of Sanctifying Grace," he added.

"I don't think so," I said.

"I saw you take Communion. You can't take Communion with mortal sins on your soul. One goes to confession. One's soul is washed clean."

I felt a certain power over this fragile man.

"If you don't believe in mortal sins, do they need to be confessed?"

Father Enright leaned against the tree. "My God. If your father heard you."

I knew he was right about Father as I walked away. For the first time, I noticed Tom Manny wasn't at the ceremony. On the church lawn, Welsh stood crying, his parents uneasy. An older boy embraced him. Welsh wiped his eyes. "I know I ain't smart," he said.

Then I saw Richard Bloom detach from a group of boys, the gown draped over his sinewy body, his eyes a piercing blue beneath a crew cut. I turned and he blocked my path.

"It's a bit late to fight, Bloom."

"I know, Ace."

"I'm sure Spoan passed you."

"He did. Listen, I think Father Spoan's a shithead. Maybe I never liked you, but I don't like injustice, either." He held out his hand and I shook it. "What are you gonna do now?"

"I don't know. You?"

"I'm signing up for the Air Force," he said. "If you stop being a dickhead rebel, you might give it a shot, Wrong Way."

"Maybe I will. Good luck."

"Thanks."

Years later, Richard Bloom would die in Vietnam, blown out of the sky after signing up for a second tour. One day, I would visit a replica of the Vietnam Wall, and, touching his name, see my reflection reaching out like a ghost. He would die in a war I would vigorously protest, and the name on the war memorial would stir tears of sorrow and regret.

Father talked to the school authorities, but Father Spoan wouldn't change the grade.

"He's a helluva guy, that Spoan," Father told me. "Maybe I made a mistake. They did educate you, didn't they?"

"Sure. To be an implacable enemy."

"I was afraid of that. You better get started, son." He hesitated. "How's Kitty?"

"Gone."

"Why?"

"She's not good enough for me or I'm not good enough for her."

"We are a pretty scary bunch."

"Maybe I should see Spoan."

"That's not a good idea," Father said.

Spoan sat behind his desk, reading *The Life of Newton*. He looked up and smiled, pointing to a seat in his organized office. Light reflected off his glasses, and his thick fingers touched over the book.

"Your father was here. Nice man. You know, you can learn a lot by copying the text—like the old Irish monks copying great literature. Or you could not finish and be delayed, and end up like Ray Reed, missing his first year of college and eventually getting washed out. I hear he drives a pizza van and drinks a lot." He looked over his spectacles. "Pity. Well, what's it going to be? You're not the kind who begs, I hope."

"You know I used the right battery."

"Really? Actually a double A would be too weak."

"Why do you hate students?"

"I don't hate students. But I don't particularly like them when they are arrogant. You are more than arrogant."

"Mr. Becker saw that my project worked."

"Did he? Well, that's too bad. He's been transferred to Arizona. Now, unless you're going to make a scene, I have next fall's classes to prepare."

"I guess you do."

I turned to go. Father Spoan spoke again.

"I am a tough teacher. No one gets out of my class unscathed, but I can truthfully say they never forget me. Years later, young men come up and shake my hand because they are out in the world succeeding thanks to the character I have helped build. Now you get the copied text to me by late August."

I left.

The priest house sat behind the school, a red brick building with a fence and a garden. The low bathroom windows were rarely locked, resting just above a line of urinals. It was a cold night when we went over the wall and Dean handed up the battery; I dropped down into Father Spoan's private toilet and placed a small metal frog in the lip of the urinal. Wires from the frog ran to a small battery. I worked in the Lysol-smelling darkness, reaching up for the window as I heard footsteps coming down the hall. There was a strange echo in the corridor, like the click of high heels.

Sitting in the window, the light came on and I saw a portly blond man wearing leather: jacket vest, full-length chaps and black high-heeled leather boots. He wore nothing else except a Nazi officer's cap resting on his blond wig, the face naked without the spectacles. Squinting, Father Spoan found the urinal. I dropped to the grass, hearing the first startled scream as I ran toward the car where Dean waited. A white figure appeared out of the darkness and walked toward us; as he crossed the lawn, I recognized Welsh, naked and carrying a pistol. He peered at us.

"What the hell are you guys doing here?"

"Where are you going with that gun, Bill?"

"I'm gonna shoot that son of a bitch! You protectin' him, huh?"

"It's a cold night without clothes," Dean said, staring at the .38 revolver.

Welsh smiled, the wind blowing over his white trembling body, and we realized we were facing a naked madman with a loaded gun. Then he looked up as a face, blond wig askew, appeared in the window. "Damn, has Spoan got hisself a girlfriend now?"

"Welsh, is that you? I'll throw you in jail!"

Welsh's hatred took over. He fired, blowing out the glass over Spoan's head. The face disappeared from the window as Welsh emptied the pistol at the priest house. The shots echoed across the lawn. Crying, Welsh finally dropped the gun to the grass.

* * *

AFTER a closed meeting, Father Spoan retired for health reasons. My grade was changed to a 'D.' In his office, Father Enright sat in a huge chair, pressing his hands to his temples.

"I guess we've lost another boy to Satan. There was no proof, of course, as to who broke into his private toilet. Father Spoan is blind without his specs...tell me, how did you wire that frog?"

"I flunked physics, Father Enright."

"If Bill Welsh didn't cause all that awful scandal with the school and the newspaper, we might've charged you with vandalism."

"Why did Father Spoan have a Nazi officer's cap?"

"Father Spoan fought in the war and collected World War II paraphernalia. I would think you'd be tolerant. And how did you happen to be there?"

"Driving by, we heard shots. Who knows, maybe we saved Spoan's life...or Bill's."

I walked to the door. Father Enright called out: "You almost flunked your entrance exam, so you're not so smart, my friend. Your father pleaded with us to admit you despite your mediocre scores."

"I don't do tests well," I admitted.

"We tried to educate you to be a soldier for Christ. Pride is very dangerous!"

"Bill Welsh's in the psycho ward. I think Father Spoan is very dangerous."

Father Enright looked suddenly tired, sitting at his desk. "You better go."

"Father Enright? I read that Merton book. You're right. He is a brilliant writer and it's a good book. He found his path, but Jesus is not everyone else's path."

"You may go," he repeated in a flat voice.

I left the office and walked down the empty corridor and out into the street, walking away from Saint Ignatius, home of the S.I. Wildcats. I remembered a similar scene from Joyce's *Portrait*. It was a good source of validation.

In a few years, I would return to find the old school building now part of a Catholic university, so not all traces of the Jesuits were gone. The original gym would serve as a private club for wealthy clients. In another part of town, a modern Saint Ignatius prep school would meet the demands of a new century.

CHAPTER FIVE

PROFESSOR MARKFIELD SAT IN HIS OFFICE SMOKING A Marsh Wheeling cigar. Militant black students demonstrated outside and no one doubted the police would crush any united student strike that threatened the school. It would start a war on campus. Manuscripts lay on Markfield's desk and adjoining chairs, and his shelves held many books, including one of his own about four Jewish men searching for a funeral and attending the wrong one. A photo of his young daughter sat on the desk surrounded by papers. He looked up from my story.

"Your typewriter has a clotted 'o'."

"Right."

"The story's not bad. Are all Irishmen this crazy?"

"Absolutely."

"Did any of this really happen in your family?"

"It may have, but I made most of it up. I really don't know much family history—particularly regarding my grandparents. I know someone sponsored my grandmother's trip to America. Even my father doesn't know any details. The old Irish played everything close to the vest or considered family histories not worth discussing."

"But it's a start. Kay Boyle doesn't think you're ready for a creative writing degree. She thinks you need to study the French school."

"What French school is that? Balzac or Camus?"

"I'm sure old French. I do think you need to avoid Hemingway and Faulkner for a while. And don't read my stuff. I'm a Jew! In one story, you got an Irishman calling another Irishman a schmuck."

"I changed that."

"Good. Keep exploring your roots. Nonfiction memoirs are big."

"My grandparents never kept records. It might be quite a search."

Markfield's myopic eyes were large behind the thick glasses; he often looked surprised. Long strands of hair covered a bald spot. His suits always seemed to be deliberately rumpled, dust on the shoulders.

"So search and research," he said with a shrug. "Mine died in Brooklyn. Find out what you can. Go to New York and check the Ellis Island records. Talk to living relatives. You got to learn to walk streets you never walked. I told the graduate committee you're working on a novel, so get me a couple of chapters and we're off to the races."

"Novel? What novel?"

"A novel novel—the one you're working on now."

We could hear angry chants across campus. It had started with the arrest of a militant black instructor carrying a nine-millimeter semiauto in his car. That he kept a gun for protection in a white racist society didn't impress the police, who demanded his concealed weapon permit. When San Francisco State fired the instructor, the black community called for a strike to block access to school until demands were met.

In the office, Markfield glanced at his burning cigar tip. "I think the radicals will abolish the university," he said. "So why aren't you demonstrating?"

"I am. I took a break to see you. My girlfriend's nervous, though. She left town."

"Afraid to get arrested? Maybe she's right. The FBI might start a file on you." Markfield leaned close. His voice dropped to a whisper. "Tell me, what would Bogie do to hippies or *The Graduate*? Would Bogart eat Dustin Hoffman for breakfast? Or what if W.C. Fields were alive? How would he handle students protesting the Vietnam War or civil rights violations?"

I tried to imagine a drunken W. C. Fields showing up on the picket lines. "I'm not so sure. Why?"

"I'm writing an article," Markfield said, "about how old movie heroes would react to our troubled sixties."

"How do you react to my stories?"

"The early one about the Irish kid and the Jewish girl was Huck Finnish—but in a nice way. I like your work, but get a novel going. You can write fiction. And enjoy your parents. Look at me. I had a real Jewish mother. She still nags, 'Wally, you got the Pulitzer, so why not the Nobel?' Gaah!"

"I realize Kay Boyle runs the creative writing graduate program, but why should I care about her criticism? She's from the old school."

"Good old school or bad old school?"

"I guess good. How can I take someone seriously who praised a book called *Being Geniuses Together*? She hates Hemingway."

"Hemingway slept with one of her girlfriends."

"I mean, she can describe dog flowers better than any writer alive."

"John Updike and Linoleum. Unsurpassed."

"If I begin a book with a guy riding a horse down an avenue strewn with dog flowers, I'll re-read Kay Boyle."

"To get into grad school, you gotta play by the rules. I think you've done enough reading. Write." Markfield puffed on the cigar. "How are you fixed with the draft?"

"My asthma kept me out."

"Lucky you. You know, Kay demonstrated recently against the Vietnam War. The cops doused her head under a faucet to destroy her nice coiffure so she'd look like the other ragged hippies."

"I didn't know that."

"Maybe her literary tastes are old-fashioned, but she's politically radical. And you're derivative, but so what? You'll find your voice. Your Irish ancestors came out of rebellion, you know." He glanced out the window, then stared at me again with his owl-like eyes. "Jimmy Dean is passé, but I'm curious. How would Dean fare in the sixties?"

"The rebel? Fit right in. Where do you think rock and roll came from?"

"I should care? Now Elvis is really passé."

"The new rockers aren't. Dylan's a major artist."

"Keats is a major artist."

"So's Bob Dylan."

"You call that music?"

"Protest music."

"Protest? And from this he makes a living?"

"Absolutely. Dylan's a legend."

Markfield shook his head and placed his cigar in the ashtray. "So's Howdy Doody," he said. He touched the story. "You got some good stuff here. If the Jews and Irish ever get together, they'll take over the world."

I turned to walk out.

"No one publishes short stories these days, except maybe a collection by established writers. So write a novel. We'll get you through grad school, but don't teach. Go to Paris or Morocco—get drunk, get laid, get arrested, join the IRA, live with some girl who casts spells, but write, write, rewrite."

"I will."

"And never underestimate a good joke."

"My stories are serious."

Markfield held up his hand like a conductor.

"A guy lives in New York and thinks some mysterious fate controls his life. Someone puts up his house when he leaves his office. Someone puts up his office when he leaves his house. He imagines his life is controlled by unseen forces, so—he goes to a psychiatrist. The psychiatrist listens and says, 'Young man, this is a common anxiety. Move to Cleveland and you'll be better in no time.' The patient takes his advice and leaves the office, prepared to start over in Cleveland. The psychiatrist picks up the phone and says, 'Put up Cleveland.'"

I looked at Markfield. He rolled his eyes comically.

"My class didn't get it, either."

"There's a divine providence that shapes our ends, rough-hew them how we will."

"He quotes *Hamlet*, no less. Revise your new story, because it's always good to have a collection of stories. We need a strong ending. Then write me a novel."

At home, I found the flat empty, despite my four roommates: Marshall, a law student who played cards in the basement of the law school; Fred, the young hippy who stayed stoned and listened to rock music on a headset; and Rosie, who lived with her dog. She had red hair and was loud at night when her private detective came to visit. All of them regarded each other with suspicion, and I was allergic to the dog. I read Kay Boyle's evaluation of my short story:

"Dear Wally, your student simply isn't ready for grad school. He's too influenced by the Americans and that phony Hemingway where café drunks can't stop talking. He needs to study the French. He tells us too much. Show us the action. His story has the quaint quality of these Irish ethnic stories like the movie, *The Quiet Man*. Now all we need are fairies and leprechauns. Please! The passive voice is to be avoided. He needs to cut, especially that pornographic reference to Montana whores. Do I care about cliché Irish immigrants? And we all need to please stop talking! (His ending drops us off a cliff with no resolution.) Wally, I do look forward to your next book. Sincerely, Kay."

It was true that I had to start a novel, but for now, I re-read the recent story.

Montana Bride

THOMAS O'Leary took the bus to Butte, Montana. When he arrived, the papers were full of the Titanic disaster. He remembered his own crossing, taking a cramped berth in steerage with foul air, and when they hit their first squall, the ship groaned and crashed into the waves; he spent a night vomiting with other passengers. At times, Thomas had wondered if leaving Queenstown, the last stop before the Atlantic, was a mistake. He said good-bye forever to his two bothers and his mother, the former Mary Sweeney; his father had died of a stroke. Thomas had to cut all ties with Ireland and strike out for America. At times, he still remembered his mother's tear-stained face.

Thomas liked San Francisco, despite the cold weather, and he had plenty of work cleaning up after the earthquake and paving new streets as the city expanded. His arms and legs were strong from five years of hard street labor. Butte was an all-Irish mining town, bleak but functional. Smoke and smelter fumes covered the city. The lower part was carved out like a huge rock quarry, and the better buildings and hotels were built into the upper level above a steep incline. The brilliant blue Montana sky faded over Butte. At the bus station, he asked after Peter Maloney who had failed to meet him.

"By Christ, I know at least ten with that name," a bus porter said. "This town is full of Micks, and a lot of them have the same name. Try the Irish bar uptown."

"What Irish bar?"

"Well, they're all Irish bars, but this one is The Irish bar. Eventually, everyone gets stewed at The Irish."

He looked at Thomas's young face and light-colored hair.

"This Maloney is a relative?"

"Of sorts," Thomas said.

"There was a Peter Mahoney shot last week."

"Shot? Some drunken brawl?"

"Federal troops. That was one strike that didn't get far. You in the mining business?"

"No. Why are you after asking?"

"This is a mining town," the porter said.

"I noticed."

"The Scots run sheep in the country and we Micks risk our lives in the mines. Why? So the wealthy Americans can declare copper is king."

"I'm an American," Thomas said. "But not wealthy."

"I guess a few wealthy hogs drowned when that big ship went down."

"And the poor below decks," Thomas added.

The porter tilted his head back and peered at Thomas's face. "So you're a Yank, eh? You been here awhile?"

"Yes."

"Who are your people?"

"Roscommon folk. And you? Cork?"

The man was distressed. "Me, a Corkonian? Never on me life! Donegal."

Annoyed at himself for talking so much, Thomas slipped on his cap and with his bag, started walking uptown. It seemed cold for April. All around him he saw Irish faces and heard many Irish accents but didn't think of home. Federal troops marched past him, and he was soon panting as the street grew steeper. The hotels were old but elegant with thick carpets and engraved windows; the bars were long and had brass spittoons. Inside, men stood at the bar drinking and others sat at tables, drinking or playing cards. All of them had the pale yet grimy faces of miners, even after a wash. A dance hall offered burlesque. The Irish Bar was in a three-story building and solidly packed. Smoke drifted in thick layers through the spacious room, and Thomas hesitated, since he didn't like to drink. He did smoke, however, and took out a cigarette before walking up to the bar itself. He ordered a beer, declining the addition of a shot.

"A shot of Bushmill's will put hair on your chest, young man."

"I bet it will." He looked at the bartender's rough ruddy face, lined with mutton chop whiskers. "Do you know a Peter Maloney?"

"And who might be askin'?"

"Thomas O' Leary."

"And what does this gentleman look like, Mr. Thomas O' Leary?"

"I don't know."

A one-armed man at the end of the bar laughed.

"I guess we're after a bad start," the bartender said. "I know a Pete Maloney. Homely fella. Thick lips, black bushy hair, blue eyes, and a Sligo accent."

"This Peter is from Sligo."

"Not a Belfast Protestant, then?"

"I hope not. Not in this town, anyway."

"We're all Catholics here," the bartender said. The bartender held his eyes, wiping glasses. Two men played dice on the long mahogany bar. "How is it you don't know what he looks like? Were you both blind from drink?"

"Does it matter?" Thomas drank his beer. "Let's say we're after having a written correspondence."

"Impressive," the bartender said. "Good to hear a few of these dumb Micks can read and write English since the Brits took our own language, Gaelic." He reached out and took Thomas's hands, turning them over. "I can see you're a working man. Have a beer on the house."

"No thanks."

"Careful, lad. You don't drink, you're no true Irishman."

"Give it to me," the one-armed man said.

"Sure," the bartender said. He slid the beer down the bar and looked at Thomas. "A lot of miners have lost arms, if not lives, to the dynamite. From your tan, I'd say you work outdoors. What kind of labor do you do, Mr. O' Leary?"

Thomas took a puff from his cigarette.

"Does everyone in Butte have to know your business? How about telling me a good hotel and one not too expensive."

"Kate's across the street," the bartender said. He winked and moved down the bar to serve other noisy customers. "I'll keep an eye out for Mr. Maloney...but quite a few fit that description."

Thomas felt light-headed from even one beer. He watched the other customers. Two of them discussed a dance called the Tarantula performed by a local female dancer named Jew Jess.

"Be Jasus, but you'd swear she's got a tarantula under her skirts as she does this Flamenco number, and one by one, off come the clothes. Then she stands in her shift, stepping on the poor spider. Of course, who's after lookin' at the spider?"

"For a few dollars, I hear you get Jess."

"And she picks your pocket clean for a few more."

"She's not a real Jew, is she?"

"God no, man, Butte don't let them in."

"Then who is Moses Singerman on East Park Street? I'm after hearing his spieler all afternoon shouting about Singerman's wares."

"Them town criers are loud," the second man said.

Thomas left the crowded bar. He looked down the steep street and blinked in the afternoon light. Kate's Hotel was an old building with peeling paint and a cool, dark lobby. Many cats played or prowled in the well-furnished parlor. A heavy-set woman with a pearl necklace around the folds of her neck approached him.

"And what can I be doon for you, laddie?"

He recognized the Scottish burr. "I'd like a room for the night."

The jowly face beneath bleached blonde hair expressed surprise. "A room? For just you? No one else?"

"You don't see anyone else, do you? Your rates?"

The woman regarded him. "Me name's Mabel," she said. "I guess we could give you a room for two dollars a night."

"That sounds reasonable. I'm looking for a Peter Maloney."

"Got a Maloney who wants to be mayor. Your friend comes in here often, you think?"

"I don't know if he lives here but—"

"Quite a few think they do," Mabel said. "I may know that name. Funny looking gent?"

"Never met him."

Mabel seemed puzzled. "Well now, that's a bit awkward. Look, if you do anything with the lassies, it will cost extra."

"The lassies?"

"Like nothing you'd be seein' in Ireland. Better than what they got at the Dumas establishment."

144

Just then, a young woman in a slip ran past them and up the stairs. Thomas looked away. "I guess she didn't have too much time to dress."

Mabel had a coarse laugh. "Who sent you?"

"The barkeep across the street."

"Malone? He's a sot. Cheap, too. Short arms and deep pockets," she said. "Come follow me."

He followed her up the stairs and down a hall reeking of cats to a small room with an ornate double bed and mirrors along the walls. Nymphs and Satyrs frolicked on the wallpaper, the bed sheets and lampshades a matching red. A single window looked across the street to The Irish Bar and other houses set into the side of the hill. Mabel took his two dollars.

"First time in Butte?"

"Yes."

"You just off the boat?"

Thomas straightened up. "I'm an American citizen," he said.

"Good for you. Don't get sore. A lot of you young Irish bucks seem really green, if ya doan mind my sayin' so. If the parties keep you up, join in. Doan worry about any traffic and your stuff during the day. No one steals from Kate's place."

"Where's Kate?"

"Died years ago. Let me know when you wanna check oot of the hoose."

Thomas put his bag on the bed and sat down, puzzled by the party remark. This was a working town. Who had time to party? He also wondered how long he could stay in Butte without finding the mysterious Peter Maloney and taking care of his business. His brother in Ireland had assured him the Maloneys were a wonderful clan and had pretty daughters. He found a small restaurant with a Chinese cook and enjoyed a meal of beef and potatoes. Tomorrow, he could check the mining office and find the elusive Peter Maloney. Perhaps the fact he now thought of himself as an American rather than Irish caused this feeling of separation from the familiar Irish workers in the restaurants and bars. He was glad he didn't work in the mines. Deep dark places scared him.

That night, he remembered Mabel's words about parties. He could hear a piano somewhere in the hotel and people running up and down the stairs; he heard male and female voices, whispers and sudden laughs beyond the walls. He tried to sleep but often a sharp laugh or shout woke him. The street outside seemed to be unusually busy. When he did sleep, he dreamed of Ireland and the last time he saw his two brothers and crying mother before taking the ship to America. He knew his brothers would stay behind in Ireland. If what young Patrick said were true about his wife, the former Bridgett Maloney, perhaps Thomas would do well with Bridgett's sister, soon coming to America.

In the morning, Mabel was smoking a cigarette when Thomas walked into the lobby. She had a cup of coffee and looked up from her newspaper. A few women sat in chairs talking quietly among themselves. They looked at Thomas with idle curiosity and wore long loose skirts and blouses that were low cut. There was mirth and a hard glint in their eyes.

"Had a good sleep, laddie?"

"Oh, Mabel, I tried. There was a bit of noise last night."

Mabel winked. "Always a bit of noise. The girls were askin' about ya. Doan wanna make them upset, ya know. They got feelings, too."

Thomas blinked. "Feelings?"

"Sure. And if no one picks them, they get the boot."

One of the girls laughed. A young cat played with Mabel's gold hoop earrings.

"You plan to sweat for the Anaconda?"

"I'm afraid of snakes."

"The wages is good," Mabel continued. "I been in mining towns where certain bosses got their kneecaps broken now and then by the Molly Maguires. Butte's safe enough—except for crazy union organizers and strikebreakers, of course. After work down in the pit, a young gent needs bit of excitement."

Another blonde woman entered with a young man behind her and walked up the stairs. Mabel drew on the cigarette, watching him.

"We need some Oriental girls here for an exotic touch, don't you think? Or a Negress."

"I suppose," Thomas said. "I'm after getting some breakfast."

"Try The Irish. You can eat or drink breakfast there. Or the Success Café."

Thomas nodded. Mabel still stared at him. "You do fancy the girls, don't you?"

"Why certainly," he said.

"I got some of the best Calico in Montana, but I run a straight hoose, you understand. Any funny queer business and you'll be out in the street but fast!"

"I'm a good Catholic," Thomas insisted.

"Aren't they all?"

Thomas tipped his cap to the girls, who smiled and waved.

"You ain't one of them outside agitators planning to strike a blow for the martyred Irish, are ya?"

"I'm a laborer," Thomas told her. "I build things."

"I got a feeling the Saint Patrick's Day parades around here will turn into riots. Too many warring Micks."

Thomas nodded and left Kate's Hotel. Across the street, it was a new bartender, and as he ate his eggs with coffee, he wondered if Mabel was right, that perhaps he was a bit green.

Jesus, Mary and Joseph, she runs a brothel and I don't know the difference, he thought. A cat house!

Sitting at the table, he became aware of someone sitting down. The man was in his late thirties with red hair and hard, cold eyes.

"I hear you're lookin' for Pete Maloney."

"I am. You are—?"

"I'm Pete Maloney. Who the hell are you?"

Thomas wiped his mouth; he took out his pack of cigarettes and offered one to Pete, who accepted.

"Thomas O' Leary."

"And who is Thomas O' Leary?"

"A union man."

Pete seemed to relax. "Are ya now? I haven't seen your name at the Miner's Union Hall."

"I'm from San Francisco. Do you have a sister named Agnes, Peter?"

"Hell no!"

He lit Pete's cigarette. "I thought so. I guess I got the wrong Peter Maloney."

"There are quite a few around," the man agreed. "We hear some

147

Federal sharpshooters are comin' in case there's a strike. You lookin' for a bride—here?"

"Maybe. You married?"

"For the love of Christ, no! We got enough widows." They sat, smoking. "Well then, I'm off to work. The Anaconda Company built this town, but it's dangerous work. You go deep enough and something happens, like a fire, they can't get you out. None of us will get rich but the owners sure will if we go to war. I thought we left Irish slavery behind in Ireland. You lookin' to dig copper?"

"I got work in San Francisco."

"Lovely city but cold," Pete said. "Of course, nothing's colder than a Montana winter." He got up. "If a strike breaks out here, it'll heat the town up." Pete gave him a salute and left.

Thomas walked to the Anaconda office and a foreman told him they had four Peter Maloneys on the job.

"They're all down in the Badger State Mine or the Speculator—except for one."

"What's he look like?"

"Doocastle fella. Thick lips, black hair, blue eyes. Why?"

"That could be himself. Why isn't he working?"

"Who knows with these Micks? Maybe he's having tea with Frank Little." A group of miners entered an elevator to ride down into the earth. The foreman stared at him. He had a thick jaw and thrust it forward as though his collar were too tight. "You're after askin' a lot of questions. You from the union?"

"Not this union. I just want to find the fella."

"He's not here."

"Good day, then."

He turned and saw a young woman blocking his way. She wore a long skirt with an old-fashioned bustle, a white blouse with leg of mutton sleeves and a fashionable hat with a broad brim. Her small hands held a parasol. Thomas felt the penetrating blue eyes engulf him.

"You're after looking for Peter Maloney?"

"Yes."

"Maloney from Sligo?"

"I believe his people are from Sligo, yes."

"And who might you be?"

"Thomas." He tipped his cap. "I live in San Francisco. You see—"

"We come across the pond a long way and Peter forgets to meet us." She pronounced it 'Pay-ter.' "It's typical of him to forget things. I hope he doesn't have a snootful. My sister and I are at the women's hotel." She shook his hand, her eyes still on his face. "And what was your business with my brother?"

"Your brother?" Before he could stop himself, he asked, "Are you Agnes?"

She withdrew her hand. "Yes. And how did you know my name?"

Thomas felt a sudden burning in his face. "Why don't we have some tea?" he stammered. "We can discuss it then."

"I think it would be better if we met tomorrow, and I'll bring along my sister, Bessie. Peter told you my name, did he?"

"Well, yes—he did."

He saw her clear blue eyes focus and look past him. Noise came from the mine and fumes swept over them.

"Nice of brother Peter to mention me."

"Yes."

Agnes put a handkerchief to her mouth and nose. "You know my name. What is your full name?"

He told her.

"My God, my other sister married an O' Leary."

Thomas saw the eyes again, glaring at him over the white cloth. He imagined her running through possibilities.

"Is your brother Patrick O' Leary?"

"I'm afraid so, ma'am. A nice fellow," he weakly added.

Agnes opened a parasol and turned. She stopped and looked over her shoulder.

"You tell Peter if you see him first that I am not some heifer to be bought and sold—or bargained for!" She turned away and then turned back again. "And you look like something the cat dragged in. Get a professional shave."

Agnes walked up the crowded street, smoke filling the sky. Thomas called out, "Perhaps we can still meet for tea?"

But she had disappeared into the crowd of workers. Five Federal troops watched from a distance.

Back at Kate's, Mabel said, "The Irish has rooms, ya know, for one dollar a night."

Thomas pushed back his cap. "But Mabel, how could I desert such a lovely establishment as this?"

"We used your room this morning. Sara cleaned it up." Mabel's eyes went bright suddenly. "You might fancy her. She's English. I know a lot of you Irish like to poke English girls and call it revenge for the rape of Ireland. I even got a Union Jack you can put over her face."

"I'm a gentleman," Thomas said. Mabel laughed, deep and throaty. Upstairs, the room was clean though Thomas imagined scents of spent lust and open bottles of whiskey. He looked at himself in the mirror, and then took out his razor and sharpened the blade on a leather strap. In the morning, he'd want a close shave. Under the bureau lay a pair of panties that he picked up and put on the stuffed chair.

"My God," he said aloud.

He was lying in bed napping when he heard someone gently try the door. The knob rattled and turned; Thomas got up in the darkened room and stood behind the door as a man entered and approached the bed. Moments later, Thomas seized the intruder and threw him against the wall. The shorter man screamed.

"For God's sake, don't hurt me!"

Thomas pulled a young boy into the light. The eyes were wide and the mouth full with thick, carnal lips.

"Who are you?"

"I'm Peter Maloney!"

Thomas released the young man and stared at his face. "You're a boy."

"I'm not so young. I got eighteen years. And how old are you?"

"Twenty-five, as if it's any of your business. Next time, knock. I talked to your sister, Agnes. She's a bit sore. Are you after selling her to the highest bidder?"

"You offering to pay?" Peter asked and smiled.

"Sit down," Thomas said.

Peter sat down. "I admire a man who rents a room in a whore house. I won't tell Agnes."

"I don't think she'd care now, one way or the other. Did she pay your way over?"

Peter didn't meet his eyes. "Another sister did."

"How did you know where I was?"

"When you ask questions about someone in this town, that someone hears quick enough. And how's me brother-in-law, Patrick O' Leary?"

"He's fine. Why didn't you meet me at the bus station? Or meet your poor sisters, for God's sake?"

"They can take care of themselves. I was at the Miles City bucking horse sale."

"Into horses are ya?"

"No," Peter said. They stared at one another. Far enough apart in years, Thomas suddenly felt even older.

"So what were you doing?"

"I don't know if that's your business. No offense, Tommy."

"None taken. Tell, me, who is Frank Little?"

"He's the man who organized the IWW."

"Which is?"

"Industrial Workers of the World."

"You weren't after having tea with him, were you?

"And who suggested that?

"The foreman at the mine."

Peter began to laugh. "That's a good one," he said "You know, thugs might hang Frank Little one day. Well," Peter continued. "I suggest you meet the two girls tomorrow—Bessie's a tough one to please, so don't mention this place—and maybe spend a day at the Columbia Gardens. They got a carousel there."

"So you ride wooden horses, then?"

"Oh sure. We had a company picnic last week but it was a disaster. The Irish and Austrian miners had a tug o' war, and when the Irish team got a bit of extra help from drunk friends, some overexcited Austrian drew a pistol. Into this rode a mounted Irishman with a rifle and shot two Austrians dead."

"Sounds like a lovely picnic."

"It was, actually."

Thomas walked over and looked out the window. A trooper was arguing with a pedestrian and pushed him with his bayonet. The pedestrian moved on. Then Thomas glanced at the young Irish boy sitting in the chair, seeing himself at nearly the same age boarding a ship for America.

"Peter? Why all the Federal troops?"

"To keep the peace. They shoot anyone who threatens the mine—or threatens scabs."

"Maybe your union could work out something reasonable and peaceful."

"Peaceful? Here?" Peter shook his head, laughing quietly. "My God, it must be lovely to work in San Francisco. Everyone gets a fair wage and takes tea in the afternoon."

Thomas took out a cigarette. He sensed a mature seriousness behind the boy's youthful appearance.

"Is the lovely Agnes even looking for a husband?"

"Of course, whether she admits to it or not. She left Ireland. Bessie left Ireland. I got other sisters who left or who will soon leave Ireland. Why start a family in that bleeding country when you can make a fortune and start a family here in America? Agnes plans to settle in San Francisco," he added. "I don't want her finding a husband here."

"What's in this for you? You expect reimbursement?"

Peter held up his hands. "God no. May I take a cigarette?"

"Suit yourself."

Thomas handed over one. They smoked in the room with mirrors and a large double bed. The piano sounded again, plaintive and sad. Peter reached behind the cushion and lifted the silky panties.

"I'd like to sample the wares here." Peter winked. "Have you?"

* * *

THOMAS heard the sirens as he sat in the restaurant having tea with Agnes and Bessie. Her sister was larger than Agnes, and she studied him, asking pointed questions while Agnes sat quietly. He had just assured them that he was not a drinking man when an ambulance drove past the windows. Both women lost their color.

"Mother of God, Peter's in the Speculator mine today," Agnes said.

Thomas stood up. "Perhaps it's not the mine."

Agnes began to sob. "We already lost a sister," Bessie said, holding Agnes.

"I'll investigate," Thomas said.

He saw people running past the window. Then he was outside and running down the hill toward the mine. Even from a distance, he could see the smoke and crowds forming outside the perimeter. A cordon of troops converged on the accident site. Men with picket signs suddenly appeared as though they had been rehearsing for weeks. Thomas saw the mine foreman shouting at workers to get back to work.

"For Christ's sake, it's only one mine in trouble. We'll get them out. We're losing money standing around."

"We're on strike as of now," a worker shouted.

The foreman blew a whistle; two men grabbed the sign and struck the protester in the face. Friends carried him away. A young woman with a child appeared and began screaming, "Where's my husband?" She was still shrieking when a group of women contained her. Thomas heard the voices running through the crowd as more pickets emerged. Perhaps hundreds of men were dead or trapped far below. Smoke indicated a fire racing up the shaft. They would never get the miners out unless they began digging and hoisting out survivors on the elevators. The dry timbers could ignite and spreading gas kill any workers crawling through darkness.

"I represent the union," a tall man shouted. "We demand you shut down all operations except a rescue operation."

The burly foreman had more men with clubs behind him and they pushed back the strikers with picket signs. Thomas walked to the entrance of the steaming mine and then scanned the crowd for Peter. He could smell smoke and the sickening smelter odor. The crowd pushed against him. As the workers left an undamaged shaft, he saw Federal troops lining up, and an officer preparing to give orders. The tall union leader and the Anaconda Company foreman were shouting at one another when an explosion rocked the ground and more smoke and dust poured out. Miners grabbed shovels and dug furiously at the earth as larger crowds arrived from town, including women with children. Thomas confronted the Federal officer.

"I can find an extra pick and shovel if you need one."

The officer stepped back. "You best watch your mouth, Irish."

Thomas heard the sound of cocking rifles. Then he saw Peter, his face blackened, standing on a rock and shouting orders through a bullhorn. As a crew worked the entrance to the mine, Agnes ran out of the crowd and embraced her brother. Thomas walked up to them. The horn slipped from Peter's shaking fingers. "A fire," he said.

"If we take the elevator down and dig toward the site of the accident, we can shore up the sides and take them out," Thomas said, thinking about his fear of deep, dark places.

Tears streaked Peter's soot-grimed face. "I was about to ride down. From the look of things, the fire ran up insulation on the cable. A carbide light could set it off. They're running out of air if they're alive. Even if we reach the bodies, the sides will cave in. There must be a hundred down there and there's gas on every level! Unless they escape to other mines, God save them."

"But can't they pump some air in the shaft?"

Thomas took a heavy shovel and began digging away at a mound of earth before the blocked elevator. Agnes brought him a cup of water. Their eyes met. Moments later, flame shot from the shaft, blowing away dirt. As a newspaper photographer took pictures of the disaster, workers raised the elevator. Thomas saw the white-hot cage and jumped back; inside laid charred bones and overall buttons.

"There's nothing you can do," Peter said, holding him. "For the love of God."

The next day, Thomas O' Leary left Butte, never to see it again. Agnes and her sister said good-bye while Peter continued the search and rescue efforts. Two months later, Thomas received a note informing him that Agnes Maloney, formerly of Doocastle in Sligo County, would receive his visit and that they could indeed have tea in San Francisco's Japanese Tea Gardens.

The End

I placed the story by the old typewriter. Fiction always changed reality, shaping it, bringing out a vision through reflections and distortions. Who were these people from so long ago? A Marsh Wheeling stub rested in the ashtray, and I smoked them for good luck, always careful not to inhale. Professor Markfield was right; it was time to start a novel. Fading sunlight glowed in the window overlooking a parking lot. As I watched a woman walking to the neighborhood store, I realized Marshall was standing in the doorway. He held a textbook.

"Marshall. I didn't know you were here."

"I've been here all the time. I read your story. It's…good."

"Really? You shouldn't read my stuff until it's finished."

"Sorry. You left a copy out. If I work for the Federal Government, I'll be investigating safety procedures in mines." Marshall put a law text on the table. "You joining the strike?"

"I have to."

"Why risk an arrest? Wait until things cool down."

"This is the age of rebellion," I said, smiling.

"If you need a lawyer, give me a call."

Two weeks later, Markfield sat in his office reading my first two chapters about a rebellious student into Pynchon, mind-altering drugs and anarchy. The hero, unlucky in love, had declared war on all established order. Markfield's windows were shut against tear gas. His magnified eyes expressed concern, though the chapters were meant to be darkly comic.

A united student shutdown strike had prompted the school president's counter attack. He was the third university president to take office during the crisis, and he was Asian, proving the university wasn't racist. Anti-strike thugs wearing blue armbands roamed the campus ambushing strikers with red armbands. Police took up housing on the grounds, eager for crowd control, shaking down students and advancing on the picket lines. Police ranks might include my childhood friend, Officer Dean. Would he arrest me? Governor Ronald Reagan beamed with confidence that the police would contain hooligans who "looked like Tarzan and smelled like Cheetah." Perhaps Grandfather had been right. There was something truly frightening about the glib, handsome Reagan. Was it the ignorance made coherent that made Reagan a too-perfect enemy? Marshall had joined black students to support the strike, and a rumor circulated that other unions would join if the teachers walked. Dockworkers on the line could make a difference.

Markfield handed me my chapters. "Not bad. You know, we might have to meet off campus," he added.

"You're against the fascist administration?"

"President Hayakawa in a beret jumped on a sound truck yesterday, and judo-chopped protesting students. My Jewish liberal guilt notwithstanding, of course, I'm against them—all of them! We lost six million in the death camps. I have a problem with Nazis, including well-educated American ones."

"The book? You like?"

"You got a novel going here," he said. "I like."

"A good novel?"

He shrugged. "Who knows? A novel."

"No jokes today?"

"I have one about the herring at Ratner's." He stopped. "No jokes today. Tell me. Thomas and Agnes in your story? You don't show us their courtship or wedding. Kay has a point. You drop us off a cliff."

"I really don't know anything about their courtship. I do know Captain Omar Bradley went to Butte and crushed a Saint Patrick's Day riot. Anti-union thugs hanged Frank Little and shot a few miners. My great uncle Pete lived through it."

"Maybe you should talk to Uncle Pete."

"He's gone," I said.

"So's my Uncle Morty. The stories he could tell."

We spent the afternoon walking a picket line with students and teachers; only a few students crossed the line to taunts.

"I hope you learn a lot in school today."

A lone guitarist played protest songs. A bus disgorged other union members who joined the strike, and a police cordon nervously watched this new development. A young woman suddenly tore down the American flag, and as the police converged to arrest her, students rushed forward to intercede. I heard the sound of a riot club striking a student as a policeman knocked the sign out of my hands. He raised his club. "Go ahead, try it."

I saw the policeman's eyes behind the protective visor. Another officer pulled him back, and I suddenly recognized the face of officer J.R. Dean.

"It's all right," he said.

He turned and lifted his baton in a salute.

CHAPTER SIX

THE DOORBELL RANG.

I opened the door, my jaw swollen from yanked wisdom teeth. Father stood in the shadowed doorway, blinking. He was well-dressed in a dark suit, and I never discovered why he came to the flat. His eyes had a slightly startled look, and heavy traffic moved on Market Street.

"Tom? Dad? What brings you here?"

"Thought I'd case out the joint."

He came in and we walked down a hallway and sat in the kitchen. He blinked a few times and grinned.

"Holly smoke, not bad."

"Are you drunk?"

"Drunk? Me? I'm dressed in a nice suit, well-groomed. Oh maybe I had a few belts at lunch, but so what? You should ask, 'Why am I not drunk?' Have any wine, that cheap rot-gut stuff?"

"Certainly," I said, "but I have to go to school today."

"Today's Saturday, and it's late."

"Right, it is late, but I should drive out there. You'll have to leave soon. Okay?"

"No, I'll give you a lift."

I looked at his handsome but aged face, the black hair combed back, glistening with baby oil, remembering those summer vacations, his body always cutting through the lakes, rivers, resort pools, swimming with that cinematic Olympic style. That was his image: the swimmer. I poured some wine.

"How's dear old Mom?"

"Still kicking," he said. "Unfortunately."

"Why unfortunately?"

"We had an argument, son. Never argue with stupid people." He drank the wine and looked around the kitchen. "Where's Dolly?"

"Out walking her dogs. Or so she said. I think one of them will be put to sleep, thank God."

"Only one? You're allergic to dogs."

"She never seems to remember that."

"Nor does your mother. Is that why you don't come around anymore? The Doberman?"

"That could be one reason."

"Ugly dog," Father said.

"Before we leave, we'll come around. Maybe freeload for a week."

"Please do."

We sat for a long time, drinking wine, not speaking.

"I shouldn't criticize your mother," he said. "Women! I like Dolly Whatshername, but she's vague, somehow, like talking to fog. Pretty girl, though. What kinda name's Dolly Ann? She from the South?"

"No." I thought for a minute. "Actually, I'm not sure where she's from. Her mother and grandfather live here. The old guy's a mean old man, badly crippled. Hates Democrats. Really hates blacks."

"Well, you are white," Father said.

"He has always tried to control her, but it never worked. God, if he only knew."

"Knew what?"

"It doesn't matter."

I knew from Dolly's other lovers and her own remarks that she had been ducking out of her house since she turned thirteen, even sneaking into porno theatres to learn more about sex. I couldn't mention her legendary clandestine meetings—in cars, alleyways, abandoned buildings or available apartments, even sneaking young boys into the house, preferably a few of color, while her racist grandfather slept. Her mother had a nasal voice, a bland, somewhat homely face, and was always polite but vague about Dolly's whereabouts, though perhaps she didn't know.

I drank, then touched my swollen jaw.

"Took out those damn wisdom teeth, huh?"

"Yep."

"I was scared when you went into the hospital with meningitis. I guess we can handle some wisdom teeth, right?"

"Right."

Spinal meningitis hit gradually in a time of school strikes and political assassinations, the disease raging, subsiding, then striking again. I resisted treatment and felt betrayed when Marshall took me to the hospital and the doctors did a spinal tap. I remembered the high fevers, the stiff neck, Father's worried eyes above the facemask. The illness took me out of life, as though I could float free from my body and watch the doctors hovering over the patient's bed. A long needle drained spinal fluid, causing body convulsions and headaches. After the fever spiked and finally broke, I escaped amputation of limbs or death. Others on the ward died. Dolly Ann also came to the hospital, and upon release, stayed with me in the same room where my grandfather had died. The progression back to health was long. I often stared at the ceiling and thought of my Irish grandparents and how the world had changed outside the house on 20th Street. Dolly Ann brought food and read from Dickens' *Great Expectations* and then stripped and lay beside me, helping me when I was too weak to respond. The disease didn't leave gently. For a period after the illness, even orgasms were painful.

"You are so lucky," she said. "I know we've had a rough time, but let's work at it."

The relationship had always been stressful, and no one thought we would last. Other people had come into our lives and left. Mother tolerated Dolly Ann's visits and Father only worried, his life briefly enlivened by shaking Robert Kennedy's hand when he campaigned in San Francisco's Castro District. Kennedy was shot four days later. Did young lovers have a chance in that troubled world?

Father offered me a cigarette.

"I'm trying to quit," I said, taking it. "So is Dolly Ann, but she doesn't last long. She sneaks a few. Maybe I'll quit drinking."

"You think you'll ever go on the wagon?"

"I can't imagine life without drink," I admitted.

Father shook his head. "Spoken like an Irishman."

He looked at me as though he had something else to say. I waited patiently.

"I worry about you, son."

"Why? I landed a teaching job in Idaho. I'm getting married."

"In a civil ceremony, not in the church."

"If it's a church wedding, I can never marry again if we divorce. With a judge, I'm considered unmarried by that same church."

Father considered this. "I never thought of that. Maybe I shoulda had some judge marry your mother and me. Then I might've had a chance to fail with someone else."

"Let's not talk about the Church or marriage."

"Or drinking," Father said. "I didn't want it for you, but I'm an old hypocrite. I love the old sauce."

"So do I."

We both laughed like adolescents.

"Your mother hates it when I get stewed."

He lifted his glass and I poured some more of the Red Mountain wine.

"Here's how," he said.

"Here's how."

We drank.

"I bet you don't care about your aching teeth anymore?"

"No, I don't," I said. Soon my head would begin drifting away.

"Are you still going to school?"

"That was just a ruse."

"A ruse? Why?"

"Because you're here and you're drunk, and I won't know what to say if Marshall or Dolly Ann, who's so paranoid about drinking, come home."

"Do I embarrass you, son?"

"No," I said, feeling embarrassed.

"Marshall's a Jew. Jews are smart." He looked at me and lit another cigarette. "Dolly Ann's worried about your drinking? Well, it did occur to me. I didn't drink during the war. Neither did Dennis's father, John. Oh, maybe we had a few on leave. We both grew up hating the British, but after Dunkirk, it was obvious they had guts and we had to help. In February of 1945, John and I enlisted and got stuck in Hawaii—a paradise. Emmett served on a minesweeper and saw lots of action, but not me. Just the Military Post Office, Hawaiian girls, and an invasion of Japan that never came."

"Despite that, it must've been a dark time. War is war."

"True, but there was sense of camaraderie, of working together for a noble cause. I was twenty eight years old, and the other recruits called me 'Pop.' I had to deck one young trainee when he pushed me into the

160

back of a truck. After that, we became friends."

We could hear traffic in the street outside.

"When did Mother leave?"

"Sometime after the war." A dreamy look came into his eyes. "You know, she met me in San Diego before I shipped out. A Philip Morris cigarette girl in short pants snapped our picture while we drank shots with beer. We knew the war was ending, though everyone feared a final blood bath. At that moment, we were in love and the future seemed so...so bright." I knew the black and white photograph showing a handsome sailor with his girl. Mother wore a flower broach with a fake diamond pinned beneath the bust of her pleated dark dress. They glowed with love, smiling at the camera. "Do you want to get married?" he asked. "You used the word 'divorce'."

"I know," I said, facing my father across the kitchen table. "To be honest, I don't know."

A friend had mentioned a rock group about to break up when a hit record forced them to stay together. At the point of an inevitable separation from Dolly Ann, I got a teaching job and our parents encouraged marriage over a living-together-without-it arrangement. Perhaps stability would change everything, though something was wrong. Dolly, whose real name was Barbara, had a friendly but remote character, asking questions but never answering them. She suggested a hidden agenda, the person who knew everyone's business, read personal mail and eavesdropped on nighttime phone calls. "I think she's a secret agent, but working for whom?" Marshall once asked. "Does she speak Russian or Chinese on a hidden short wave?"

It had been what Hollywood called a 'cute meet,' Dolly working at the post office where I stuck endless letters into slots. At night, I rode a motorcycle along the freeway feeling the wind in my hair, thrilled with the rumbling cycle. Other bikers waved to me as I wove through racing traffic. One afternoon at work, she came by to collect mail and saw my leather shirt over the stool.

"You ride motorcycles?"

"Yes," I said. "Dangerous, but I love it."

"I like danger," she said, smiling. "I've always wanted to ride one."

Her platinum hair was twisted in a popular beehive fashion, but the eyes had a direct stare that suggested another world. A nervous laugh greeted probing questions. That weekend, she clung to me as we rode up Twin Peaks, taking the winding narrow roads. Dolly Ann sat on the back, calmly doing her make-up while leaning into tight curves at high speed. It was a pleasant afternoon. One day, I opened the door and she was just there. Then she stood by the mirror, shedding her clothes in the small room I rented off Market Street.

"I live with someone," she said, "a musician, but Doug will never know. He's stoned most of the time."

"So you like deception? Secret affairs?"

She didn't answer. Why should anyone complain when she made love like a porno star? She was a musician and the male organ was her instrument. A man could feel like a god as she worshipped between his thighs. Sex banished all doubt at night, but then daylight came and a painful dread that something didn't fit. If questions were asked, the handsome face with slightly bulging eyes under bleached bangs went passive. The eyes held secrets, giving none. When I eventually joined Doug in an ill-fated rock band, it was never mentioned that we once shared the same woman.

I had kept a journal and often embellished my adventures. It was my training as a writer. A chance bar meeting with a female became a wild orgy, with poetry recited naked beneath a brilliant moon. One afternoon, I came home and found Dolly Ann reading through my journal. It was easy to break into the small furnished room since a skeleton key opened the lock. Squatting, she glared at me over the pages.

"So you had…you had other women?"

"And you haven't seen other men? What are you doing here?"

She didn't answer.

"Why are you reading my private journal?"

"You describe me as some blonde bimbo painting her face?"

"That was someone else."

The anger tightened her jaw. "Someone else?"

"Why are you reading my private stuff?"

"Because I check everyone out. You're deceitful, like all the others!"

"What others?"

She hurled the pages at me and left.

162

It should've ended there, but one night I opened the door and Dolly Ann stood in the dimly lit hall. She smiled and came into the furnished room. Laurence Olivier on an album cover of Shakespeare readings watched from a shelf. A streetcar passed on Market Street. She liked to undress slowly, dropping her clothes and kneeling to undo belts and unzip pants. It was a fluid, sensuous ritual, hands pulling down cotton cloth, lips pressing against tumescent flesh in a carnal sacrament.

"You might think I'm abasing myself," she said, "but I'm in control."

A month later, we shared a flat on Market Street with Marshall and others, including non-students. When Dolly left for work, the anger returned.

"While you're sleeping through class, I'll be filing letters."

"I'm in grad school," I argued. "I can't work. I've got an agent who wants me to revise my novel and that's work."

"That's fun work!"

"If it makes you feel any better, we'll wear sackcloth and ashes while you're at the post office processing mail," Marshall said. "We can beat each other with whips."

It didn't make her feel better.

Now Father questioned our marriage plans, a striking admission. Would I become a person who would "never know"? One clear evening, I rode the motorcycle along the Great Highway parallel to the ocean. Later that night, thieves stole it while I slept, which might have saved my life. Officer Dean, off-duty the next morning, stood in the doorway shaking his head.

"Your Harley's gone," he said. "Forgot to lock it again, right?"

We had made nightly runs roaring up San Francisco hills, recalling our high school adventures. The motorcycle brought many thrills, but after escaping two near-collisions, I knew a third might be fatal.

I was still remembering the chopped Harley when Father's rich voice continued and I realized he was asking questions. "Answer this. Are you happy living with her?"

"I could do without that awful woolly white dog," I said. "He barks at everything. How could anyone name such a useless puffball Rex? You name a king Rex. As for Dolly, she wants to get out of the city, see the country."

"That's no reason to get married," Father said, "and San Francisco's a lovely city."

"Right."

"The Irish took it over, thank God. Don't get me wrong, she's a nice young woman."

"I know."

"Maybe all your fights are healthy. Our family can't exist without heated discussions, right?" Father paused. "Have you played around, son?"

"Some, but we always reconcile."

"Because when you marry, it might be over. Then you have to go through the pain of divorce. She is smart."

"You think she's smarter than I am?"

"She gets better grades."

"But I graduated. I wrote a novel for my MA. Got an agent."

Father was truly puzzled. "A novel? What about? How can you write a novel? What have you done? Hemingway, at least, went to war."

"So did I—at school. And I saw a man shot going over the Berlin wall."

"Oh yes, you saw a death in Berlin," he said. "I've seen a few deaths myself, son. I could write a novel, if I ever sat down and tried. Maybe I should read yours."

"It's in the library at San Francisco State. What's left of the library, that is."

Father was suddenly angry.

"I supported the teacher's union, but when those radical students nearly destroyed the library, they shoulda been shot—or given a scholarship somewhere else."

He drained his glass and I refilled it.

"It was a sad day," I agreed, remembering the students running through the burning library, pulling down books, tearing them up, throwing bits and pages out the window, a protest reminiscent of Nazi book burning. Somehow, the revolution had gone sour. Was there a point when we became the enemy?

We sat, drinking.

"Still want me to lam outta here?"

164

"No, stick around."

"Women want men who have things. Money. Power. What do you have, except Irish blarney and your novel?"

"I got a lot of gall and some scorn."

I was getting tipsy with the wine and pain medication. Father looked at my swollen jaw, shaking his head.

"The gall of a burglar? Listen. I have another question," he said. "Last month at supper. Why did Fran throw that bowl of milk in your face?"

"You had a bad fight, started bawling, and I called her an old hag."

"What?" Father was stunned. "Jesus! Was I loaded? I cried?"

"Maybe not. You did have a few drinks."

"What a house." For a moment, he said nothing. "I guess I better take Shank's mare home and do battle. She will sniff the wine and be furious, you know."

"Good. Let her be furious."

"I'm tired of fighting. I may not be around much longer."

"Sure you will."

In the dying light, Father looked pale and tired; he took slow, deep breaths and rubbed a hand over his chest. I paused before speaking. "Tom? Maybe you should lay off the cigarettes—and booze."

"I think you're right. I get pains in my chest now and then, but it could be indigestion."

"Remember, Grandfather died of a heart attack."

"And he was tough as nails. Died in the house he built to raise us all. I might die there, myself."

"I hope not anytime soon."

"Tell me, will I ever see a grandson?"

"Dolly Ann doesn't want children."

Father gently touched my shoulder. "Maybe it's a good idea for now. It's terrible when parents break up. You're lucky your grandmother, may she rest in peace, took over your custody when your mother left."

"She was a lovely woman," I said.

"That she was," Father agreed, suddenly moved. A spirit seemed to enter the room. "Dear old Agnes. A saint! Why don't you write about her?"

"Maybe I will. We know so little about her. She appears and then fades in my memory."

"I heard some of the old stories when I was a child, but I've forgotten them. Minnie Kennedy came over first, a young girl, and she worked and made enough to bring the others, one by one, including Agnes. My parents left their native country to come here; they worked hard and survived a depression. They were traditional and fell in love and raised a family. They had a bond with their kids. Then one day they died and were buried side by side." He paused for a second. "Those marriages seem old-fashioned now. It's too bad you and your mother have never had a close bond. In fact, your mother and I have rarely been close. We had that one night in San Diego. I guess every couple has a night when everything seems…beautiful. The moment passed but we had a child…you." For a brief moment, his eyes had a distant quality. He pushed his glass away. "I wanted you to have a better life. Do you?" I wasn't sure how to answer. "I better go," he said, sadly.

"Let me walk part way with you. We rarely have a chance to talk."

"See, it was good I came by."

Fog covered Twin Peaks. We walked down the wind-blown street, Father trying to walk steadily, blinking against the bright glare on the sidewalk. At the corner of Market and Church Streets, a cab nearly hit us as we crossed on the yellow light. Father stood in the street, confronting the driver sitting behind his steering wheel; Father's eyes narrowed with anger, his body suddenly young and tense again, waiting for the driver to step out of the car. I pulled him to the curb.

"It might have been our fault."

We saw the driver's white eyes in the black face. His passenger sat up.

"Look at that," Father said. "Damn smoke nearly ran us down!"

"Let's walk on."

The burly driver glared at us, waiting for a moment before gunning his car as horns honked. His fat white passenger looked out, drunk, waving a flask. As the cab drove off, I realized the driver was an old high school friend, Tom Manny. He had not graduated from Saint Ignatius. The drunk was Ray Reed. I wanted to talk to them and catch up after all these years—but the cab was gone. We walked on toward Dolores Park.

"On the other hand, if I were black, I'd run over a few drunken Irishmen myself," Father said. He walked, running his hand along the wrinkled suit. "John's drinking heavily again. I hope he doesn't wind up on skid row."

"I'm afraid he has."

I had gone to visit one afternoon; John's once huge arms were thin, his hair long and white; John sat on the unmade bed with a scrawny woman missing teeth. The room was small and cluttered. People walked the halls at all hours. Winos sat in the lobby watching television. John and the woman drank Muscatel wine, and I reluctantly bought them a second pint before leaving.

"He was a good man," Father said. "Could he sing 'Danny Boy'."

We stopped just below Dolores Park. "You want me to walk in the house with you?"

"No, I can face the music. You come to dinner tomorrow night. Spend sometime with us before you leave."

"You're coming to the wedding next month?"

"And the reception, of course! But come by besides those necessary occasions."

"Certainly."

We shook hands, and I watched as Father walked up the path through the park toward the house on the hill. A J streetcar passed and went up the tracks. San Francisco was his country. He seemed to grow smaller as he moved, walking away from me and out of my life, for soon, I would be in another state, and we would have separate lives. There was so little time. Dolly was not in the park with her dogs. I walked back to the flat, feeling the throbbing in my jaw.

The wedding ceremony was a month away, but I could see us being led into a chamber before the judge, his mouth beneath the broad nose and large eyes reading from a prepared text, the other couples moving like cattle through a chute. Mother would remain passive, and Father would watch the parade of Mexican, black, or racially mixed couples, possibly feeling for the first time that he was an ethnic minority.

Years later, I would view the film of the wedding reception, wondering why such a mistake had been performed and recorded for posterity, the uncertain smiling young couple cutting the cake and appearing so vulnerable. There had been magic once, but didn't we know it was lost? The marriage would last three years until she found a radio announcer who eventually cheated on her. There would be no discussions over morning coffee to assess past mistakes and ask why. Barbara Dolly Ann would change her name and secrets would remain buried. There would be no children. We would never lie in adjoining graves between two oak trees. Father made his final appearance in the wedding movie, dancing with two women—one on either side—waltzing off into eternity but leaving us with a happy image.

But this was all in the future as I walked to the flat, wondering why Father had shown up tipsy, since he liked to drink alone or with friends. What did he have to say that required a drink first? Was it just to reminisce about the family? I sat in the kitchen when Dolly Ann returned, and when I didn't ask the usual questions, she finally noticed the silence.

"What's up?" she said, releasing the dogs. "You okay?"

"I saw Father today."

"He came here? Was he sober?"

"Of course."

"Were you?"

"We had a pleasant talk over wine. He suggested I write about my grandmother. It might not be a bad idea."

"So do it."

"Do we have a problem here?"

She said nothing, watching me, then glanced down at the white Maltese. He had a limp, a fatal sign. The other dog, a Beagle, was happy to be inside. I felt my breathing grow tight and shallow.

"Rex's teeth are really bad," she said. "I think we have to put him to sleep. I know you hate his yelping, and when they limp—it's time."

"One fewer dog—at last." I took a hit from an asthma inhaler. "Where did you walk them?" She didn't answer. "You were gone a long time. The park?"

"Nowhere in particular," she finally said. "Yeah, the park. Why do you ask?"

"Because you rarely tell the truth!" I had to stop. "Sorry."

I waited for the familiar signs: her lower lip quivering, the eyes going hard and strange, then the mask appearing only without the nervous giggle. Perhaps there would be an explosion and she would accuse me of being paranoid again. This didn't happen. Without warning, she began to cry. She never cried.

"You're crying over that yapping mutt?"

"No," she said, a fire in her eyes. "My father died."

"Your father? Air Force, right? I didn't even know he was in the picture."

"He wasn't. My mother got a call last week—"

"Last week? And you're telling me now?"

"—last week from another woman with the same last name. Seems fly boy Dad had another wife and family."

"Wasn't your mother divorced?"

"Separated." Dolly controlled her sobs. "It gets worse. He had a third family in England—and never even took me there! I could've seen the world with him."

"How did your mother find out?"

"On his death bed, he confessed to his Florida wife."

"What killed him?"

"Cirrhosis of the liver."

Dolly took out a pack of cigarettes and lit one.

"Are you angry about his secrecy?"

"No. What do I care about his other families? He could've spent time with me. I knew there was a reason he didn't."

"You must have half brothers and sisters."

"I suppose I do."

"It might be fun to see them."

"I don't want to see them."

I had never seen a photo of Dolly Ann's father, but only knew her cruel overprotective grandfather, humped over like an old bird, leaning on his cane, sputtering about irresponsible teenagers, liberal Democrats and "niggers."

Dolly wiped her eyes. "I know you don't care."

I got up and held her. "No. I actually do care," I said. "Why don't we ever discuss these things?"

"I don't know. I guess I just can't help it." She picked up the Maltese and gently rocked him, kissing the trembling dog and murmuring quietly. "I've always had to protect myself," she finally said.

"From what?"

"I'm not sure."

"Look. I know he ignored you, but I am sorry about your dad."

"So am I." She looked at me and smiled. "I'll get better—I promise."

"Sure."

She put the dog down. "Someone has to take Rex to the vet."

"I will."

"Thanks."

Suddenly, Dolly put her hands to her face and quickly left the room.

When I took Rex to the vet, dogs were barking in distant cages and I held my breath against the rush of dog dander. An older woman held a cat with a broken leg. In another room, Rex finally lay on his back, his mouth tied shut, and we could see fear in the dog's eyes. As the needle went in, I felt a rush of sorrow. It would be hard to explain if I cried over a dog.

CHAPTER SEVEN

THE ENGLISH DEPARTMENT SECRETARY HELD MY EYES: "Your dad died."

When I visited him earlier that final summer, Father lay on his back in the hospital room after receiving a pace maker, his face a little sunken, the voice still strong and resonant. We joked that day, ignoring the fact that the man who raised me was going to die even if he quit his twin habits, alcohol and tobacco. We all had to pay, and a family heart condition finally caught him off base. He would not quite make his fifty-fourth birthday and become nothing more than a retired social security number.

That it should come to this.

"It was a friend of your mother's who called," the secretary added.

I went home and poured myself a drink. Then, after a few minutes, I called Mother, who confirmed the news. Her voice sounded remarkably calm. As she went on about Father dying "drunk and happy," I convinced myself it was for the best. This illusion would fade with the passing of time, and the grim reality of that bridge finally smashed. Whatever last moments we shared were now gone, and there would be no returning from any undiscovered country he had traveled. Outside, a moribund autumn littered the streets with dead leaves.

One night, we strolled in Dolores Park walking their new dog; it seemed ironic that it would take a dog's needs for us to have a last conversation. Most of the words were lost. Much of the discussion would disappear with failing memories and the passage of time. Do people ever realize the significance of farewell conversations when they are happening? Still, we walked the dog through the park and talked, aware that there wasn't much time. The setting sun turned the clouds a deep red. It seemed a third presence walked with us, but there was no third person; was it an invisible Mr. Death himself, patient as always? Dolores Park was open with grass-covered hills.

"Do you remember when you stepped off the plane from Europe?

171

I didn't recognize you with long hair and a beard."

"I remember. You took me home for a haircut."

"And what would the neighbors think if they saw my beatnik son?"

"Screw the neighbors."

"Typical answer."

"I was different. So what?"

Father looked up at the bridge over the tracks where his father had lifted him as a boy to watch the trolley passing underneath. "So what?" he repeated. His voice was low and resonant, with no need to project. "'So what,' he says."

"Europe changed me. Gave me a new perspective. Even the rock and roll was new and exciting. The Beatles in England, Dylan in New York."

A young man played guitar on the grass.

"There's just as much poetry in Crosby's 'White Christmas' as anything by that nasally Dylan. Presley could at least sing."

As we walked, I remembered an image: father, son, both drunk—listening to "White Christmas" and "Tambourine Man" in an effort to determine which lyrics had the most evocative power. Perhaps the white, bland Bing Crosby represented a safe artist to quiet the paranoia of World War II.

"In the old days, fathers and sons enjoyed the same music."

"You remember your childhood hero, Johnny Weissmuller?"

"He wasn't my hero. Oh, a great swimmer, of course, but I beat him."

"He got booed off the stage at the college."

"Why did they boo him?"

"The student body considered his *Tarzan* movies racist."

Father stopped and looked at me with a quiet outrage.

"Racist? Ridiculous. The movies were entertainment."

"Perhaps." We walked on. "What are we gonna do?"

Father looked at me. "About what?"

"Your health."

Father's handsome face had new lines, the black hair thinning; holding the struggling dog, he took a long, labored breath.

"I feel terrific. Never better."

"Do you still swim?"

"Haven't in a while. Too old for that shit."

"Stay off the booze and cigarettes, you'll live to be a hundred."

"How are you fixed with the sauce?"

"Great. I can get it anytime I want."

Father shook his head. "It will kill you in the end."

I couldn't argue. "We have to make sure you get well."

"I was up at Lake Tahoe, and bending over to tie my shoes, suddenly felt pain in my chest and left arm. I couldn't breathe, I felt nauseated. Son, I was scared." He looked up at the house on the hill. "I could still use a smoke."

"No more smokes. Stay scared."

He suddenly seemed pensive. "Death? What's it like?"

"Let's hope you don't find out for awhile."

A passing dog started a fight, so we took Mother's new dog home; it had disappeared by the time of the funeral that early winter, and I didn't ask why.

The old days of Irish wakes with ice lifted off the corpse for drinks had passed. Now it was only a rosary, and relatives listened to the priest reciting before the open coffin. I wondered if the Vikings weren't right to put the body on a ship and riddle the vessel with fire arrows, rather than lay the body out for morbid viewing. I couldn't accept that plastic-looking empty husk as my father, Thomas. It was too much of a contradiction, a furious denial of what he had been in life. Where was the person who took the wheel of his brother's boat and waved at the home movie lens? When would we hear that warm baritone again with its Bing Crosby resonance?

During the funeral, I sat in Mission Dolores Church like so many Sundays before with a devout dad, his face always in profile, hair smelling of tonic. The emptiness of the ritual honoring the flag-draped coffin seemed complete; to an arrogant unbeliever, the priest saying mass resembled a bad actor in costume. The smell of wax and candle smoke filled the big church, the flowers suddenly too sweet. For a moment I thought I was going to faint. Perhaps Sister Ann Maureen would hear salvation in the hymns and find comfort.

As we filed out of the church behind the coffin, I saw my old chum, J. R. Dean, well-dressed, standing to one side. He looked like an actor playing a handsome plain-clothes cop, gun in shoulder holster, hands folded. He winked at me as we passed. Mother waved at a few guests.

After the trip to the cemetery, we had the customary gathering. All the relatives were there, including Emmett, whose first wife had died of cancer. He was remarried now and had been there the weekend of his brother's fatal heart attack. Father's younger brother, Jim, had arrived, his square, handsome face smiling beneath a military styled crew-cut. The discussion turned to recent assassinations.

"The Kennedys were pigs," Jim said, speaking like a proud Irish traitor. "Not our Kennedys, I mean, the ones who produced J.F.K."

"How can an Irish Catholic liberal say that?" someone asked.

"I'm a right wing Republican," Jim said, grinning, holding a drink. "I know Tom was a dyed in the wool Democrat, may he rest in peace. But in Orange County, California, I saw the light."

"What light was that?" I asked.

"Let's not be after forgetting the bastard men of Orange in Ireland," another angry voice said.

"Never," Emmett said, pouring another drink. "Let's just perpetuate stupid wars."

Mother, cheerful, entertained her many guests: Mary, Father's older sister, bearing an eerie resemblance to my grandmother, Agnes; Veronica, the mysterious Vee once again in public, a bit older, the teeth still bad, the brown hair still plain, the quick laugh covering any intimate feelings.

"My, your hair is so long."

"I should cut it," I said. "It no longer makes a political statement, and they are cleaning out the English Department anyway."

"It looks good on you," she added. "I'm now working at the post office."

Looking into Vee's eyes, the sense of early kinship seemed gone. She had never married. I couldn't ask with whom she was living, if anyone. Perhaps I had grown into a young man unfit for the family. Only Emmett was nonjudgmental.

"The other day," Mary said, "my husband, Ed, wanted to promote a fellow named Murphy because of his excellent record and good Irish name. When Murphy showed up, he turned out to be black."

Jim was amused. "A big black coon?"

"Black as the ace of spades," said Ed, a large, florid man laughing around his cigar. "An Irish jig named Murphy. Is nothing sacred?"

Jim watched me as I gulped my drink.

"I bet you're a free spirit—like my daughter. She joined some cult. What are you doing with yourself?"

"Teaching."

"You also worked at the post office before that?"

"Yeah. And I was a civil rights worker." I met his eyes. "I'm partial to niggers."

"Good," Jim agreed. "It's about time the jigs were freed. Then maybe they can free us white folks who pay for jig welfare."

Once again, the Irish were pitted against the blacks. Emmett took me to one side. "How's your writing?"

"Phony, as usual. I'm a liar by trade."

"So what? Keep writing."

As the party continued, Dean arrived. He looked around, pulling at his necktie, and finally spotted me. "Jesus," he said. "Nice hair. Barber die?"

"No, it's a protest against the complacent middle class."

"How compelling."

We sat, drinking together.

"How the hell are you? How's your wife? I always liked Dolly Ann. She's got a lot of class. Helluva gal."

"We're getting divorced."

"You're better off."

"God, I feel terrible."

"About the divorce or your dad?"

"My dad."

"Why is everyone so happy? I feel kinda sad."

"I'm sure everyone here does. It's a family tradition to never be too expressive about one's feelings, unless one is drunk, of course."

"Which is most of the time."

"Well then, maybe they *are* happy the old boy's gone."

"I finally decided to track my old man down. He disappeared when I was about two, but when I finally found an address, he had died two months before. All I have now are some old letters, work papers, a passport and a pair of specs."

Dean lifted his glass and drank. The party continued. These people would never be together again until another death.

"I keep waiting for some kind of epiphany, but no dice."

"What the hell's an epiphany?"

"A moment of enlightenment."

"You intellectuals," Dean said. "Think of positive things."

"Like what?"

The front room and the bar alcove were filled with conversation as relatives made connections. Layers of smoke drifted and turned. For a moment, the deceased was forgotten, but I remembered Father attending a surprise birthday party for me—my 24th—and how he sat in his dark suit, sipping a drink and watching young guests with long hair and beads and brightly dyed clothing as though he were observing exotic wildlife. A bit of dialogue came back to me.

"I play lead guitar, man. You old guys play jazz, right?"

"I play shoe horn," Father said. "Or on the floor."

Dean's voice brought me back to the post-funeral party; we reminisced European adventures including a mysterious Italian woman named Franca we met on the night train to Rome. She was something out of an Italian art film: beautiful, sexual, wild, elusive—breasts spilling out of a low-cut, mesh net bra.

"She walked into our hotel room in a slip," I told Emmett, "and took Dean out while I lay on the bed, staring at the ceiling."

"Sounds exciting," he said. "For someone."

We continued talking. Mother put on some music for dancing. A tall older woman suddenly appeared beside me, something familiar in her eyes. She held out her hand.

"Hello. My name is Ann Haley."

"Hello, Ann Haley."

"I hear you're a writer."

"I write some."

"My mother was Minnie, your grandmother's sister. Someday when you want the family history, I may have a few details."

"The famous Minnie. I'll long to hear them," I said, pouring another glass of wine.

Later that night, I sat on the patio of the backyard, the garden paved over with cement, "Welcome" crudely drawn upside-down in the concrete. I remembered the flowers and vegetables Grandmother Agnes raised. Mother was a little tipsy, the hair platinum blonde, her face a tightly drawn mask from cosmetic surgery. The house that contained so much history remained, but things had changed. She finally met my eyes.

"I know you miss him, but he's gone. That's all there is to it. We have to get along, so don't hate me."

"I don't hate you."

"Are you sure?"

"I don't hate you."

"He was no great shakes as a husband, you know."

I could still see him sitting in the backyard, intoxicated, with the inevitable tee-shirt hanging out and wearing his hat with colorful fishing lures, though he didn't fish.

"I don't doubt that," I said.

I drank some cheap, syrupy wine.

"You drink a lot," Mother said. "Like him."

"That's a fact."

"Suit yourself." Mother nodded to herself, her charm bracelets rattling as she took a drink. A streetcar rolled by on the hill behind the house.

"We buried some champagne in the garden one night. Remember?"

"When you was getting married. Otherwise, that old dog would've lapped it all up. Middle of the night, burying magnums of champagne in the backyard. What a house!"

I looked at her. "The night he died. What happened?"

"We was drinking at an Irish bar and he got into a fight, so Emmett and his wife drove back to Modesto. We came home. He got up around midnight, took something out of the refrigerator, and I heard a noise in his bedroom sometime after that. He didn't get up for work and I phoned in. When I finally checked—"

"You don't have to go on."

"He had a half-empty bottle of wine under the bed."

A spirit of death seemed to pass over the patio.

"His face was black. Scared me half to death."

"Maybe it was his last touch of revenge."

"Revenge, my ass. He was a pain, if you ask me. Always drinking, always starting a beef. He loved to argue."

"So do you."

"I think he's better off."

I stood up. I wanted to throw my glass against the back wall.

"Better off? I don't think so. He was too young to die!"

"Oh please. Don't be so melodramatic."

Mother might grieve for a lost pet, but moments of real feeling, even tragedy, struck her as melodramatic. Even public laments over the murders of Martin Luther King and the Kennedys were melodramatic. I felt a sudden bite in the air.

"Melodramatic? I see."

"By the way, I found a lot of the guests rude. They're so special, they don't know who I am?"

"No," I said. "They don't. Who are you?"

Mother poured herself a drink. "I might be your best friend," she said. Mother looked past me, her expression suddenly empty and bland. Another streetcar rattled above us. "Either we part friends or the worst of enemies," Mother insisted.

For the first time, she seemed old, the bright hair and taut face giving her a surface youth that was mocking and a little pathetic.

"I don't want to be anyone's enemy." I walked toward the house. "I'm staying in a motel tonight."

"Suit yourself. And something else. He never made no will, so if you're expecting big bucks, forget it."

"I never counted on any inheritance."

I sat alone and drank much of the night in a motel room. Alcohol did bring a temporary relief, and with it the sounds of alcohol flowing into glasses and the rich colors: the amber Scotch, the dark Bourbon, or in this case, the clear Vodka. I didn't need friends and preferred recreating conversations with imaginary people who had the answers. I thought of Father and our summer vacations, waiting for the tears, but none came. Toasting the spirits of those dead and gone did not conjure them back, and I slept a dead sleep without dreaming. In the morning, I woke fully clothed on the bed, feeling dry and sick. It was dark outside and the glowing clock face said it was five in the morning. Evidently, I had not gone out in search of a woman. After a night of drunken fantasies, the morning brought its harsh reality. In the lamplight, an empty vodka bottle sat on the table. I tried to remember where the motel was located and it came to me: Lombard Street. The room had the neutral colors of any motel room, with a painting of bulldogs playing poker. I couldn't get back to sleep so I lay on the bed, waiting for first light. It often happened that I woke up too soon and had to wait through a trembling dry period for the day to start and the bars to open.

I drove down Geary Boulevard to the Cliff House and looked at the museum with relics of so many childhood trips. Playland at the Beach survived only in photos; its craters were covered over with snack shops and high-rise apartment buildings. Seal Rocks rose from the ocean as they had for centuries, the distant seals barking a morning chorus.

I didn't feel hungry, but the first drink of the morning was always the best, preferably the bright brassy depths and sharp taste of beer catching one by surprise. It was a sudden liquid rush. Hands stopped shaking. Frayed nerves relaxed. I watched strangers talking, drinking and eating in the bar, a picture window facing the bright sea.

Why did mother lie about Father's last night?

Emmett had described a relatively quiet evening spent at a celebrated Irish bar, with Father sitting in the corner, well-dressed, drinking little, talking to two young immigrant Irishmen. Perhaps Mother needed to invent her own scenario.

I sat, drinking my pint of morning beer.

"Maybe you need a shot with that," a woman's contralto said. "Or are you just a one pint man?"

She had dark, close-cropped hair, a youthful, handsome face, and a wide but somehow bitter smile. She wore jeans and a blue sweater with black outlines of reindeer. There was no self-consciousness. The accent had a Celtic lilt.

"What a great idea."

I ordered a shot.

"I was just kidding."

"Never kid an Irishman about drink."

"I should know. May I?"

"Sure."

She sat down.

"You sound either Belfast Irish or Liverpool. Which are you?"

"My name is Dervla. Dervla O' Connor. I was born in Killy Begs, grew up in West Belfast. If you keep that up, you'll have your liver in your lap."

"I came back to San Francisco for a funeral. It's been a hard day."

"Wonderful. A special occasion, especially a sad one, gives you fecking Micks a great excuse."

"I don't need an excuse or a nursemaid."

Dervla laughed and looked away. Her face glowed with rugged health and sensuality, but the eyes were hard. For a moment, her expression softened.

"You were born in San Francisco?"

"Yes."

"I shouldn't intrude."

"Please do."

"I will."

"Why?"

A light burned in her eyes, so direct and challenging.

"I'm attracted to drunken Irish louts. God knows, I've had a few in my day. I'm actually supposed to meet someone else here—another drunken Mick. When are you leaving San Francisco?"

"Two, three days."

"To where?"

"Idaho."

Dervla looked over at a sloppy man who had just entered the bar. "Oh shit," she said.

I looked more closely; it was Richard Boyle, a cigar between his teeth. He looked older, his belly distended, the hair still dark and curly, the eyes red-rimmed. He leaned against a brass rail, grinning when he recognized me.

"Jesus Christ," he barked, the teeth still bad. "You old fuck!"

"Boyle, you slob." Patrons looked up.

"Jesus," Dervla said, "you two reprobates know each other?"

"Further back than I care to remember," Boyle said, laughing hoarsely.

I had known this man since grammar school, first as someone who terrorized the nuns, then as a person who drifted into my life every five years, boasting of plans to cover this or that revolution, and writing generic articles about them. Boyle's greatest talent was his ability to drop into hostile territory and escape at the last minute, being there when friendly troops moved in to rescue stranded Americans. But then, another friend once argued, what would jungle guerrillas do with a raving Richard Boyle? His articles would be published, and a future film would nourish Boyle's gonzo journalist legend.

In my mind, he would be always standing on a nude beach at the Russian River, huge belly dwarfing his genitals, a cigar in his teeth despite asthma—our shared affliction— holding a whiskey bottle and bellowing a Marxist message to other nude bathers whom he suspected were capitalists. Stay drunk and get laid was his true message.

"We have to go," Dervla insisted. "I work for a living."

"What brings you here?" Boyle asked.

"My father died," I said.

"I'm sorry to hear that."

For a moment, he seemed sincere, and I remembered our conversation so long ago when Grandfather died.

"What are you up to, Boyle?"

"I'm moving out tonight. Tomorrow I'm going back to Latin America. That's where it's happening. El Salvador, Nicaragua, Chile. Revolution, man. War! I'm gonna write about it."

"You can't write."

"You can? I thought you were an actor."

"I'm a better writer."

"Another writer. Just what we need."

Boyle sucked on the cigar, then coughed. His lungs rattled.

"Hey, remember SAM? Sister Ann Maureen's working as a nun in El Salvador. Still looks good after all these years."

"Say hello for me. "

"I will. Let's talk, soon."

Boyle rubbed his head vigorously as they walked out the door and up the street, and then Dervla came back into the Cliff House Bar. "We won't move much of his trash. Boyle just wants to sit on my face." She handed me a card. "Call me about ten tonight."

I was feeling an alcoholic morning glow. I left and walked along the littered beach to the distant zoo, another place I had visited as a child with Grandmother Agnes and even my mother on one occasion. If the memories were dim, the photos in the family album provided proof that

181

she took my cousin and me to the zoo one long ago afternoon. I look happy, Dennis looks angry, and Mother smiles at the camera, her platinum blonde hair shining in the old black and white photo.

I visited monkey island and then took a bus to Fisherman's Wharf for lunch. The day seemed remarkably warm, and though the faces were different, San Francisco still maintained its old Victorian charm. If the main actors had vanished, the set remained the same. I called that night and Dervla came on the phone, her accent more pronounced.

"Boyle's gone. I work tomorrow at the museum near Civic Center. Why don't we do lunch? Noon. Take the five bus."

I had another night to get through. I also knew the bus that traveled on MacAllister Street leading to the museum and library. It was through the bus window that I saw her waiting on the corner. She nodded and got on.

"Was Boyle upset?"

"About what? I don't think he takes you seriously."

"Does anyone? Besides, we're only having lunch."

"That's right. I can't just pop in bed with you, buster. You have so much pain."

Her brown eyes were full of a happiness that contradicted the harsh, biting tone of her voice and the tight line of her mouth. "Boyle is a glorious asshole."

"So am I," I said.

"You're buying lunch, so you're not cheap."

"I'm buying lunch?"

"I haven't read your work, but I suspect you romanticize women. Maybe you even have an Oedipus complex."

"God forbid."

"That's a relief. Though spiritual, I suspect you don't believe in God."

"Very perceptive. My church is the theatre."

"Well, that's promising. Boyle operates on one level…anything that can't be drunk, eaten or fucked is worthless."

"I'm not sure I disagree."

Dervla smiled, her teeth straight and white. "I bet you've been burned by religion."

"Of course. I'm Irish."

"I have a feeling we'll be on the same bus, but with different destinations. Boyle will show up when his money runs out."

"Then what?"

Dervla laughed deep in her throat. "He'll hit us both up for a loan. Listen, if we play, we play by my rules."

"Fine. Let's eat."

We ate in a small bar-restaurant and exchanged stories, histories.

"When my parents died, that meant for sure I was off to America. I was overjoyed. I hated Ireland. I hated the poverty. I hated the Irish drunks. I hated all of it."

"I hear Ireland's changed. The economy's better. Peace might be a possibility. Even leprechauns and Irish fairies now own personal computers."

"Good for them." She took a bite. "Maybe I can help you."

"Help me? How?"

Dervla sipped her coffee, watching me. "Are you so naive? You're a lonely guy, uncertain. You're messed up, but it's a poison I recognize."

"Dervla? What do you want?"

"I don't know," she finally admitted. "Boyle is fun in his own way. The landlady made a big deal about how I wasn't the only one to share his bed while he was drinking and trashing the place. I shocked her when I said I didn't care. We did have some brutal fights."

There was a strange malevolence in her eyes, even though she was smiling.

"I usually win. I grew up freezing and hungry so I take what I want."

"Good."

"That may include you. I'll take you, squeeze you dry, and spit you out."

"Do I get to sit on your face, too?"

"Maybe." Dervla sipped her drink and cut another piece of meat. "I also like Irish poetry. Fecked up as we are, we're not boring."

"You talk a tough game, but you're really quite sensitive. I think you need a cultured Englishman."

Dervla laughed, spitting out some food. "You make me laugh," she said. "Tell me about your early childhood. Not *Oliver Twist*, I hope."

I told her about growing up and my grandparents.

"So Grandmother Agnes was a saint, eh? What about your mother's parents? You didn't mention them."

"I never really knew them. Mother's mother was a bland, gentle woman and her father was a German named Charlie Mundagle. Charlie was strange. Thin, wiry, white hair, missing teeth, he raised raccoons, rarely worked but could steal electricity. Mother liked him, her sister didn't."

Dervla cocked an eyebrow theatrically. "Or he preferred your mother. I smell a rat."

"I bet you do. Look, I was raised by—"

"I know. Your dad, his dad and Saint Agnes. She escaped, at least." Dervla looked away. "Look, maybe tomorrow you could lend me a hand moving Boyle's trash."

When we parted, there was gentleness in her handshake. She could have been any other Irish Colleen smiling at a friend. The next day, I helped Dervla move Boyle's stuff: greasy boxes, old jeans, a few books, gun magazines, Asian porno pictures, girlie posters and a baseball card collection. It took most of the day to move them into storage. It was like a composite of Boyle's vagabond life, including old letters, scribbled postcards, an outdated passport and a few photos. Dervla found one of us as teenagers, wearing leather jackets and posing arrogantly in Dolores Park.

"Young bucks," she sneered, "with an attitude."

It was so typical of Boyle just to clear out of the city, leaving responsibilities, driving off in his unregistered car with shark's jaws painted on the side.

At noon, we had lunch at the Japanese Tea Gardens. A fog was rolling in, the day cold and overcast. Shadows covered the trees. Dervla was strangely quiet, contained. Perhaps she was missing Boyle, the wild fights, or wondering what might have happened if their Irish energies had not clashed in such an explosive way. There was a resignation in her voice.

"I'm glad I'm out of that, but I feel a little sad."

I reached across and took her hand, a gesture that seemed unusual with someone like Dervla. She didn't resist.

"Why's that?"

"I find that I am drawn to crazy, messed up men, particularly

Irishmen who are mad as hatters."

"But *you're* mad as a hatter."

"True. Everyone says I'm too venomous, but that's my nature." For a moment, her expression changed. "I remember starving and finding rotten potatoes in the bin. My father thought of me as a servant. I hated the men I met, since they were as bad off as I was—though I might use them now and then. No priest would keep me a virgin until I married some drunken slob past his prime."

"Life's unjust. Get over it. Or start over."

"I will—in another life."

A calm came over her. There was a curved bridge over a goldfish pond near the tables. She looked away toward the ornamental gardens.

"I used to stop a certain young man riding his bicycle down the road. We'd leave and lie down by the river." She laughed. "Then he became a priest. Oh well. I did like him." She glared defiantly at me. "What about the women in your life? Tell me about all the romances you ruined."

The question actually caught me by surprise. There had been so many women in my life after the bad first marriage: gifted women, sensuous women, literary women, but they all had faded. One night, there always came that fatal choice: to sit in a bar until closing time or go home to a woman lying in bed or waiting up; then came the inevitable fight. One day, there would be no home or woman left. The faces seemed to blend into one face—always attractive, always sensual, and always with some defeat in the eyes. When the anger and sorrow turned to pity, it was time to go. A year later if we connected, it would be as though we had never met.

"They're all a blur."

"I bet."

"Tell me. Do you miss your parents?"

The hard queer stare came back into her eyes.

"You want more history? I trained to be a legal secretary. Mom and Dad thought I was lying. Why would a helpless colleen like me learn to type legal documents? Sure, wasn't I out drunk somewhere or screwing a Protestant? Mother was too beaten down to imagine any other life. Then before I could wave my boat ticket, a fever took both of them. I had an aunt in Boston to sponsor me and enough money to travel the States when I got there. My sisters stayed behind."

"Think you'll ever go back?"

"Why would I want to go back to Ireland?"

"To see your long lost sisters."

"One of them is a born-again Christian, which in the south, is worse than being a Protestant." Her eyes burned with a sudden anger. "The other had seven kids. That will never happen to me. I won't be a slave to some drunk's children." She pushed her plate away. "Times have changed, maybe, but the Irish have a worse history than the American Indians. Think about it. We've been buggered for eight hundred years."

I remembered Grandfather reading aloud about the Easter rebellion of 1916, Irish citizen rebels shooting from a commandeered post office at the British army, killing over a hundred soldiers until the English fired eighteen-pound guns into the streets and took control. Executions began. They shot the rebel leader, James Connolly, sitting bound in a chair, wounded in the ankle and unable to stand.

"Our history is violent." I searched her face. "Did you have any brothers?"

Something in the space between us seemed to change. "Maybe." The mask was up, defiant, cold, hard. "We better call it a day," Dervla said. "We can get together later."

"Would you like that?"

This time, her smile had no trace of anger. "I would like that," she said. "I am sorry about your dad."

That afternoon, I visited the cemetery, full of sunlight now. Father's gravestone lay clean and fresh-looking. It named his dates of birth and death; fifty-three years seemed so short. Then I walked to Molloy's Tavern. It was dark inside and had only a few patrons. I thought about Father and felt a little funny; why couldn't the dead past stay dead? Then I started drinking vodka and tonic.

After midnight, the Golden Gate Bridge opened up like a beautiful runway, the lanes glowing in the yellow fog lights, "A Day in the Life" blasting on the car radio. I finished a pint of bourbon and pressed on the accelerator as a huge plane with flashing red eyes soared up behind me; I got the old Chevy up to ninety, roaring across the bridge, the car shaking, the plane now a police car, the siren rising to a crescendo over the Beatles' orchestra. I pulled over; a block-like policeman demanded

I step out. His face was stern in the flashing bubble gum lights.

"I want your license."

"Certainly."

"I want you to walk a straight line."

"Officer, certainly you don't think I'm drunk? You're joking!"

"Walk a straight line—now!"

Then I was singing the alphabet, rather than reciting as requested; when I bent over the car to write out the alphabet, something happened to the letter "L." Was it a cousin to the capital "I"? I lingered for a moment, skipped on to "M", then felt the cold iron cuffs tightly closing as he pulled my wrists behind me.

"I insist on taking the breath test," I said at the station. "This is entrapment. I'll have your jobs!"

"Good," the cop said. "Blow into this."

I blew twice into a long tube; numbers came up on tiny windows. It registered .26. "You're more than drunk," the cop told me.

"It's a lie!" I said. "The machine's wrong."

A second test registered the same count. The strip search was swift and efficient.

"Turn around and spread your cheeks," the officer droned. I did so, nearly falling. The harsh light in the cell made my nakedness somehow more degrading. "Turn around and lift up your scrotum. No drugs hidden under your balls?"

"I'm in for drink, not drugs."

"Shut your mouth." He saw no hidden drugs. "Good," he said, leather creaking. "Follow me."

Then I sat on an iron cot in the drunk tank with snoring, heaving bodies lying on the concrete. The tank smelled of sweat, alcohol, cigarettes and dried vomit. A fat man with dark hair watched me through the bars; his round face and light-colored eyes reflected more curiosity than disapproval.

"You must have some serious health problem or extraordinary tolerance to alcohol to be awake with a count that high. Another point and you'd be legally dead."

"I'm an Irishman. We can hold our liquor."

The jailer paused. "Why aren't you comatose?"

"I'm a man," I said.

187

"Soon to be a dead man. Maybe your liver is sluggish and not processing the alcohol. Did you drink a lot tonight?"

"No, for once, I didn't," I said. "I don't think I did."

Later, the electric door sprang open and I entered a dark cell with strangers. A burly man with a scarred face gripped the bars, staring across the brightly lit corridor at large rugged-looking women with red and blonde wigs.

"Hey, sweetie, I wish I was in your cell."

"Fuck you," one of the women said in a deep voice.

I looked again. The scarred man turned toward me, laughing.

"Queers," he said. "Fruits. Guys dressed as girls. The worst kinda faggots!"

In the partial darkness, an old man sat against the wall. For a toilet, there was a hole in the center of the cell.

"They got niggers in the cell next to us," the scarred man warned. He had a cut over his left eye. "Spear-chucking boogies. Watch your back."

"Sure."

I heard a raspy whisper: "You got a cigarette?"

I looked again at the old man and noticed his burned clothes. "No," I said.

There was an iron bunk and I lay down, hearing echoing voices. My street fighter cellmate raved about "spear chuckers" and "jungle bunnies," holding up his white arm as exhibit A. "The white race is the superior race," he screamed. Angry voices called back. I went in and out of sleep hearing curses and psychotic screams of anger.

"Shut the fuck up, Whitie. I'll settle with yo' ass, tomorrow."

"Oh, I'm so scared! Ugga Bugga gonna settle wid me."

In the morning, they fed us from a trough and herded prisoners into a huge holding area. A young man in a three-piece suit ignored the other prisoners. The old man told us he was tired and stretched on the cement floor. I leaned against the concrete wall and saw clearly the filthy face and slightly mad eyes of the pugnacious cellmate. He glared at the black men across the holding tank. One of them detached from the group and walked toward us; he put his arm next to the scarred prisoner, now quiet.

"I got red blood in my veins, just like you, cracker motherfucker.

188

You wanna call me names now?"

The street fighter stood up. "Blow me, Buckwheat."

"Sure," the black man said. He struck the white man a hard blow, and they began fighting; guards rushed into the cell and pushed them apart. The white man had a broken nose and blood gushed down his filthy shirt. He began cursing.

"That's enough," a guard said. "You all go to the judge's chambers when your name is called."

Then I saw the old man lying on the floor, unnaturally still. His tattered, burned clothes covered nothing but fragile bones, and he didn't seem to be breathing.

"Someone better check on him."

The cop leaned down and felt for a pulse. "This old timer's dead."

Before they carried the body out, my name was called and I walked past two muscular skinheads who guarded the bleeding racist. Black inmates had retreated to an opposite wall, and the stout transvestites smoked in another corner. I telephoned an old friend and walked into court, feeling hung over and unclean in the bright chamber. Behind the elevated bench, the judge sat, a small man with a narrow face and pale blue eyes.

"Your count is pretty high, sir. You want counsel?"

"I called a friend who's a lawyer, but not to defend me."

"All right. Drunk driving. How do you plead?"

"Guilty."

"You're lucky. The new law next week would send you to jail with a heavy fine. Today, you get a light fine and traffic court. Can you handle that?"

"Yes, your Honor."

"I never want to see you here again with an alcohol related offense. Is that clear?"

"Yes, it is."

Marshall waited outside, wearing large glasses. He had gained weight and his hair had turned gray; he now worked as a Federal lawyer in San Francisco.

"I couldn't believe it when you called me from jail."

"Neither could I."

"That old demon rum, eh?"

"I guess so."

"I like to drink now and then."

"How's the world of law?"

"Well, I once wanted to defend truth, justice and the America way. Now I'd settle to make dough." We drove into slowing, heavy traffic. "Jesus, how was jail?"

"Noisy. Fights. An old guy died in the holding tank." I could still smell a lingering jail odor. "I need to take a shower."

"How's your mom?"

"Feisty as ever."

"There's less there than meets the eye," Marshall said.

"Thanks for picking me up."

"Remind her you don't have Jewish friends for nothing."

Marshall found my parked car and then drove on. It was another quick meeting and quick good-bye. I drove home and showered, washing away the jail smells, then went to bed. Mother had left, visiting friends and a travel agent. I slept for twelve straight hours and woke up in darkness, desperate for another drink. I finished a quart of 7-Up and ate a late breakfast. After sitting in the yard, staring at the concrete, I went back to bed. I didn't dare go out or call Dervla. I knew any date could eventually end in a bar. The cycle would start again. Perhaps only a professional counselor could stop it.

In the morning, I went into the basement and saw Father's old library with out-of-print books, including many first editions, a few missing dust jackets. I found the players edition of Shakespeare with pictures and drawings of celebrated actors over the centuries. There was a collection of the Tarzan and Mars series by Edgar Rice Burroughs. *Look Homeward, Angel*—Father's favorite book—gathered dust. A few items had disappeared, including an electric Lionel train. The wedding photo of my grandparents was also missing.

A photo of my cousin, Dennis, lay on the floor. He wore boxing gloves, and I saw again an afternoon fight beneath the redwoods staged by Father who had praised Dennis. Dennis was "a man's boy." Dennis liked the Friday night fights. Dennis could defend his younger brother against larger bullies. We put on the gloves. Dennis was short but tough and he tried to duck under my longer reach but failed, and I caught him with a right uppercut and then a left hook that smacked

Dennis in the face. He looked surprised and went down hard, bleeding from his mouth.

"Take it easy," Father said. "He's shorter than you." But I could see approval in Father's eyes. I had lived in my imagination and in new books but found a strange joy in knocking down another human being. Dennis got up furious, but there was no rematch.

I put the faded photo on a shelf. The basement smelled of dust and mold.

On another level sat a thick baby book; on the glossy cover a multicolored air balloon floated over blue and green mountains. Inside was a dedication to Mother written in Father's beautiful hand, one of his few remaining signatures. The photo album chronicled my birth and family history, windows into a past life with pictures of my younger parents and Grandmother Agnes smiling at the camera. In an old black and white photo, Grandfather frowned defiantly in front of a black wooden fence in the backyard, Father draping an arm around him. With the progression of photos, the hair styles and clothes changed over the years. The most striking photo was of Father holding a ten-day-old infant in his arms. Father's hair is thick, dark, and combed back lion-like; he wears a white shirt with a black vest and spotted tie. The baby looks unhappy in the backyard light, but Father, his face slightly turned away, smiles. It's a sunny day but war is raging, and soon Father will join the navy.

After examining the books, I decided to take the photo album and the Shakespeare edition with me, the same book I had searched as a child. Beautiful actors in costume holding crowns or skulls or posing in old sketches, peopled these plays. The strange exotic language still held secrets. Theatre had opened up a new world of drama and poetry, from the time I played Sasha the bird in *Peter and the Wolf* to Tuzenbach in Chekhov's *Three Sisters*, a college production staged by the advanced acting class. Why did Chekhov's doomed sisters haunt the imagination more than my real family?

Mother got up and cooked a wonderful breakfast. It was amazing how adjusted she had become, taking care of business, pensions, arrangements. Her voice sounded happy on the phone as she talked to friends.

"I'm selling the house."

"Why?"

"The roof leaks. The real estate agent thinks he can get a good deal."

"Keep the house. This is history—our history."

"Your history," she corrected. "It's mine and I can do what I want. You got any objections?"

"No." Then: "I have to go."

"You want a glass of wine?"

"No. I'm drying out for at least a year."

"Good luck," she said. I didn't mention my drunk driving arrest. I knew I could take the traffic court in Idaho.

"I'm going to soak in a hot tub before I leave, and then it's back on the road."

"Don't drink in the hot tub. It's bad for you."

"I know."

"Watch out for fruits. They love the public baths."

"I will."

"I want you to send me cards on Christmas and my birthday."

"Cards? That's all?"

"Ain't that enough?"

"I guess so."

We kissed politely. Mother seemed suddenly calm. She looked at an old photo of Father at eighteen, dressed in a tux for the senior prom. The brooding, dark good looks suggested a modern American hero on the road.

"He was a handsome man, your father."

I nodded that he was. "What happened with you two?"

"Whadda ya mean, 'happened'?"

"The troubles...fights. All that."

Mother shrugged.

"Nothing happened—except he sucked life outta the bottle. Same old story. He did manage to sober up raising you. I'll grant him that."

"Where did you go?"

"Where did I go when?"

I hesitated before asking the question. "When you...when you left us. I guess I was three?"

Mother's face brightened. "Hawaii. It was just after the war and it was wonderful! No drunks. No kids. No more blackouts and sirens.

Your dad served there. It's a paradise. The water's so pretty and it's always sunny. You should go there."

"Maybe I will."

I remembered a photo of Mother in Hawaii, blonde and beautiful in a one-piece bathing suit. A photo of her Siamese cat, George, sat on a living room table.

"Well, so long," I said.

I left and drove to Folsom Street near the Bay Bridge. Leather bars lined the wide street. A number of public gay bathhouses had appeared in San Francisco; soon, the plague of AIDS would sweep through the city creating a new holocaust and closing targeted bathhouses. There was one establishment where anyone could rent a private room with a hot tub, and often couples brought wine and made love in the wet, steaming environment. The hot bubbling water swirled and it was relaxing to soak, empty of thought. The knock on the door sounded light, hesitant.

"Who is it?"

"Dervla. Let me in."

"I thought Irish girls were afraid of naked men."

"Who said you were a man?"

Dervla entered, wearing jeans and a jean jacket; she leaned her elbows on the tub.

"Do American men really have smaller dicks?"

"How did you know where to find me?"

"I called your mother, and she mentioned you wanted a soak before leaving. It was a process of elimination. I'm an idiot, but I wanted to see you before you left."

"Here I am. Why don't you come along with me?"

"No, that'd be disastrous."

"We might have fun on the road."

"I don't think so."

"Then hop in."

Dervla disrobed. It was almost like a dance as she stepped out of her clothes. She had large breasts, tiny surgical scars underneath for size reduction, lovely hips and smooth thighs. There was nothing quite as beautiful as a naked woman revealed, and every time felt like the first time. She lowered herself into the swirling water, beads of moisture on her forehead, black hair wet and close to her skull. She grinned at me.

"We don't have to do it."

"I've forgotten how."

"It's not disrespectful if you do. It's just a release of tension."

"How clinical."

"You think all Irish girls are virgins or sluts, right?"

"In the old days, maybe. Dervla? Was there another reason you left Belfast?"

She held the washcloth like a weapon. "My brother blew up an English barracks."

"I can't tell if you're joking or serious."

"—and I hated the poverty and ignorance."

"Why are you here?"

"San Francisco?"

"No. The bathhouse."

She ran both hands through her raven's hair. "I like you. I can open up to you, knowing today's the last day we'll meet."

Dervla lay back on the swirling water, breasts visible above the foam. It was getting hot. Steam rose off the water, her face like an apparition through the mist. Dervla ran one hand down her wet belly and between her thighs. She closed her eyes, feeling gently with her fingers, moving up, pressing in. "Kiss me," she said, eyes still closed. Her fingers moved.

"All right."

Her lips were soft, moist, her tongue probing. "Kiss my breasts."

The nipples grew suddenly hard, erect, and her breath came in short rapid gasps; her body tensed, relaxed, and then she was quiet for a few minutes.

"Not every woman gets off with just a penis banging around inside her vagina."

"Clinical, again. I bet you're a nurse."

"When the ER needs me, yes. Let's get out."

We got out and lay on a mat near the door. My hands began shaking; I felt a numbing fatigue, and desperately wanted to either drink or vomit.

"Here, I got a soda in my bag. Sugar calories cut the withdrawal."

The sweet soda did make a difference. I gulped it down and the shaking stopped.

"You need professional help, chum. Start with a liver enzyme test."

"Funny you should say that," I said. "A jailer suggested the same thing."

"You got busted. I knew it," she said, cackling.

We lay there together, hearing piped-in Beatles music that should have sounded old-fashioned but didn't. Laughter rang from another part of the bathhouse.

"Did you get off?"

"Yeah. But I can always get myself off. I wanted some human contact. I may even want to get you off."

"Give me about a month."

I looked at her, lying naked on the mat. "Did your brother really blow up a barracks?"

"He did. He was part of the IRA. I believed in the cause, but I didn't approve of the way they got there. Have you ever seen a street covered with torn bodies, including children? Turn in the bloody killers, you get your fecking kneecaps blown off."

"Boyle and some IRA chums wanted to spill green paint off the Golden Gate Bridge onto the British fleet. Nothing happened."

"Really? The Brits shot my brother."

"My God," I said.

Dervla sat up, her arms around her knees. "Do you have any idea what that kind of world is like?"

"I think so."

"Do you now? It's a world of blood hatreds. It's not Bing Crosby singing some phony American Irish song. Yeats can't do it justice."

"You don't have a monopoly on pain, you know. And they can't fight forever."

Dervla said nothing. Her dark eyes were moist, glittering, and she turned away, suddenly crying. Over sixty years had gone by since my Grandmother's migration, yet Dervla faced the same nightmare. She looked at me as though staring across a battlefield.

"I'm sorry," I said.

"It's all right. I hate sentimental weakness. I hate it!"

"You're not weak to cry for your brother."

"He ran down an alley into a police ambush. I lifted his head off the pavement. I had his blood all over my hands."

She made despairing choking sounds deep in her throat. I reached out and held her, rocking gently. Crying, she pushed me away.

"Father thought he deserved it for being reckless. Damn it, why am I digging all this shit up? I'm in America."

"Naked—in a bathhouse."

She began to laugh through sobs. After a moment, she regained control.

"Dervla? Will you be all right?"

"Sure. I'm fine. I'm just your average snippy, fecked up Irish spirit. Now you see me, now you don't."

Dervla's eyes were luminous and a little frightening up close. Her large breasts pressed against my chest. She touched my lips with her fingers, and then slid a finger into her mouth. The music had stopped.

"I'll be gone, tonight, Dervla."

"So will I."

For a moment she seemed to be gazing into another world, her eyes suddenly compassionate, even calm. Perhaps she was once again a young Irish girl waiting for a lover on a dirt road, a river running through fields green from a soft rain. Our eyes met. Her voice was low and soft. "Lie back. Face the other way."

Our bodies stretched out, then slid together. It was like an erotic Swedish film from years before: mouths slightly open, eyes closed, a taste of soft, giving labia, the feel of closing lips, a female moaning with a sudden ripple through lower stomach, a quick springing of seed. She rolled on her back, wet cheek pressed to thigh. Foamy water swirled in the tub.

* * *

WE dressed and said good-bye outside the bathhouse. Dervla turned and walked away without another word, seeming to fade, to sink into the crowd. Our final moments were gone.

That night, one hundred miles away, I sat out on Emmett's patio, gulping a soft drink, thinking about whiskey and Dervla. Fading red light glowed on the horizon. When I called, her number was already disconnected. Mother remembered talking to no one; perhaps Dervla

196

was an Irish ghost, vanished into thin air. Emmett fixed himself a drink and sat down. I had spent many summers here when Father was alive, swimming in the canals or playing in the rubber pool in the garden. As it grew cold, an opaline mist moved in over the city.

"How's your mother?"

"The same. You don't like Fran, do you?"

"I don't make judgments. Are you writing?"

"Not nearly enough."

"Will you write about your mother?"

"I don't think so. Shaw's mother was crazy and he never bothered to write about her."

"Bernard Shaw was more concerned about socialism and poverty. Is Fran crazy?"

"I'm not sure."

Emmett sipped his drink. He had lost even more hair and now wore glasses.

"Well, if it's something you don't have to write, why bother?"

I drank my ginger ale. Electric lights cast shadows and the crickets were quiet. Down the street, a hospital was going up in a former cow pasture.

"It's hard to imagine my father gone."

"I know. I feel the same way. He was my brother. We went to Ireland together."

"Maybe you could help me write his story."

"No, his story—or our story—will be written by someone else. I'm a journalist. I write features. He deserves more than a feature article. I don't write biographies or fiction. If you want to write bad enough, the words will come."

I looked at Emmett's face. "You don't seem very sad."

"We all grieve in different ways. I certainly don't cry when I'm sad. What do you do?"

I didn't have an answer.

"I found out last night where my name, 'Emmett', came from. I thought it was the Irish hero, Robert Emmett, but according to Ann, my mother's niece, there was a second Kennedy brother named John Emmett."

"Agnes had another brother besides Uncle Pete?"

"Yes. He was killed in the Dardenelles straits during World War I. He must've been on a ship or in a submarine. Or maybe he died at Gallipoli, but they were mostly Australians. An Irish Mick in the British navy. Amazing."

"He died and Agnes never mentioned him?"

Emmett looked at me over his drink.

"Maybe the old Irish folk just don't like to talk about themselves—or their relatives. There might be a story there."

"There might be," I said, remembering stories of the fierce fighting in World War I: the hand-to-hand combat, the mustard gas and hot machine guns slaughtering running troops. Why had I never heard of this patriotic brother who gave the ultimate sacrifice?

"It's cold. Let's go inside," Emmett said.

The next morning, I left Modesto, eventually driving across Nevada. A nacreous sky spread over the desert landscape of tall cactus plants. Passing through Carlin, Nevada, a sad country song came on the radio. Someone was lamenting his momma and his daddy in prison, and I started to cry. I pulled over near a bar with a gravel parking lot and drive-in restaurant. I felt like a drink but pushed on toward Wells, Nevada, then north to Jackpot and the Idaho border.

The next afternoon, the English Department chairman, wearing a white matching suit, his hair stylishly cut, informed me that all MA instructors were being released. Russian novels filled a shelf. The chairman leaned back in his leather chair. "We're upgrading the department with Ph.D. candidates. I'd like to build a great English Department in the wilderness." He folded his hands. "Oh, my condolences on your loss. I just heard."

"Thanks."

"What will you do now?"

"I don't know," I said. "Maybe work a Shakespeare festival in Utah. Maybe work with the tribe at Fort Hall."

The chairman smiled nervously. He had a rich, lilting voice. A photo of Leo Tolstoy with a battered hat and full white beard stared at us from the wall.

"If you get a summer job with Indians and Upward Bound, that would be just ducky."

"If not, I don't know what I'll do," I said.

"Get your Ph.D.," the chairman insisted with some reproach. "I mean, really, you need a terminal degree."

"Sounds like a disease. I suspect I need a break from higher education."

I shook his hand and left. A few students walked across the familiar campus quad. With Dolly Ann gone, there was no furniture; it felt unsettling to enter a house that echoed. That night, I tried to call Dervla, but there was no new number.

"Operator, give me all the Irish bars in San Francisco. That's right. All of them."

The bartender at The Irish Abbey Tavern called out, asking for Dervla O' Connor. A moment later, I heard the rich, slightly raspy voice with the Belfast inflection.

"Hello. Who's this?"

"Me."

"Who the hell is 'Me'?"

"Who do you think?"

There was a long pause, with the sounds of people drinking and talking over a loud jukebox. I imagined her face over the phone, the eyes dark and mischievous.

"It's over, my Irish Yank friend."

"Why?"

"That's part of the magic. Look, I'm washing out my mouth with good Irish Bushmill's. When you come back, who knows?"

"How will I find you?"

Dervla cackled. "I'll find you, like I did last time."

"Really? How's Boyle?"

"Drunk in El Salvador. Maybe he'll get his ass shot off."

"He'll always survive."

"He called to tell me some nuns got raped and killed. One of them was your old eighth grade teacher."

I felt something tighten and drop inside me. For a moment, I saw Sister Ann Maureen's pretty face beneath the wimple. She was standing in a cemetery looking at a boy's picture and covering her smile with a dainty hand.

"SAM? Oh my God."

"It was a bunch of fecking fascists. Hey, will you cope?"

"She was a good person," I said.

"I'm sorry to tell you." For a moment, Derlva's voice had genuine concern. The house band began playing in the background. "Look, it's been lovely, Boyo, but I got some heavy drinking to do."

"Why don't you drink here?"

"Are you fecking crazy? I escaped one hell with Boyle. Be glad we connected."

"Let's connect again."

"I have to hang up." There was another pause. She sang over the phone: "Good-night, Romeo."

"Dervla?"

This time, the Belfast lilt had a cutting rasp.

"Don't be a sap. I'm a one-night stand, okay? If we lived together, we'd fight, and soon, you'd be sucking up morning beers and writing worthless novels until you died of cirrhosis. Sober up, love someone practical, and write your ass off." There was another pause. "Just make sure it's honest, unlike Boyle's self-indulgent crap."

"Dervla, who the hell are you? A dervish? A banshee? A witch?"

I could hear her sniggering. Then a pause. "I might be a witch. Maybe a good witch. Maybe a bad witch." Her accent went into a mock Irish rhythm. "Good-bye, and may the luck o' the Oirish be with you." There was a click and a dial tone.

The following night in Pocatello, a university town divided by a railroad yard, a film class presented Orson Welles in *Lady From Shanghai*. It was a clear and crisp November night; November was the month of dead souls. Train cars screeched in the distance. Dead leaves littered the street as I walked toward the school, feeling somehow like an unseen stranger. I wanted to see again that fleeting glimpse of San Francisco's Playland at the Beach as Orson Welles strolled past, walking away from a finale of murder and death. It was the only cinematic record left of that magical place where I spent so much of my childhood.

EPILOGUE

MARSHAL AND I DROVE ON THE NARROW TWO-LANE highway.

"The Hemingway Memorial is just up the road past Sun Valley," I said.

"I only read one book of his. Empty. All these people sitting around cafés drinking wine when they weren't fishing or watching bullfights." Marshall gazed at the countryside of hills and cottonwoods. "Why did he kill himself?"

"I don't know. Depression maybe."

"I mean, he had a lot of money and fame."

"I love his books," was all I could say.

"You know, I always get a map and see the sights," Marshall said. "I really like Craters of the Moon. All that black lava rock. Very existential."

We took a turn on the road, with a mountain to our left. In the winter, skiers would soar down Mt. Baldy. One Christmas Eve night, we watched skiers holding torches crisscross down the mountain, a magical pattern of lights. In Sun Valley, young Mormons in formal dress sang Christmas carols, their faces earnest, only the unmotivated smiles betraying a routine. Ice sculptures lined the narrow paths. Tourists crowded into the lodge away from the cold. With summer came the heat and winter seemed a remote dream.

"How are your kids?"

"My girls are fine. The oldest will be going to Harvard."

"So you're pushing them to get an elitist education?"

"Define 'push'," Marshall said. "It's pretty hard to fail when you graduate from Harvard. After Harvard, half of life is just showing up." He looked over at me. "Hey, Groom, how do you feel?"

"Good," I said. The tie felt uncomfortable, but I knew the sport suit was impressive.

"You look good. Looking forward to getting hitched?"

"Of course. Karen is herself a dowry," I said.

"What play's that from?"

"*King Lear.*"

"Just what we need—more Shakespeare. Give him a rest. I'm also tired of Noel Coward's frivolous people, Ibsen's fjords and Chekhov really bores me."

"Chekhov is great."

"Sure. 'Ah Ivan, let us beat a serf to relieve the boredom.'" Marshall paused for effect. "What serious writer names a play after a bird?"

"Ibsen and Chekhov both did."

"I rest my case."

Marshall continued his comic diatribe against classical theatre. After he finished with the great writers, he trashed the modern playwrights.

"Please. No more Stanleys breaking dishes."

"I like Tennessee Williams."

"And that boring Beckett. Gaah!"

"I directed a Beckett. I think he's very funny."

He looked over at me, pensive. "Beckett's funny? Maybe you need order, so you're better off married."

"It'll be better than the first one. What a disaster."

"What ever happened to your ex—Dolly Ann?"

"I'm told she's remarried and teaching Mormon children in Salt Lake."

"I heard all bad Americans when they die go to Salt Lake."

"You may have heard right."

"Well, the cold war's over, so we know Dolly wasn't a spy."

"Maybe she was. A lot of people we knew back then got arrested."

"A few deserved it."

We drove on. The windless air grew warmer and would be hot by noon. The wedding guests would stand on a slope facing the memorial. New golf courses with manicured green hills covered the Sun Valley landscape. Occasionally, famous faces filled the bars and restaurants; they built new houses though they didn't stay in Ketchum much of the year. Higher prices were driving out the local residents. Morning buses carried Latino workers in to clean the condos of rich Anglos.

"Why can't your mother make it to the wedding?"

"She's resting after her Amazon cruise."

"Good old Fran," Marshal said. He had stopped running and now had a potbelly. The thick crow hair had turned solid white. "She does do things her way, though. If she tries to screw you out of anything, I'll be your lawyer."

"I may need you. She'll probably leave her money to her dogs."

I tried to imagine Mother as an explorer of the Amazon. Perhaps she sat at a sidewalk café, drinking, looking across the Amazon River at the thick green jungle; it would be like gazing through an aquarium, the air heavy and moist, distorting the riot of rich colors: red, green, yellow, jet blacks. The photos from her African trip showed a small, thin blonde woman, walking among colorfully dressed African blacks. Back humped, face pale and taut beneath the blonde wig, Mother seemed alien under the fierce African sun.

"She made it to Africa and the Amazon. If she flew to Boise, I could've picked her up. I've been thinking about my father lately. I know he would've been here." Faces and images crowded my mind.

Marshall spoke: "My parents were nervous I was marrying a Shiksa until they found out her father was a judge and rich. 'Not Jewish but not bad,' my mother said. After the wedding, we had a softball game, the Jews against the Wasps."

Alongside the road, many cyclists rode on the paths.

"Sorry to hear about your mother, Marshall."

Marshall shrugged.

"Ovarian cancer," he said. "She was eighty, complaining up to the end. Don't drink, don't smoke, don't play cards. This hospice has terrible room service."

"So an era is gone."

I imagined my ashes and the ashes of my new bride eventually scattered on the little brook that ran in front of Hemingway's bust and plaque. The plaque contained words Hemingway had written for a hunter killed in 1939. Now they served Hemingway's memory as well:

"Best of all he loved the fall
The leaves yellow on the cottonwoods
Leaves floating on the trout streams
And above the hills
The high blue windless skies
Now he will be a part of them forever"

Karen waited with guests by the memorial; it would be good to exchange vows before Papa's bust that faced those same hills. A few friends could not make it, or—like Lynn and Dervla—had disappeared. A few were gone forever.

"A lot of eras are gone," Marshall said. "Including ours. Whatever happened to your friend, James R. Dean?"

"He was diagnosed with MS. Then he had a personal tragedy recently. One of his daughters was killed in a car crash. She survived Gulf War combat and came home to be killed."

Marshall shuddered.

"God, if that happened to one of my kids, I'd go insane. What about Boyle?"

"Last I heard, he was drunk in Rome."

There were fewer trees and many hills, brown in the July heat. We could no longer see the green golf course and the river that ran below. The bicycle path had ended. No other cars drove on the road leading into more open country.

"Something is wrong," I said.

"What could be wrong?"

"Good God, I think we passed Ernie's memorial."

Marshall laughed. "What? You're not only late for your wedding, you get lost?"

"We got lost!"

"But we're making good time at least."

I turned the rented car around on the narrow highway.

"Just like Wrong Way Corrigan," he said. "Don't expect a reprieve from me. I came here to see a wedding. Mazeltov—or congratulations."

"So we got lost. I get there eventually."

"Mazeltov actually means 'congratulations' with the suggestion that 'it's about time.'"

We drove back toward the memorial where the guests had gathered to see an outdoor ceremony. We were moving fast. A lone Indian in jeans and a buckskin jacket stood by the road. He was short with a square, rugged build, and he waved us down. I slowed the car. His broad face with a headband appeared in the window.

"Just going to Ketchum," he said.

"Get in. I can take you at least a mile."

The Indian got in and sat in the back seat.

"You look real pretty, Tybo."

"Thank you. Going to a wedding—mine."

"Good," he said. "My name's Claude Bronco, Bannock-Shoshone warrior."

I introduced myself and Marshall held out his hand. "I'm Marshall, federal lawyer. I defend truth, justice and the American way."

"Hello, Marshall."

"What's a 'Tybo'?" Marshall asked.

"'Tybo' means 'White Man with a Camera,'" Bronco said.

"Is that good or bad?"

"Good. I even know a few good white men."

"Glad to hear that," Marshall said. "I even have a camera."

Bronco's hair was black and coarse, like a horse's mane. His brown face resembled a Mayan carving. He leaned over the seat and took my free hand, studying the open palm.

"You have a long love life," he said. "Many different friends at the wedding."

"Yeah, if we ever get there," Marshall said.

"You'll get there," Bronco said. "But no parents. Just no good."

"My father died some years ago. My mother couldn't bother to attend."

"I saw that," Claude said. He closed my fingers over the palm.

"My mother's dead," Marshall said. "His will live to be a hundred."

I watched Claude Bronco's face in the rear view mirror. He met my eyes.

"I saw one parent gone, other—not so good."

"My mother's alive and well," I insisted. "Not that it ever made for happier times."

"I saw that too," Bronco said.

"Really? What do you mean, 'not so good'?"

"She's a sad lady."

"Due respect, Mr. Bronco, my mother's never sad. She lives for a good time."

"She does. She did. When happy ladies get too old, they get sad. When they get sad, they don't eat. They don't eat, they die. It happens to some people. Life just isn't fun anymore. In the early days, old

Indian women stayed behind to starve. The tribe moved on."

"My mother loves a good dinner," I said. "She won't starve."

"Not today. Not next month. But soon."

"I don't think so."

Bronco looked out the window at a blonde woman on a bicycle towing a child behind. She wore spandex and bent low over the bars. He finally spoke.

"She makes you angry. Too bad."

"Oh please. Due respect, I don't believe in fortune tellers."

"I know you don't." His bulk seemed to fill the car. "But I'm an Injun. All Injuns are mystic. I'm stopping at the Casino Bar. Gimme a buck! Two bucks."

"Here, take a five spot," I said.

"Bless you, Tybo," Claude Bronco said, waving his hand like a bishop. He looked down the road. "This was our land, you know. That's why I drink—to forget."

"I drank a bit in my day," I said. "Did you see that in my hand, too?"

Claude Bronco's dark Indian eyes revealed nothing. Then he smiled.

"It's all a trick," he said. "I hear Irish name, I see Irish tribe of drunk warriors telling stories, so I make up stories."

"We haven't heard any stories yet," Marshall said.

"I know a few, gentlemen, but I don't believe in fortune tellers either."

"How did you know my father was gone?"

"A lucky guess," the Indian said.

"All the same, maybe you could read my palm," Marshall said. "Tell me I'll make a difference in the world and that my kids will always be happy."

Claude Bronco put his big hand over Marshall's, then pulled away. "Not today," he said. "It's just a game."

"I like games."

I saw the weathered sign for the Hemingway Memorial to my left and slowed the car. The road continued toward Ketchum.

"When is the last time you heard from Fran?" Marshall asked.

"She sent me a card on my last birthday. Her sister, Harriet, would call me if she was that sick." I looked at Claude Bronco in the back seat. He was slipping the five spot into his shirt pocket. "Isn't that right, Claude?"

"Right. She would. It means nothing," he said. "Only entertainment."

"So entertain me," Marshall said, reaching in his pockets. "I'll pay you another five spot."

"No."

"Then come to the wedding," I said.

"Crowds of white people make me nervous," the Indian told us. "Have a good life."

Claude Bronco got out and started walking down the road. Soon he would pass new construction. The Sho-Ban Indian seemed awkward on foot, and I imagined him astride a horse, leading a charge against uniformed cavalry trapped on a hill. Gunsmoke would cover the warriors, the air itself hailing arrows.

A group of people stood in the clearing near the Hemingway bust. We walked down the cement path toward the monument. The sky was clear and light blue. Karen wore white with a broad-brimmed cream-colored hat trimmed with a blue veil; she and the best man stood next to a black-robed judge. Karen saw us and smiled. The air was hot, but a breeze began blowing through the cottonwoods.

"God," Marshall said. "Why wouldn't he read my palm? You think Claude's on the level?"

"You said it. Fran will live forever."

"This is true. Maybe you better call later."

"Sure," I said.

"If I don't get a card on my next birthday, I'll call. I guess I can't imagine my mother sick or giving up. The phone works both ways, you know."

"It's not good to hate a parent," he warned. "Fran is actually admirable in her own way."

"What way is that?"

Marshall thought for a moment.

"If shallow, she's honest about it."

"She doesn't know me."

"So what? She tries in her own way to connect."

It was true that while I attended the American Film Institute in Hollywood, Mother saw some value in this artistic pursuit. That was never possible with my theatre work. Father died before my first play was produced, but Mother never saw them and truly wondered why anyone bothered.

"Your mother's a bit theatrical now that I think of it," Marshall said. "Write a play about her."

Seeing the bust of Hemingway made me think of an actor named Joe Gistirak whom I directed in *Krapp's Last Tape*, a Beckett play about an old constipated banana addict and alcoholic listening to birthday tapes of himself thirty years before. Joe was a rugged veteran actor with a commanding stage presence—bearded with hollow eyes, high cheekbones and a husky, sinewy voice. Alone at his table in a circle of light listening to a younger voice bragging that he wouldn't want those lost years back, Joe created a devastated yet defiant human being, solitary in his den and memorable. When the play opened along with Pinter's *The Dumbwaiter* directed by Peter Coyote, something magical happened. Joe then appeared as the bitter old man—Dodge—in Sam Shepard's *Buried Child*, which went on to win the Pulitzer Prize though without Joe in the New York cast.

We met one last time to discuss a production of Moliere's *Tartouffe*; Joe was uncertain about playing the lead role at his age, and also struggling with an inner darkness not unlike Beckett's tramps.

"Look around you," Joe said. I saw young gay men at various tables in the Bakery Café, Joe's favorite place in San Francisco's Castro District. "The gay community is obsessed with youth. I'm just an old has-been. An out-of-date fag."

"You were brilliant as Dodge. No one could have done that part the way you did. And who said you're too old? You have that macho late-Hemingway look." It was a warm, pleasant day and Joe seemed amused at the comparison. He sipped his coffee while I nursed a white wine, for once again, I was back on the bottle. "Joe, you're beautiful."

"Thank you for that," he said.

"Let's work on *Tartouffe*."

"Sure. But first, I want to take a long rest."

A few days later, I read of Joe Gistirak's suicide. He had become the tormented characters he played on the stage. I might commiserate with other theatre people, but I couldn't express the devastation I felt at Joe's death to Mother, who would dismiss him as just another dead actor—all the more pathetic for being old and not famous.

"Fran as Tallulah Bankhead," Marshall said. "A showboat performer."

Perhaps we did have a connection. Mother knew movie stars. She smelled money and saw glamour in film. Monthly checks with no note came to help pay rent on a small Los Angeles apartment with no furniture and a sleeping bag on the floor. It was a mark of the LA professional to be rarely home. Answering machines talked to one another across the seductive Hollywood, full of fleeting hopes and invisible gold. Perhaps she secretly hoped I would marry a film star. I knew that playwright-turned-actor Sam Shepard was becoming famous when Mother spotted his name in the gossip columns. That I worked with him one summer elevated my status.

"Show time," Marshall said.

A few wedding guests turned and smiled at us.

"Joe gave up," I said. "Fran would never do that."

"Who's Joe?"

"An actor I knew some years ago."

"Good," Marshall said after a pause.

The crowd parted as we walked toward the small open space. The judge held a Bible. Lou Valentine Johnson played a classical guitar piece. The brook flowed past the monument as I reached out to take Karen's hand.

Ellis Island

WHEN THE ELLIS ISLAND RECORDS WENT ON LINE, I searched for my grandparents. I don't know why I had to know just when they came over, and after two months waiting for the millions of Internet hits to subside, I finally got through. Any answers only raised more questions. Agnes Kennedy appeared nowhere on any ship's records. Emmett had written a brief note tracing her family history. My grandmother's mother was also named Agnes...Agnes Burke who married Patrick Kennedy. I tried to imagine them standing by as an Irish priest baptized the infant Agnes in the Sligo church of the Sacred

Heart. John and Mary Leonard stood as sponsors. Who were those people from late 19th century Ireland? I haunted the Irish church in my imagination, and one day would visit the place myself.

I regularly called Hazel, Emmett's widow, and one day she told me about a vital family contact.

"You want information about the family? I know Ann Haley is still alive."

"I forget. Who is Ann Haley?"

"Her mother was Agnes' sister, Minnie."

The name, Minnie, resonated in my memory, whispered and spoken so many times as I grew up. "Right. The famous Minnie."

"She might answer your questions."

When I telephoned Ann Haley, I expected an old voice; instead, I heard a young, vibrant voice despite her 86 years. For a few moments, she didn't remember me.

"I have a nephew named Michael," she said. "You sound different."

"Really? Someone else has my name?"

"I'm afraid so."

As we talked, some of Agnes Kennedy's family history came into focus. Of course, it began with Minnie.

"Minnie was the oldest Kennedy daughter, and maybe the strongest."

"How so?"

"She came over first and lived with an aunt in Boston. Minnie attended school but hated it since the other kids made fun of her Irish brogue. She went to New York and worked as a cook for a wealthy Jewish family. My mother became a great cook over the years. Then she returned to Ireland for a visit and brought Bessie and another sister named Ann who died in San Francisco at the age of twenty."

"Twenty? What happened?"

"Some mysterious illness. In 1906, Minnie and Bessie settled in San Francisco, working for a family on California Street. The quake hit and the family's house was destroyed, so both sisters took a carriage out of town. They escaped the fires and quake but lost everything."

"But they survived?"

"Yes. Barely. They were homeless and without work for a month."

The story continued like a chronicle from another time. I tried to see the two Irish women on a carriage leaving a burning city.

"Minnie eventually returned to San Francisco and made enough to bring out Kate and Agnes. There was also a cousin named Matt Burke who one day took off for Alaska and was never seen again. Then Minnie met Patrick at your grandfather's marriage to Agnes. Patrick was Thomas's cousin. Minnie married him two years later in 1916."

"Cousin? You mean my grandfather's brother?"

"No, he had a cousin, also named Patrick."

"So that's one mystery solved. Agnes was not married through any arrangement. How did she come over?"

"I don't know," Ann said. "Maybe by ship directly to San Francisco. Those records are harder to get."

"So there were two Patrick Corrigans?"

"There were a lot of Irish people with the same names," said Ann, laughing. "Not much imagination there. I think I remember you—the long-haired kid at your dad's funeral, correct?"

"Probably."

"Minnie and Bessie lived through that terrible '06 quake," she repeated in a sad voice. There was a pause on the phone. "Minnie often talked about Ann. To die so young."

"What kind of illness?"

"Probably pneumonia. Mother said Ann Kennedy went out one cold San Francisco night in a skimpy dress and got a chill the next day. Somehow, they knew something bad would happen. Perhaps Ann was just...fragile."

"Did she die before or after the quake?"

"I don't know. Maybe after. Maybe the terror of the earthquake and the new country was too much."

I tried to remember the name and any childhood story about this ill-fated Irish woman. Occasionally, stories were buried in sudden silences or averted glances. Where was Ann going that night? To met a secret lover, perhaps? I could imagine a young woman lying on a bed in a small room lit by oil lamps, her face pale and ravaged in the weak light, while her healthy sisters hovered over her. She would not live to see the new century.

"My grandmother never mentioned her," I finally said.

"Agnes may have been too far removed, or it was too painful. Ann was the gifted, beautiful one."

"More so than Minnie?"

"My mother looked up to her. Cherished her memory."

"I'll look up Minnie on the Ellis Island records."

"But not under Minnie. She's under Mary Ellen Kennedy if she's there," Ann said. "Came over at age twelve."

"Twelve?"

"Yes."

"She first arrived in America at the age of twelve?"

"Correct."

It was another startling portrait, a single female child exploring a new world. "That explains some of Minnie's legend."

"Her aunt in Boston sponsored her. Still, she was young to make that trip. Can you imagine a girl alone on a ship full of desperate immigrants? But she prospered and sponsored her sisters who finally brought over Pete, the youngest brother. Uncle Pete loved to boast and talk, but Minnie and her sisters led the way, you know."

"So Peter was the last child?"

"After Agnes. And he was the only brother to reach old age."

I could still hear Uncle Emmett's voice as he talked about the other Kennedy brother slain in the first great war.

"Tell me about John Emmett Kennedy."

"All we know is that he fought in World War I and died at the Dardenelles. My mother said it was a big battle, but I don't know which one."

"But still no one knows exactly when or how Agnes came over?"

"No. We probably never will."

"Thanks for the history," I said.

It struck me that both my grandmothers had famous maiden names: Kennedy and Joyce.

"My memory is going," Ann said. "Sometimes voices come back to me, and the next day, I forget. Despite the Celtic gift for talk, or because of it, very little was ever written down. If you find out anything about your grandfather, let me know."

"I will."

We promised to keep in touch, a promise often ignored.

The search for Grandfather proved frustrating and exciting. Fifty-six

Thomas Corrigans had passed through Ellis Island between the years of 1892 and 1924. Most of them could be dismissed as candidates, but one passenger stood out. In 1907, a Thomas Corrigan from Ballaghaderin in Roscommon left Queenstown for New York. 'Ballaghaderin' was an old spelling. He traveled on a new steam ship called the Caronia to meet a cousin named McGreal living in the Mission District of San Francisco, his final destination. I never knew of a cousin named McGreal. Names and conversations have faded over time, but that name never surfaced in family histories. This Thomas was the same height as my grandfather, 5' 9", and had the same fair hair, even though I only knew my grandfather as bald. The man was a laborer, the common occupation of my grandfather and most Irishmen who were leaving Ireland. The ship's list or manifest had problems. The second page, which should have included names of relatives, was missing. The passenger's age was also inaccurate. This Thomas Corrigan was 27 when my grandfather would have been 20 in May of 1907, judging from a California death index that finally revealed his date of birth: March 21, 1887. Ironically, 27 nearly fit the incorrect date on the Holy Cross grave marker. Could Grandfather have lied at some point about his age, or was the 'seven' meant to be a 'zero' on the ship's manifest, scrawled hastily in a tiny hand?

I imagined immigrants lined up at huge tables in a giant room with little light; each carried their meager belongings only to meet a relative in New York or elsewhere and begin a new life. Immigration officers scribbled information in black ink. Beyond the island was the Statue of Liberty, but what did she promise? Did New York excite dreams of wealth or inspire terror? The ship's list broke down the passengers by ethnic groups: Polish, German, Spanish, and British. "Hebrew" was a classification for a race and noted carefully. A separate passage explained that any appearance of black blood qualified a passenger as "Negro." Cubans were differentiated from Negroes. Irish, Scotch, Welsh and English passengers were grouped together as British citizens; my grandfather would have carried a British passport at the time since Ireland was not independent. The names were numbered and not in alphabetical order. All immigrants were asked if they were anarchists or polygamists. They wrote who paid for their fare and how much money they carried. Thomas was wealthy with $75 dollars. They all noted their health was good and none were scarred or crippled. The officer guaranteed none were "idiots, paupers or criminals." The process was repeated, one ship's manifest after another listing displaced passengers from so long ago seeking the elusive American dream. Each name in every column carried a bitter history. The Caronia, a relic from another era, was scrapped in 1933.

If this Thomas Corrigan wasn't Grandfather, it was interesting to think he lived in the same Mission District. Did they pass each other on the street, noticing their common Irish heritage but not recognizing their shared names? If 1907 was the correct date, were all Grandfather's stories about the 1906 earthquake just tall tales? Minnie and Bessie had endured the natural tragedy, but he had not. I like to imagine that tragic April morning did find Grandfather in Union Square with a traveling John Barrymore, still dressed in a tuxedo from the opera the night before, and the star—Enrico Caruso himself. Legends claim Caruso sang an aria from *Carmen* out the window of the Palace Hotel to ensure he still had a voice, the operatic tones soaring over the ruined city. The true horror was about to begin. The army came in and shot looters and those suspected of looting. That Grandfather drove a carriage to the Ferry Building to ship the Italian tenor home made an exciting story. It was a ride through hell; fires and explosions finished off what the earthquake began, the destruction of San Francisco. As a child, I never asked where Grandfather got the horse-drawn carriage. If the earthquake story isn't true, Grandfather did rebuild the city and pave its streets, and at some time met the Kennedy sisters.

One can stare for hours at old records and ship's lists, hoping to find an ancient name scrawled on the page that reveals some meaning in the family history. One can look for patterns among the columns of names and make up histories. Families appear, including old immigrants seeking a final exploration. The man whose name appears above Thomas Corrigan is Coleman, another Thomas from Roscommon. Did they travel together and have long discussions on the deck as they crossed the Atlantic? The 1916 uprising was still nine years away. After Corrigan and Coleman is Maggie McDermott, a County Mayo girl of 19 who listed herself as a servant. Coleman went to New York and McDermott to New Jersey. Perhaps these three nodded to each other on the dock before parting forever that spring day.

It was sad to think that Agnes died on the 20th of March 1954, a day before my grandfather turned 67. He greeted his birthday without his wife of forty years. The true identity of the Ellis Island passenger meeting his cousin McGreal in San Francisco will never be known, but there was one bit of proof. I requested and received my grandparents' marriage certificate. On 15 July 1914, they married at Saint Mary's Cathedral in San Francisco. Though not mentioned, Patrick the cousin and Minnie the sister watched the ceremony. One of the witnesses listed was my grandmother's other sister, Bessie Kennedy. The second witness was a man named John McGreal.

* * * * *

Printed in the United States
1089200004B